Filmmakers Thinking

Adrian Martin

Foreword by Radu Jude

Sticking Place Books
New York

© Sticking Place Books 2024
© Adrian Martin
© Elías Querejeta Zine Eskola
© Foreword by Radu Jude

This book was first published in a limited edition by Elías Querejeta Zine Eskola (www.zine-eskola.eus) in 2022. It has been produced within the framework of the EQZE studies programme.

Cover image: © Cinémathèque française (Fritz Lang collection)

Adrian Martin's website: www.adrianmartinfilmcritic.com

Designed by Goran Tovilovic

www.stickingplacebooks.com

All rights reserved.
No part of this book may be reproduced, stored in or introduced into a retrieval system, or transmitted, in any form or by any means (electronic, mechanical, photocopying, recording or otherwise) without the written permission of the publishers, except in the case of brief quotations embodied in critical articles or reviews.

ISBN 978-1-942782-77-3

para Cristina

Contents

Thinking Machines by Radu Jude	ix
Prefatory Note	xi
Introduction: The Filmmaker's Dialogue	xiii

Part One: Ideas of Cinema

1. Ways of Invention	1
2. Preserving the Core	7
3. Metaphors, Fields, Semantic Maps, and Horizons of Reference	15
4. What is Cinema? The Most Essential Things	19
5. Origin Tales	29
6. The Famous "Invisible Style" Defence	37
7. Invisible Imaginary Ubiquitous Winged Witness	45
8. Chance and Destiny	53
9. A Genealogy of Inspiration	61
10. Magical, Secret Ingredient	69
11. Nailing Down the Parameters of Cinécriture	75
12. Cool, Clear Water	83
13. The Power of Negation	91

Interlude: Statements of Intention

14. Chantal Akerman: *Almayer's Folly*	99
15. Philippe Grandrieux: *Sombre*	105
16. Jean-Luc Godard: *Vivre sa vie*	111
17. John Hillcoat: *The Proposition*	115
18. Jacques Rivette: *Daughters of Fire*	123

Part Two: Ideas About Cinema

19. Pure and Impure Vocation	133
20. Do It and Show It, That's All	141
21. Plunging Down into the Unreally Real	149
22. Stepping Off a Fast Train	157
23. Time Imprinted	165
24. Mythical, Infantile Substratum	173
25. Asynchronised Strike	181
26. In Suspense	187
27. Past the Photographic	195
28. Featureless White Screen	201
29. The Proper Spectator	211
30. Denuded Music, Moving Positions	217
31. Occult Alternative	223
32. Short Preface to All Criticism	233
33. A Dream is a Thought Expressed in Images	245

Index   251

Thinking Machines
by Radu Jude

Adrian Martin is someone who loves thinking. The proof is this book, but also his long-term online audiovisual essay series *The Thinking Machine*, where he and his partner/collaborator Cristina Álvarez López take cinema seriously as a tool for thinking – exactly as someone like Jean Epstein did some 100 years ago.

He is also a teacher, and this book, "short and punchy, composed in relatively brief fragments," as Martin aptly describes it, is indeed the book of a teacher. So, at the very beginning, this can be a turn-off. But then it becomes, in my opinion, something else completely. Because what kind of teacher is Adrian Martin?

Well, he is one of the most honest and, because of that, annoying teachers – because, when asked a question, he doesn't give you an answer, he gives you 100 answers, and invites you to think and to study.

So, what is the question, then? I guess there are many, but all converge on the old one, the one which André Bazin made famous: "What is cinema?" And the answers of filmmakers are confusing as hell. Maybe this is true for other arts or disciplines, I don't know. The great merit of the book – and this is related to its brevity – is that it functions as a survey of most filmmakers' approaches to their art. And only the fact that the book doesn't go into too many details makes this diversity visible.

As a (very confused) filmmaker myself, I found this book tremendously useful. I began with the feeling that I already knew most of the ideas in it, but actually discovered many new ones, and I have already started researching some of them. I want to stress that this book belongs to the category of books that send you away to study more. As I am a filmmaker so unsure of himself (and maybe, because of this, I am in the best position to appreciate this book), I tend to split everything into two categories: things that liberate me and things that block me.

The theories of artists have the same effect on me. Andy Warhol, for instance, liberates me, while someone like Carl Dreyer doesn't – his perfect cinema makes me feel horrible, while admiring it all the way. Rembrandt is so great that he makes me feel like a nobody, but someone like Cy Twombly or my beloved Isidore Isou encourages me. (A personal side note: any book which mentions the criminally unknown film by Isou, as this one does, has my immediate sympathy!) So, of course, while reading, I tended to favour these types of filmmakers' ideas.

But in the end, finishing the book, I discovered something else: that all these ideas need each other. Not only is cinema a tree with many branches, as Jonas Mekas liked to say, but these branches oppose each other, and this opposition keeps the tree in balance. I understand now that S.M. Eisenstein needs George Miller, that Pedro Costa needs Ridley Scott, that even Jacques Rivette needs Gillo Pontecorvo, and that Godard needs everybody else.

Showing this need is the great, hidden idea of Adrian Martin's beautiful book. And, if I may say so, this need still makes cinema exhilarating.

Prefatory Note

In its English-language form, my title suggests a double meaning: *Filmmakers Thinking* indicates an active, ongoing process – filmmakers in the process of thinking. But it also implies the possessive *Filmmakers' Thinking*, which conjures a body of work that can be consulted, a series of texts (of various kinds) in which these artists' thoughts have been set down and captured, and so are available now for our study and enjoyment. I intend both meanings, for both are at play in the pages that follow.

This book has an unusual structure, and an unorthodox intention. It does not present a fully argued-out thesis or commentary coming from me. It follows no strict chronological order. It boasts neither footnotes nor a bibliography. It is not an ordinary, linear book of film analysis, criticism or history. It does not pretend for a second to be an objective survey. Rather, it arises from a simple but passionately held conviction: that we need to pay more attention, and more respect, to the words of filmmakers. To that end, it presents, in a particular sequence that I have chosen, the writings, statements and reflections of many filmmaker-thinker-artists.

But neither is it a straightforward anthology of filmmakers' texts (some books like that, all useful, none comprehensive, already exist). Rather it is (to use a culinary metaphor) a kind of "taste sampler" or a smorgasbord spread – selected quotations interspersed with my own notations. For each filmmaker, I usually pick one major text – or some part of that text. Sometimes I offer contextual background, at other times I suggest connections or contrasts between the various stated or implied filmmaker positions. I occasionally even criticise someone's statement, but almost always sympathetically, in order to somehow redeem it. I want us to imaginatively inhabit the world of filmmakers thinking, not stand apart and judge it from outside.

There may be the faint outline of a particular "film culture" or cinephile culture (mine) etched into the pages that follow, but I never make that too explicit. If there's an underlying or subterranean form to this book, it arises discontinuously, in flashes – just as it might in the successive weeks of a classroom seminar, which is exactly how this project began: as a series of PowerPoint slides, some dating back over a decade. My mind works (as I have discovered) like a sequence of PowerPoint slides, bullet points and all.

I lay out the documents I have collected, present them, and annotate them in passing. Sometimes a text (like a film scene) requires slow, step-by-step or phrase-by-phrase reading and re-reading. At other times, I pick at morsels, out of chronology, like a magpie. I jump from one thing to another, across time, across nations, across forms, modes and genres. Hopefully, some themes will add up, gathering together in the swirl. As Samuel Fuller might have handwritten on its final page: *The end of this book can only be written by you!* And that's why it's short and punchy, composed in relatively brief fragments.

This book can be read as a stand-alone text, but it does not only stand alone. It arose from, and accompanied, an intensive, one-week lecture course that I gave annually at the Elías Querejeta Zine Eskola (Film School) in San Sebastián between 2019 and 2023. Within the curricular vision proposed by EQZE's director, Carlos Muguiro, this focus on "Filmmakers Thinking" was initially among the core subjects for all students. Now that the book is written and distributed to each new year's student intake, the course will evolve in different directions – which may, in the future, give rise to another book. And so it goes. I am deeply indebted to Carlos for this orientation within his overall pedagogical schema, and for choosing me to explore and convey it in my own personal way. In 2024, I am also now grateful to Paul Cronin of Sticking Place Books for offering a way for the book to be accessible to a wider, international audience.

To any reader who is not lucky enough to be enrolled in the wonderful institution of EQZE, I strongly recommend chasing up the films and scenes that are mentioned in the course of these chapters, and to view them closely and repeatedly, as we do in the classroom.

Introduction
The Filmmaker's Dialogue

In his 1997 essay "The Documentary World," German filmmaker Hartmut Bitomsky (born 1942) adapts anthropologist Claude Lévi-Strauss' notion that any artist is "engaged in a threefold dialogue." The first dialogue – the one with an audience, real or projected, is swiftly dismissed by Bitomsky as "confused and erratic," and thus hard to properly gauge or theorise about. Discussion of it, according to Bitomsky, can serve to pinpoint only a necessary and inevitable "element of unreconciled opposition and conflict" between artist and audience. Whether or not we agree with Bitomsky on this, let's stay with the drift of his thought – as we will endeavour to do with every filmmaker discussed in this book.

Bitomsky regards the next two types of dialogues as crucial for any filmmaker (not only documentarians, as his essay title might suggest). There is the dialogue with "the depicted things, the represented objects, the model… From a broad perspective, this is a dialogue with the world and with reality." Then comes what seems, at first, an uncontroversial and even unremarkable statement: a filmmaker is in dialogue with "the artistic material that the artist has, or does not have, at his disposal, the material that he must select or master."

But what are these materials exactly, what constitutes them? It is here that Bitomsky will stage a leap, and stake a greater claim. He begins with a simple, unarguable list – "For the filmmaker this artistic material consists of the camera, the lens, filters, light, sound and editing" – and then casually adds: "plus the whole history of film and all methods of making a film that exist or that do not yet exist."

The whole history of film, and all methods of making a film that exist or do not yet exist! This implicit injunction to all film artists truly boggles the mind in its far-reaching, even Utopian totality. Yet Bitomsky's statement seems to me to sum up, admirably, the theoretical interests and intentions of many filmmakers – the diverse thinking that is the subject of this book.

Filmmakers are concerned with the immediate tools (camera, microphone, editing equipment, etc.) and what can be done with them, expressed with them. That seems an eminently practical matter. At the same time, there are numerous, overarching possibilities already laid out for all of us by cinema history – as well as possibilities as yet unthought of, yet to be explored. Possibilities of form, format, structure, combination of diverse media, new technological capabilities and infrastructures – not to mention the ever-changing environment or atmosphere of the modern world that we intimately experience and process, that creates new perceptions and subjectivities.

This book is structured on the loose division between two kinds of "filmmaker thoughts." The first kind is what I call ideas *of* cinema: how an idea within a specific film project is arrived at, developed, worked through, executed. This is the realm of *craft* as well as of *art* in cinema; of *poetics* as the science of "how to make" something, not to mention the *poetry* of expression, meaning, emotion.

In my selection of texts and extracts to discuss, I have avoided what filmmakers are generally called upon to talk about – their own careers and lives – and aimed instead to extract those special passages where filmmakers dare to talk about their more general intuitions and explorations into the aesthetic principles of filmmaking. Not "rules" – for "there are no rules in cinema, and that's why we still love it," as Jean-Luc Godard has his alter ego Jerzy say in *Passion* (1982) – but provisional principles, working methods, experiments.

The second kind of filmmaker thought concerns ideas *about* cinema: the more general, theoretical, sometimes fantastic reflections to which many directors are attracted. What is cinema as a medium or art form, what elements constitute it, what has it done, what is still left for it to do or discover? Some filmmakers find themselves looking into a crystal ball to predict the future of cinema; if they are thus compelled, it is because they believe there are still possibilities it has not yet fulfilled.

In between, as a bridge between the two parts of the book, I have placed sample presentations/discussions of five filmmakers' Statements of Intention – documents (often invisible to the public) indicating how they conceived a project they intended to make (and, in almost every case, did). I find them particularly revealing of the true, sometimes secret thoughts and processes of filmmakers.

The theoretically inclined reflections of filmmakers (whether written, spoken or somehow assembled) are not always treated with respect or taken seriously. The assumption is often made that when a filmmaker such as Sergei Eisenstein, Agnès Varda or Raúl Ruiz speaks in general terms about cinema, they are really only speaking about their own films – or about themselves, their personal temperament and (perhaps eccentric) obsessions. The least charitable version of this account sees these directors involved in a furious act of self-promotion, "talking themselves up," creating the audience for their work and instructing it on how to react.

I reject this distinction. What filmmakers think about cinema comes from a special place that intermingles practical experience, constant reflection on their *métier*, and very often a lifelong cinephilia of loving, watching and critiquing films – even if that inner discourse is rarely expressed in the typical format of film reviews or analytical essays.

Moreover, I think that, even armed with the best of intentions, we must take care not to see filmmakers' thinking about cinema as *primarily* (or only) useful in elucidating their own styles and works. It is too easy, finally, to read (for instance) Godard on montage and then flash up some dazzlingly edited sequence from his own career, as an illustration of how he resolved his questions and preoccupations into a personal mode of making films. The greater and nobler challenge for us is to take what filmmakers think and apply it to the *cinema as a whole*, or specific traditions within it. And not necessarily the most seemingly "appropriate" traditions, either. The Russian theories of montage, for instance, can illuminate many things beyond strictly Russian films of the 1920s.

For the same reason, in this book I hold to the principle of only referring directly to filmmakers' thinking – not to secondary commentaries on, explications of, or critiques of their thought. So, there are almost no citations from film critics or theorists (which, in my own case, is very different from my previous books), and no recourse to well-worn, synoptic histories of cinema theory. (Therefore, you won't read much about André Bazin, Stanley Cavell or Christian Metz, except fleetingly.) At the same time, I have endeavoured, for each major piece cited, to situate its context, to give some sense of the history it inhabits.

Only one previous book, to my knowledge, has travelled any distance along the specific road chosen here – Jacques Aumont's excellent *Filmmakers' Theories* (2002), which exists in French and Spanish editions – but, as I am sure Aumont would agree, that work can now be extended in many directions, and with a much wider range of examples. For the realm of "theory by filmmakers" is sometimes reduced to a handful of weighty books – Eisenstein's *Film Form and The Film Sense*, Andrei Tarkovsky's *Sculpting in Time*, Ruiz's *Poetics of Cinema* series, Stan Brakhage's *Metaphors on Vision* – and some key essays by Maya Deren, Artavazd Pelechian, and a few others.

Yet not all filmmakers have an ambition to concretise their thoughts in the seemingly systematic form of a book (or several books) – a form we tend to (still) overrate in the hierarchy of culture and learning. Filmmakers express themselves, not all at the same rhythm, in various ways. Some (like Glauber Rocha) write manifestos; others (like Godard) call press conferences. Some develop a single lecture or short course that they present around the world to represent their ideas; Varda finally made a film, her last work, from her own lecture of this type. Some (such as Jacques Rivette and Luis Buñuel) look for a special interlocutor to transcribe, edit and shape their spoken thoughts on the page.

So, I propose widening this field to include all manner of publications and statements by filmmakers: memoirs, interviews, occasional reflections, catalogues, "artist books," blogs, teaching notes, scrapbooks, occasional invitations, award acceptance speeches, introductions to screenings, masterclasses, and working documents of various sorts, some accessible only in special archives. We often need to dig for the most profound reflections in the least likely and most ephemeral of places.

Sometimes, filmmakers – especially those of a terse or secretive temperament – tend to speak in shorthand formulations; or they compose texts comprised solely of seemingly discontinuous, poetic aphorisms (the most famous and influential book-length example being Robert Bresson's 1975 *Notes on the Cinematograph*). We must grant these condensed, high-voltage forms the honour of the imaginative, intellectual expansion they deserve.

I have sometimes even secretly smuggled in a nugget of wisdom that I learned while on festival jury duty in the company of a filmmaker – perhaps one not prone to writing, or to publicly sharing their thoughts on the work of their contemporaries. Such reticence within the industry is perfectly understandable (some filmmakers only agree to talk openly if they know it will not appear in print in their native language), so at times we need to decrypt the suggestive signs using whatever intuition we possess. Speculation, peppered with expressive anecdotes or a dash of gossip, can go a long way toward infiltrating the mind of a filmmaker. Both the creation and appreciation of film are thoroughly human processes, after all, and all the more pleasingly complex for that.

My survey is not systematic, and it is far from exhaustive. It does not aim for encyclopaedic balance (of nationality, gender, etc.), and it shamelessly betrays both some of my own cinephilic obsessions, as well as my individual limitations in terms of the world's multiplicity of languages. In a deliberate way, my selection of filmmakers to discuss could even be considered arbitrary; there are many others whose words I use in the classroom version of this work, and still others awaiting me, whom I've not yet looked into. This haphazard arrangement is intended as a provocation to all readers: go out and find your own, further examples!

All the same, the *Filmmakers Thinking* project does have a focus: to uncover not the memories of a filmmaker about their career, or their immediate impressions of one or other situation they find themselves in, but rather the *reflections* that have arisen from their multi-form engagement with cinema as both maker and spectator. Sometimes these reflections will be embryonic, a sketched trace of a thought, a glimmer of something that we can ourselves expand. At other times, we will discover, on inspection, that they are surprisingly deep, the fruit of a lifetime's engagement with film.

Source: *Hartmut Bitomsky Retrospective*, a catalogue booklet published by the Goethe Institute of Munich in 1997, edited by Bruno Fischli and Carola Ferber. Bitomsky's wide-ranging essay "The Documentary World" appears, in both German and English, pp. 10-19.

Part One
Ideas of Cinema

1
Ways of Invention

Sergei Eisenstein (1898-1948) offers us the special case of a filmmaker who reflected deeply on the process of filmmaking both before and after the fact of producing each of his works. He would frequently return, in his writing and teaching, to sequences from his own œuvre, but with a definite objectivity – almost as if they had been made by somebody else. At the same time, Eisenstein was able to enrich these analyses by plumbing the subjective dimension: stories of how a particular scene or detail came to be, as only he could tell the tale.

The following is a story of Eisenstein's *creative process* – a theme that will pop up again – as conveyed in an account of the making of his film *Alexander Nevsky* (1937). His term for creative process is "True Ways of Invention" (also translated as "true paths of discovery"), which provides the title for his 1946 text. We could also phrase it as the question: *where do cinematic ideas come from?* As with all the texts of filmmakers' thinking referenced in this book, it will be summarised, rearranged and cherry-picked in light of the points I wish to draw out. I recommend, in every case, a complementary reading of the entire text, referenced at the end of each chapter.

Nine years after completing *Nevsky*, Eisenstein traced the path of invention, by himself and co-writer Pyotr Pavlenko (1899-1951), of the figure of Ignat the armourer (played by Dmitry Orlov): "This is how, in an *organic* way, there arose the living traits of a new character in a work of art." The road to Ignat is a long and winding one indeed.

That is because, before Eisenstein and Pavlenko realised what function needed filling by such a character, they had to solve an entirely different narrative problem. The historic story of Nevsky depends upon a central, spectacular event: the Battle on the Ice. The military leader deployed a manoeuvre that was, at the time, novel and unprecedented: complete encirclement of the enemy (on ice), cutting it off and boxing it in, followed by a "pincer movement," an attack from both sides simultaneously.

It was, as legend has it, a "stroke of genius" on Nevsky's part. Yet the filmmaker was well aware that strokes of genius are very hard things to convincingly dramatise on screen. "We had to show a 'Newton's Apple' ... Such situations are extremely difficult to invent." Clearly, simply having the hero stand up and declaim "Eureka! I've just had a great idea!" will never do the trick. How to show the birth of an idea and its formation in somebody's head?

So Eisenstein appeals to the need to work through an "organic and effective process" in order to arrive at the best cinematic solution – to "live through the theme in your imagination" and "gradually crystallise the formula of the concept (thesis)." This solution will assuredly not be a plain "illustrative thesis"; Alexander cannot just see in his mind's eye the pincer movement on ice that he will later make reality.

Eisenstein and Pavlenko together seek a scene, a situation, an image. They start from the formulation "the wedge cuts stuck" – and then imagine an axe stuck in wood. "A good beginning," Eisenstein recalls. "But there the imagination trickled out. No colour in it. Not plausible. Both of us felt ashamed." The following day, they worked on the idea of "thin ice" – and arrived at the image of a cat breaking the ice with its weight. Another false step: "The stupidity of our reasoning was unbearable!" Eisenstein recounts that he could not sleep for days and, when he could, his nightmares were eloquent: "I imagined axes breaking ice, and cats stuck in wood."

Even in asides or jokes like these, Eisenstein is eloquent. We could say that he is silently correcting here the simplistic caricature one often reads of "Soviet montage" – that it is just a matter of editing-in an extraneous shot of an axe or a cat to heavily signal a metaphoric association external to the action. At the same time, Eisenstein is signalling the unconscious processes (dreaming, criss-crossing or jumbled-up associations) that are going to have to be respected if a genuine artistic solution is to be reached.

Then, the chance element of *serendipity* – which frequently plays a part in the creative process, and must also be respected – intervenes. In his insomnia, Eisenstein reaches for a beloved book of Russian folk tales, and re-reads "The Rabbit and the Fox." In this tale, the larger animal that is the hunter gets caught between two birch trees – allowing (in a splendidly vulgar punch line) the rabbit to circle back and penetrate the fox from behind, gloating with revenge! "How could I have forgotten one of my favourite tales?" the filmmaker wonders. (Recall that his own, somewhat infamous drawings are full of outrageous and fanciful erotic "puns" conveyed purely visually.) "I've got it!" His own Eureka moment.

Eisenstein and Pavlenko confer and decide that a character should *tell* this tale at a propitious moment in the film. Not Nevsky himself; he needs to *hear* this narration, thus receiving a "valuable hint." So now a new phase of the process begins: inventing the character of the tale-teller. This will be Ignat, dressed in a costume that suggests rabbit skin.

Ignat begins to take shape as a functional and also symbolic figure. He attains specificity as an armourer, someone who is *wiser* than the other soldiers around him. He will *always* speak in proverbs and tales: material to be judiciously spread throughout the script. (This is what Russian narratologists of the Formalist school referred to, in Eisenstein's time, as the process of *motivation*: not the psychological motivation of a character, but the "planting" and hence justifying of a motif.) Specifically, a scene early in the script is rewritten in order to give Ignat an "identifying" association: his armour is too short for his body. This detail, however, does double duty, because it prefigures the manner in which he will die, wounded in the spot that the armour does not cover. "The ridiculous might become tragic," comments Eisenstein.

This is, in itself, a dynamic aesthetic principle of changing both the function and mood of an object within the fiction: something pathetic (the armour) can become deadly serious. Italo Calvino commented sagely on this principle in literature (in his *Six Memos for the Next Millennium*), and it pertains equally to film.

> I would say that the moment an object appears in a narrative, it is charged with a special force and becomes like the pole of a magnetic field, a knot in the network of invisible relationships. The symbolism of an object may be more or less explicit, but it is always there. We might even say that in a narrative any object is always magic.

Eisenstein would surely have agreed with Calvino. For his mind, too, naturally moved from the particular creative instance to the general theoretical "lesson" that could be drawn from it; as Australian filmmaker and theorist Helen Grace (a noted Eisenstein expert) has observed, incidents that are first related as anecdotes can become "part of the invention of the method." Much of Eisenstein's writing and teaching was devoted to pursuing such lessons in method. "The pleasure of finding the needed image was so great that I almost completely missed the general lesson to be drawn from the experience." From an idea *of* cinema, he will move to an idea *about* cinema – indeed, about art as a whole. Yet on this level, also, Eisenstein will surprise us with his agility and inventiveness.

"We could achieve nothing while we sought to substitute plastic prototypes… for the plastic image of battle." In this context, plastic refers to elements that are visual, graphic, pictorial (such as a cat or an axe). "Then came a suggestion from material of another plane – a tale, a story." This corresponds to what would later become known as *lateral* thinking: a "moving sideways," a displacement from the seeming centre of a problem, in order to find an unexpected or unlikely solution. Eisenstein was a brilliant lateral thinker.

Eisenstein reaches the point of formulating (or discovering) what he calls an aesthetic *law*: "The suggestion must come from the dynamic scheme underlying facts or objects, not from the details themselves." Metaphors in a story cannot be too direct or illustrative; they must travel a path of poetic *inference*. They must leap from one level to another – as, in this instance, from the spoken word of Ignat to the mental idea or image inside Nevsky. Again, a lateral and multi-planar process.

Why should this be so? "If the facts of objects belong to a different plane, say, to the plane of sounds and not plastics, the sensation produced by the dynamic scheme becomes more poignant, the mind capable of translating it to another plane must be sharp, and the effect becomes stronger." Here, Eisenstein is evoking not only the mind of Nevsky as character or himself as creator; he is also saluting the (hopefully) agile mental activity of the spectator as he or she "puts the film together," across all its levels, as it unfolds. This is the spectator's share in creation.

Source: Sergei Eisenstein, *Notes of a Film Director*, published in 1970 by Dover in English, originally selected and assembled (as we are informed in Richard Griffith's introductory note) by Eisenstein himself in 1948, and bolstered in this edition by further, subsequently written selections made by the English translator, Xenia Danko. "True Ways of Invention" is on pp. 43-52. It has recently been reprinted (and re-translated) in the latest edition of Eisenstein's open-ended memoirs, *Beyond the Stars, Part 2: The True Paths of Discovery* (Seagull Books, 2018). Helen Grace's commentary on Eisenstein is at http://www.apparatusjournal.net/index.php/apparatus/article/view/242. The Calvino passage is taken from the second chapter, "Quickness," of his *Six Memos for the Next Millennium* (Penguin, 1988).

2
Preserving the Core

> How can you explain the way an idea for a film is born? When and where does it come from? What bumpy and mysterious route does it travel?
>
> Federico Fellini, 1980

In 1954, the great German-born director Max Ophüls (1902-1957) wrote an elegant, musing essay titled "The Pleasure of Seeing: Thoughts on the Subject Matter of Film."

> A film story only exists for me when I can visualise a succession of images. What prompts me to do so can be almost anything: a novel, perhaps a play, or even a poem. It can start with something that happened to me, or an event that someone recounts to me; it can start as a daydream, or it can come from a piece of music, or from looking at a picture. The inception of a vision is everywhere and nowhere at all.

In any event, a film story must come to be, in the course of its development, "unalterably fixed in a succession of images" within the mind of its director.

Italian cinema's *maestro* Federico Fellini (1920-1993) believed something very similar. In his remarkable *Making a Film* (1980)– a book that he was nudged to write by his collaborators in order to clean up a previous hodge-podge publication of his scattered interviews – Fellini takes us through what he calls the "mechanisms," or stages, whereby an initial idea eventually becomes a finished film.

Fellini regards the film in process as both *his* (belonging to him) and *not his* – in the sense that it detaches itself from him and becomes its own entity in the making, sometimes coaxing him, at other moments rejecting him. He enters into an ever-shifting and complicated game with it: a relationship constituted, at different phases, by seduction, aggression, indifference, surprise.

"What is a film in the beginning?" Fellini asks.

> A suspicion, a conjecture about a story, shadows of ideas, vague feelings. And yet in that first intangible contact the film already seems to be fully itself, complete, vital, and extremely pure. The temptation to leave it like that, in this immaculate dimension, is extremely strong: it would all be simpler, perhaps more just. But you can't...

Next comes, for Fellini, the fairly disagreeable phase of "agreements and contractual conditions" – the putting together of the finance for the production. But also for the director himself, who needs to go on making a living. Meetings are held; deals are struck. "Like a pimp, the film reveals its sinister character more and more: but it's captivating. It makes you pocket some money, and this provides some comfort."

The third phase is the screenplay – and Fellini is rightly suspicious of every process that threatens to reduce the richness of cinematic images and sounds (whether those already made, or those yet to be made) to a fixed, literary sequence of words. Yet there needs to be at least a basic map drawn up of the narrative possibilities inherent in the original idea. "It's the moment in which the film draws closer and pulls away," Fellini observes. "It's like the film is being pulled by its hair in this third phase, and it resists. You have to coax it somehow." He and his writing collaborators play a sort of hide-and-seek game with the task at hand: avoiding too serious work, dividing up the scenes for the different hands to script. (Another chapter in his book takes the monologue form of a freewheeling script "summary" addressed to Brunello Rondi, a co-writer on *8½* [1963].)

Fellini well knows that, in the end, a screenplay "has a literary rhythm anyway and a literary rhythm is different, incomparable to the cinematographic one." As John Boorman (born 1933) also cautions in his memoir *Conclusions* (2020): "Don't make the script too good." A filmmaker must not be too tempted by its literary quality on the page; the goal, eventually, is to find one's way back to what Fellini calls "those first images, not triggered by anything in particular," images that are "confused, contradictory, scornfully clear." Fellini concludes this part of the process: "I need a flexible screenplay, faint and at the same time very precise, where the ideas have finally become clear."

In the next phase, "I open an office." (This is a crucial, even magical moment for many filmmakers. Australia's Paul Cox [1940-2016] once advised young directors that, if you want to make a film, hire a room and put the project's title in large letters on the door. It *will* materialise.) For Fellini, opening an office means to begin lengthy pre-production; this is a joyous time for him, perhaps his favourite part, and he spends four pages evoking it. "The film opens up to all possibilities, it confronts all the unknown factors." He looks for striking faces, details of costumes, mannerisms of behaviour in the hundreds of people he observes in casting (which involves no ordinary auditions or script-readings); what he encounters at this phase may well end up changing certain characters or altering the course of the screenplay. It is a period in which Fellini feels free – indulging in the incessant drawing that he describes elsewhere in his book, his "graphic notes."

> It's a way of looking the film in the face, to see what kind of movie it is, the attempt to focus on something, however miniscule, bordering on insignificant, that nonetheless has something to do with the film and speaks to me about it in a mysterious way.

Eventually, this playful work, which could go on infinitely, meets a cold, hard, principle of reality: the looming production schedule. Now his visual ideas must find their preliminary, manifest, material form: the sets must be built, colours must be chosen, dimensions and perspectives must be fixed. It is a disturbing moment for Fellini. "Everything is losing its allusiveness…"; he loses faith in the film and (as he puts it) the film loses faith in him. Fellini stresses the importance of holding onto the initial idea: "I quixotically continue to defend the ambiguity, the blurred outlines, the temptations, the assumptions that controlled it, its vital right to be kept in a dimension of ideal accessibility."

It is most likely in this phase bridging pre-production and the very start of the shoot that many filmmakers generate the tool known, variously, as a workbook, image book, "lookbook" or ideas book. It tends to be a collage of written notes, quotations, and images: something that will communicate the director's "ideal projection" – impossible to fully express in a conventionally "literary" or verbal way – to his key collaborators in cinematography, production design, sound, and costume design. (We will return, in the middle of this book, to a related type of document, the Statement of Intention.) Bertrand Bonello has recently explained his own process in this regard.

> What I do, and while I'm writing [the screenplay], is that I keep a separate document that holds my notes. It's not a shot list. It's different. It's where I write questions – or answers – about a scene. For example, do I need one shot for the scene, or several shots? Am I close to the scene? Or am I far? Music, or not music? What kind of colour works for the scene? What is the heart of the sequence? What is the thing that I shouldn't miss when shooting? Is there something I am overlooking in order to understand the scene? So, I have this big, big document, like – I don't know – sixty pages that I give to my DP, continuity person, and assistants. And then we have all the questions we need to prepare the scene before shooting, including how do we deal with the space,

> the tempo, and stuff like that. I'm quite precise about all this… I do several drafts of this document.

Let us return to Fellini to round off his account of the entire filmmaking cycle. The first two weeks of shooting prolong the experience of Hell for him; "I endure them with a bitter taste of self-destruction, a suicidal thrill." But "one fine day," the filming becomes relaxed, familiar, enjoyable. "From that point on the film is a friend; the movie takes it upon itself to direct you who are directing it." The film must "invent itself step by step." During shooting Fellini refuses to watch the dailies, because he does not want to be haunted by any sense of discrepancy between the ideal image he holds within, and the external results coming out of the camera. "Having this continuous point of comparison to the movie you're really making, the film you wanted to make risks changing, fading, and might disappear altogether."

Fellini admits: "This cancellation of the movie you intended to make has to occur, sure, but only at the end of shooting, when in the projection room you'll accept the film you made and the fact that it's the only film possible." The gradual bringing to a close of the shoot has a ceremonial atmosphere, a ritual of slowly bidding adieu to his dream, and putting it aside forever. Fellini's appointed time to deal with the real, material film then happens in the editing room, the "moviola phase" as he calls it. "The relationship with the film becomes private, personal: I have to be alone with it and the editor." He is not without one, delightful regret: he sometimes wishes he could preserve the fully raw soundtrack, with the actors babbling nonsense, the sound of the crew at work, the whole "life on set" (think of Apichatpong Weerasethakul's fond ode to this sort of processual chaos in his 43-minute video *Worldly Desires* [2005]). Fellini also enjoys watching the film-assemblage completely silent.

But then another happy phase, collaborating with music score composer Nino Rota, begins; the final farewell to the finished product is not far away. "Now the film is complete," concludes Fellini. "I abandon it in irritation. I've never watched a film of mine again in a public movie theatre." In this, he is the opposite of Éric Rohmer who, his biographers tell us, liked to constantly re-watch all his films on videocassette, and enjoyed sharing that experience repeatedly with his closest friends.

Fellini is openly wary of most intellectual theorising about cinema, but he betrays a fine theoretical mind of his own in the following reflection.

> The translation of a fantasy (in the precise sense of a "phantasm," in other words something very precise but in a completely different dimension, light and impalpable) in plastic, solid, or physical terms is a delicate operation. Now the greatest appeal of these fantasies lies in the fact that they're undefined. By defining them you inevitably lose the dreamlike dimension, the air of mystery. You must plan on preserving it at all costs because the success of the operation, the proof of its viability, originality, its poetic outcome, lies precisely in managing to preserve as much as possible of that evocative, sincere, cropped, floating, blurred aspect there was in the imagined (fantastic) image.

The message to filmmakers – indeed, to any artist who must work in a collective team – could not be clearer: *preserve the core idea*. Andrei Tarkovsky (1932-1986) certainly believed so: "The problem has always been to keep the initial inspiration intact and unadulterated as the stimulus for work, and as a symbol of the finished picture" – he referred to this as the process of keeping a film firm to the "axle of its own idea." Even George Cukor (1899-1983), in his far more classical Hollywood context of the 1930s, held to this principle: the director is the person in the crew who maintains "the central line and integrity of purpose without which no work of art, nor even of efficient storytelling and entertainment-making, is possible."

Source: I am mainly quoting from Chapter XIII of Federico Fellini, *Making a Film* (Contra Mundum Press, 2015). Note that this is the only complete edition in English written and authorised by Fellini. Max Ophüls' essay "The Pleasure of Seeing" is translated into English in *Ophüls* (British Film Institute, 1978), edited by Paul Willemen, pp. 31-32. Bertrand Bonello's remarks are in the 2019 interview by Joe McElhaney and David Gerstner, "*Zombi Child* and the Spaces of Cinema," *Cineaste* magazine online exclusive at https://www.cineaste.com/spring2020/zombi-child-spaces-of-cinema-bertrand-bonello. Andrei Tarkovsky's words come from his book *Sculpting in Time* (see Chapter 23) and George Cukor's from his essay "The Director" reprinted in *Hollywood Directors 1914-1940* (Galaxy, 1976), edited by Richard Kozarski, pp. 322-331.

3
Metaphors, Fields, Semantic Maps, and Horizons of Reference

How should we read the statements of filmmakers? Beyond their evident or suggested propositional content, we need to become – as in the approach to any text, written or audiovisual – detectives. In particular, detectives of history, of the historical context that informs any statement. In this brief methodological interlude, I want to suggest four recurring tropes worth attending to in all the material we are examining, whether dating from the recent, familiar present or the distant, alien past.

First task: to be aware of the *metaphors* that filmmakers invariably use to describe, illustrate and incarnate their reflections on the cinematic medium. Often a very different set of metaphors from one practitioner to the next. Metaphors are sometimes looked down on as illusions, masks, lies or deceptions, as if the pure, unadorned reality of things could simply be touched – but nothing could be further from the truth. Metaphor is a principal form of poetic reflection, and filmmakers naturally love to use it. (I will continue to use metaphor as the umbrella term for all constructions of this sort: analogy, simile, symbol, comparison, homology, etc. – you can sort out those distinctions yourself, if you believe they are useful.)

We need to learn to recognise certain clusters or "families" of metaphor. Some filmmakers like to use nature metaphors (such as the four elements: earth, water, air and fire); others prefer science metaphors (from all possible branches of science). There are architectural metaphors and bodily metaphors; linguistic metaphors and thermodynamic metaphors; psychoanalytic metaphors and spiritual-religious metaphors; animal metaphors and landscape metaphors. The list is truly endless, and open to perpetual reinvention by anyone who thinks, speaks, writes or makes films. Metaphors are truly the lifeblood of filmmakers' thinking.

Every time a metaphor is deployed, it is a vital clue as to where a filmmaker is "coming from," the basic premise from which they conceive cinema and their relation to it – their essential *world-view*. Our role, at least in the first instance, is not to judge or critique the orientation suggested, in each case, by these metaphors – but to perceive it, extend it, follow it out as far as it will go. To inhabit that world of their imagination.

Another way to help us chart this world is the tool of the *semantic map*. It is a simple tool, but it can reveal much about a filmmaker's thinking. So, task number two: to figure out the list of "opposing terms," set into a diagrammatic, binary formation, that a director tends to use. These oppositions are not necessarily where they will arrive or conclude in their reflection, but it is the point from where they start – and from where, perhaps, all thinking starts, on its (hopeful) path to complexity. Pier Paolo Pasolini distinguishes the cinema of poetry from the cinema of prose; Maya Deren defines horizontal and vertical dimensions; Jacques Rivette opposes the "secret" to the "law." When we bolster each side of a semantic map with all the metaphors and adjectives that accrue to it – day/night, strong/weak, natural/artificial, and so on – we begin to get a vivid sense of their orientation.

Our third task is to identify, to imaginatively reconstitute and occupy, the historical *field* in which a filmmaker stands at the moment they utter their statement in public or commit their thoughts to the page. (A field could also be called a context, but I prefer the spatial, cinematic images of maps, fields and horizons!) How old are they at the moment of making their statement (biological age has no fixed psychological characteristics, but it's important to know if the speaker is 20 or 60)? At what point of their career are they – beginning, middle, end? What is going on around them in their immediate social environment? What cultural movements are they affiliated or associated with? Who are their personal comrades (and did that connection last the test of time and the changing tides of history)?

And then: what movements are our filmmakers *against*, what forms do they regard as outmoded, what perceived tendency do they resist? Sometimes the "enemy," the feared or despised Other, whether human ("the bourgeoisie") or cultural ("realism") or media-specific ("theatre"), will only be an implied presence in the text. Sometimes the Other is a specific individual who stands for something (fairly or not) that is abhorrent in the filmmaker's mind – and if *not* named or cited at all beyond faint allusion (as Isou, for example, shuns all mention of Bazin), then the insult is all the greater! We may need to speculate, to sniff out details such as these like a guard dog. Our ultimate goal is to arrive at a snapshot of the filmmaker's personal "culture."

Fourth task: what I call the *horizon of reference* that any filmmaker draws upon in their specific time and place, and in their individual experience. The horizon that "wraps around" them – and that they draw into themselves. This is closely related to the general field notion just proposed, but it is more specific. Here, it's a matter of the explicit *references* or allusions that the artist makes – sometimes perfectly clearly, sometimes only cryptically: names dropped, works mentioned, movements and eras gestured toward.

These citations can cover a vast field: everything from a film, exhibition or TV program just viewed and a book just read, to whatever was in all the newspapers that week, or a distant, associative, involuntary memory that has somehow been mysteriously triggered. Some of these references, like distant stars, will have become extraordinarily obscure by the time they reach us today, and may require due research to re-illuminate their once-upon-a-time significance. Political and social references may also (given the filmmaker) play a major role on this horizon – recall, for example, how often Pedro Almodóvar (born 1949) has declared: "Each time I begin a new movie, I try to imagine how the story would go if Franco had never existed."

Our task here is not simply to enumerate (or ferret out) these diverse references but also, in each case, to intuit – if we can – the logic or coherence of the whole horizon line. What picture does it add up to?

Metaphor, field, semantic map, horizon of reference: four heuristic tools that will aid our *historical imagination* – a tool that is itself also richly useful in order to understand our present day.

4
What is Cinema? The Most Essential Things

There is one crucial area where "ideas of cinema" and "ideas about cinema" overlap in the thinking of filmmakers: the way every one of them posits – explicitly or implicitly – what they consider the *most essential elements* of the medium of cinema. In a sense, this constitutes their response, different in every case, to André Bazin's immortal question: *what is cinema?*

To map this zone, we can begin with the simplest distinctions and proceed, by degrees, to the most complex. For many filmmakers, for instance, the *image* – the visual realm – is the most essential aspect of cinema. For others (such as Lucrecia Martel, Chantal Akerman or Abigail Child), *sound* is equally, and possibly more, important. Often, we will discover such opinions at the level of *assumptions* – things that a filmmaker simply takes for granted, rather than spelling them out as a unified or conscious theory *per se*.

If a director assumes, for instance, that "cinema is storytelling" – that there is (or should be) no kind of cinema *beyond* storytelling – that is because the culture around him or her assumes this, and has ingrained it as a common sense idea. Like any of us, filmmakers emerge from a sometimes restricted field of reference and experience. We don't necessarily need to criticise them for that (within their own framework, they may ponder conventional assumptions sincerely, deeply and revealingly), but it does help us to detect and identify the particular tracks along which they are travelling.

As we shall see in the second half of this book, some filmmakers make the more properly theoretical move of attempting to define what makes cinema *specifically cinematic* by enumerating its major elements. Here, assumptions are brought to the surface, laid out, presented and justified as a system. When Sergei Eisenstein, for instance, worked in the last years of his life toward the elaboration of a *General History of Cinema* (the notes and drafts for which have been recently translated and published in English), he had a grand, global system of the history of art, media and aesthetic forms in his head, from cave paintings and the first musical instruments to the gradual invention of film.

To begin, let's take three very different examples of directors who have stated – in an abbreviated, even laconic fashion – what were, for them, the most essential elements of cinema: Luchino Visconti (1906-1976), Alfred Hitchcock (1899-1980) and George Miller (born 1945).

At the age of 37, in 1943 (still relatively early in his film career), Visconti composed a brief statement on what he termed "Anthropomorphic Cinema" – cinema based, above all, on the human element.

> I was impelled toward the cinema by, above all, the need to tell stories of people who were alive, of people living amid things and not of the things themselves. The cinema that interests me is an anthropomorphic cinema.

This conviction led Visconti to one of the most famous statements of his life – virtually a manifesto of a certain type or ideal of cinema.

> I could make a film in front of a bare wall, if I was able to find the true material of humanity to place against this naked, cinematographic element: find it, and tell it.

Is there a note of provocative, polemical or poetic exaggeration in Visconti's vision of anthropomorphic cinema? Undoubtedly. Even in his 1940s, neo-realist period (*Ossessione* [1943] and *La terra trema* [1948]), Visconti rarely reduced a scene to simply placing a single actor in front of a bare wall. And in the stage and screen works he went on to make for the rest of his life, from *Senso* (1954) to *L'innocente* (1976), the lush, baroque, often deliberately smothering décor is a key part of his artistic and social intent, as Glauber Rocha (1938-1981) and other commentators quickly grasped. But let us not read Visconti so literally or programmatically here. His point is clear, and he takes it in intriguing directions.

> The most humble gestures of man, his bearing, his feelings, and instincts are sufficient to make the things that surround him poetic and alive. The significance of the human being, his presence, is the only thing that could dominate the images. The ambience that it creates and the living presence of its passions give them life and depth. And its momentary absence from the luminous rectangle gives to everything the appearance of a *nature morte*.

The emphasis is strong, and this manifesto-like statement was presumably launched by Visconti in reaction to other trends in modern art that he found repellent or objectionable: to assert that "the human being, his presence, is the only thing that could" – or should – "dominate the images," implies that another wave in cultural production was devaluing the human being and, inversely, overvaluing the world of "things," props, objects, buildings (a decade or so later, he might have aimed this critique at his compatriot Michelangelo Antonioni or the French New Novelists like Michel Butor and Alain Robbe-Grillet).

As it happens, the "actor in front of a bare wall" functions as a phantom ideal, a kind of vanishing point in Visconti's own cinema. We can momentarily glimpse it, for example in the slinky dance of Silvana Mangano in his episode of the anthology film *The Witches* (1967): for a brief passage there are only the actor's movements and gestures before an indistinct background. But where that scene eventually goes indicates the other, reverse side of Visconti's creative sensibility. His allusion in 1943 to *nature morte*, the painting genre of "still life" in English but, literally, "dead nature," points to what will become a genuine and generative obsession in his work: death, decay, ageing, literal and physical corruption. This is, in his increasingly dark vision, the other side of youth, beauty and "purity" – including his stated ideal of pure cinema.

Visconti brushed over the question of how to convert the ideal spectacle of an actor before a wall into a fully fleshed-out narrative – the "telling," as he puts it, of the "true material of humanity" (although we will see later how other filmmakers have literally generated a story from such a primal, guiding image). For Hitchcock, by contrast, story values are the main thing he addresses in his 1939 lecture at Radio City Music Hall on "melodrama and suspense." Already, at the end of the British phase and beginning of the Hollywood phase in his career (he was 40 in 1939), Hitchcock had become well known, at least in industrial and educational circuits of the film world, both as an entertaining showman and a "master" of craft secrets in his favoured crime-thriller-mystery genre. For instance, he preached – as Billy Wilder also practised – the notion that "your film must end on its highest note. Then it is stopped," which is a far cry from many dribbling-out endings in today's mainstream cinema (especially in tele-movies). It is always fascinating to observe exactly when the best conventions of yesteryear suddenly seem unreal, artificial or contrived – or, as in this case, too abrupt – for the sensibility of contemporary practitioners.

Hitchcock begins his 1939 lecture with an arresting formulation governing "the method one invariably uses in designing a motion picture script" – and of the ideal *shape* that a film should trace from conception to execution to ultimate reception. He cautions against wanting to somehow capture or translate the density of a rich novel; instead, one should begin from a single page summary of the plot and action – particularly identifying what we might call its central *motor* (e.g., as in several Hitchcock films, mistaken identity). Filmmakers should "build up" from that skeleton, not scale down from *War and Peace*.

After the film has been made and seen, Hitchcock reasons, and one prospective viewer asks another "What's it about?," the summary that emerges spontaneously from the spectator's mouth should (if all has gone well) very closely approximate the content of that original page – indeed, it is "what you should have had on the piece of paper in the very beginning." He concludes this point: "That is the complete cycle I like to aim for, as far as possible, and that is the process one works on in designing a motion picture script."

Hitchcock took the *motion* in that term "motion picture" very seriously indeed. Looking back nostalgically to the silent era, he praised the genre of melodrama because of "its obvious physical action and physical situation. After all, the words 'motion picture' mean action and movement." By contrast, in the sound cinema of the 1930s, "we have lost what has been – to me, at least – the biggest enjoyment in motion pictures."

For his entire career, Hitchcock practised what he himself described as "the wrong thing to do" – at least in conventional definitions of dramatic construction. He chose to decide upon specific "backgrounds and incidents" *first*, before building up the chain of character motivations and cause-and-effect linkages. This was a challenge that often drove his hired scriptwriters crazy. Hitchcock's example, from his own filmography, is of the original *The Man Who Knew Too Much* (1934).

> In *The Man Who Knew Too Much*, I said: "I would like to do a film that starts in the winter sporting season. I would like to come to the East End of London. I would like to go to a chapel, and to a symphony concert at the Albert Hall." […] [It must] appear to be quite natural that all the events have taken place in those settings because it was necessary for them to do so.

In cinema history, the opposite of stereotyped characters has usually been posed as "three-dimensional" characters (as understood within a 20th-century framework of psychological motivation and free will), operating within a naturalistic context of events (life as it "ordinarily" flows). Hitchcock displays an ambivalent relation to psychological characterisation of the modern kind (as his "spectacle first" method shows) – part of a code of *realism* that is another *sine qua non* for many mainstream filmmakers, especially post 1960. Hitchcock commented that, from the "cardboard figures" or stereotypes of silent cinema, we have evolved (by 1939) to "more delineation of character," and "obviously, in the long run, that is what we are going to rely on." In fact, Hitchcock came to rely more on an element he doesn't mention here, as it may have de-emphasised his own creative role: the given personae of great movie stars like Cary Grant and Grace Kelly. A star in cinema is something between a two-dimensional figure (a *type*) and a dramatically individualised, three-dimensional personality.

In the effort to *combine* action and character, however, we must not (according to Hitchcock) rely too heavily on spoken *dialogue*. "The two rhythms – of action and dialogue – are entirely different. The problem is to try and blend these two things together." Hitchcock issues a stern warning: modern psychological novels and plays, in his judgement, have "a tendency to abandon story" – whereas, in popular cinema, "we do need a lot of story."

Many filmmakers, including Fritz Lang and Billy Wilder, grappled with this challenge of blending action and characterisation during the classical period of Hollywood cinema (roughly 1920 to 1960). Some (including Josef von Sternberg) more or less ignored it as a problem by embracing high artifice, or finding their own, distinctive path into modernity (as Samuel Fuller did). Comedy filmmakers (Ernst Lubitsch, Frank Tashlin, Howard Hawks, Jerry Lewis) were able, right up to the mid-1960s, to successfully balance visual and physical gags with verbal humour – we are still far, in that period, from the overwhelming, often baleful influence of television situation comedy (almost completely reliant on dialogue) on film or, at the other extreme, the more freewheeling, experimental approaches to fluctuating comic/dramatic tone pioneered by Elaine May (born 1932) and other giants of her generation.

What Hitchcock, in his preferred genres (action, adventure, crime-thriller-mystery, horror) added to sheer action and movement was the surplus value of *suspense* and *intrigue*. His justification for this was the necessity of "keeping the audience occupied mentally." As in the classes of Alexander Mackendrick (see Chapter 7), sheer involvement in the unfolding plot, or even close identification with fictional characters, was not enough for Hitchcock; there had to be another level of engagement to hook that part of the viewer's brain which is more detached, wandering off, evaluating the streaming, variegated mass of the film's details. On this point, Hitchcock was decades ahead of many commentators (including scriptwriting gurus) on the nature of the storytelling process. *Immersion* in the screen was not a supreme value for Hitchcock, as it is for many today; he conceived the mental (cognitive) activity of the viewer a bit differently. In modern parlance, we could well say that Hitchcock's precise target was the perennially "distracted" spectator.

In fact, deploying a splendid metaphor, Hitchcock described the relation of film to viewer as the former supplying the stimulation of drugs to the latter in order to keep them awake: "The audience gets tired after an hour, so it needs the injection of some dope"! The imagery of dope injection returns Hitchcock to his more-or-less "mechanical" starting point of "action, movement and excitement."

Let's compare Hitchcock's attitude with that of a contemporary director of spectacular cinema: George Miller. The first *Mad Max* film was made spontaneously and intuitively in 1979 but, once that film became an international success and he travelled the world, Miller was exposed to a level of theorising about narrative that he eagerly embraced, and even "institutionalised" within his own working practice at the company Kennedy Miller.

Beginning with *Mad Max 2* (aka *The Road Warrior*) in 1981, film narratives were no longer considered by Miller and his collaborators as simply sensational, popular entertainments within neatly defined movie genres (like action, science fiction or Western); they were universal, timeless *myths* of heroes and quests as described within the framework laid out by literary analyst Joseph Campbell and his many acolytes. Other filmmakers, including John Boorman (*Zardoz*, 1974) and George Lucas (the *Star Wars* cycle), have also come under the influence of this orientation.

For Miller, immersion and emotional involvement are indeed the goals of filmmaking today. He declares: "You can't, for instance, do anything to exclude the audience, such as being esoteric, introspective or self-indulgent" – a stance that, logically, excludes a great deal of non-mainstream cinema. Like Hitchcock, Miller aims for the spectacular excitement of "great dramatic events" – just witness the car-chase set-pieces in all the *Mad Max* films – and he is deeply aware of their effect on an audience.

However, whereas Hitchcock's idea of the audience tends to be an assortment of canny individuals, Miller opts for what he calls the "collective rhythm" of a mass crowd. Indeed, his central comparison for the kind of cinema he makes is with grand theatrical events (like circus and opera) and stadium-size musical performances. In this model, the audience is intoxicated, fused into a single, collective entity – part of the Campbellian appeal to (one understanding of) Carl Jung's notion of the "collective unconscious."

Miller gives few interviews that allow much real insight into his rigorous working methods (particularly at the script level), and he does not write essays or books about his creative process. He believes in the value of a certain professional secrecy (as many filmmakers do) and keeps his distance from industrial and cultural organisations devoted to cinema. However, near the end of the 1980s, he and his colleagues did open up and offer (in a series of candid interviews) some tantalising indications.

Miller and his professional partner Byron Kennedy (died 1983) set up an in-house "collaborative laboratory" that Miller described as "an ongoing investigation into the nature of drama," so a general or theoretical ambition is evident there. Classic Hollywood films were closely studied, as was the work of Akira Kurosawa. More particularly, every original script idea within Kennedy Miller (renamed Kennedy Miller Mitchell since 2009, to incorporate Doug Mitchell) is workshopped intensively, pulled apart, rewritten, combined with other possibilities; there is no "ownership" or sovereignty of concepts, and people within the company can switch roles. Miller's resident dramaturg Nico Lathouris, for example, assigned to work with the actors in early productions after himself appearing in the first *Mad Max*, eventually became credited co-writer of *Fury Road* (2015) and *Furiosa* (2024).

Miller likened his company's collective creative process to that of Steven Spielberg's Amblin Entertainment or (to a lesser extent) Roger Corman's B movie companies since the 1950s. Other examples could be cited in Steven Soderbergh's projects for film and television, Sergio Leone's career, or the many teams in Hong Kong cinema (such as Johnnie To's Milkyway). In Hollywood, we tend to think of a credit to many screenwriters as a sign of conflict, discord, brutal revision, but it is common in Italy or Hong Kong to have teams of half-a-dozen writers, with individuals sometimes having responsibility over particular areas (dialogue, plot construction, characterisation, etc.). Even a highly identifiable "art cinema auteur" such as Philippe Garrel uses this method today (women write the female roles, a novelist brings in their perspective, Jean-Claude Carrière is mindful of overall cinematic structure, and so on).

In the 1980s, Miller proclaimed: "I think there are almost rules you can use to define" cinematic drama. He didn't spell them all out, but he did offer this nugget as an example.

> You have to very early on find some common ground and then lead the audience into the world of the drama – what we call "weaving the circle." And pretty soon they become one with the screen.

Miller is here referring to a narrative technique that Pascal Kané analysed in depth during his years as a critic, before he made the transition to filmmaking: what he calls the detached or initially *uninscribed* hero, who is outside of the social situation he or she witnesses, but gradually enters into it, becoming a part of it – in the process, changing both themselves and that world. The mythically ambitious *Mad Max* films, beginning with part 2, fit this model perfectly – with the added twist, borrowed from Westerns, that the hero will usually walk away at the end and thus "uninscribe" themselves, preparing the way for another sequel. Many political dramas also depend on an "innocent" or uncommitted central figure finally arriving at a crucial moment of "raised consciousness"; the same is true of LGBTQ tales in which a character eventually discovers and admits to their true sexual orientation. Just as in Miller's model, this provides a point of identification for the viewer, and a gradual "awakening" of awareness. The circle between film and spectator is thus woven.

Source: Luchino Visconti's essay-manifesto on anthropomorphic cinema first appeared in the magazine *Cinema*, no. 173/174 (September/October 1943). Hitchcock's 1939 lecture is available at https://the.hitchcock.zone/wiki/Lecture:_Radio_City_Music_Hall,_New_York_City_(30/Mar/1939) and in the book *Hitchcock on Hitchcock* (Faber and Faber, 1995), edited by Sidney Gottlieb, pp. 267-274. The interviews with Miller and his collaborators (including writer Terry Hayes) are in *Back of Beyond: Discovering Australian Film* (UCLA catalogue, 1988), edited by Scott Murray.

5
Origin Tales

Closely related to the question "What is cinema?" is another, more fanciful one: "Where did cinema begin?" This is not the strictly historical inquiry of "*When* did cinema begin?" When filmmakers rhetorically ask "Where did cinema begin?" – and then proceed to answer – they are not asking literally when the first camera was cranked, or when the first frames flickered into life through a projector. It is another way of defining *real* cinema – the *essence* of cinema, as each filmmaker sees it – by appealing to the moment, recorded or unrecorded in the history books, when the cinema grasped its truest vocation.

In other words, we are dealing with an *origin tale*, usually couched in the language of myth: "One day someone picked up a camera and pointed it at [*fill the blank*]... [or:] One day, someone juxtaposed two photographs on a table top... [or:] The first time that a child accidentally flipped a series of drawings in their hands, giving life to an animated movement... On that day, cinema was born!"

In some origin tales, the birth of cinema begins even before cinema – in what is known, amorphously, as *pre-cinema*. And this pre-cinema exists wherever you can convincingly find or imagine it. For example, in the shadows that long ago conjured the movements and stories of figures: the shadows projected on the wall of Plato's Cave that chained prisoners were cursed to watch, or the puppet-shadows of Balinese theatre, or the humble family games in which people form animal figures with their hands and use a handy torch or lamp to throw and exaggerate those figures upon a surface.

Whichever story or image is chosen will highlight one particular element at the root of cinema as a medium: its propensity to tell stories, or to show bodies in movement, or to materialise our nightly, unconscious dreams...

Sergei Eisenstein devoted the last years of his life to sketching out the epic project of a *General History of Cinema*. He intuited the pre-history of the cinematic apparatus in what seem to be the least likely forms and places: in the ornamental designs of ancient architecture or a belt for the waist (like successive frames of a film strip); in the structure of musical percussion; in the elaborate *mise en scène* of a religious procession; or in the montage of materials woven into a Persian rug. Wherever Eisenstein found evidence of *seriality* – of a repeated pattern of motifs, slightly varied as they proceed – he saw signs of the cinematic medium waiting to be born.

In both his video *Scénario du film Passion* (1982) and in his multi-part *Histoire(s) du cinéma* (1988-1998), Jean-Luc Godard evokes a legendary era in the early days of silent filmmaking. This mythic tale told by Godard sits somewhere between a tall story, a fable and a joke – it may even have some slim basis in anecdotal truth. Accordingly, it is now available (like the "immortal story" of Isak Dinesen and Orson Welles) for anybody to expand or contract at will. I shall now retell it in my own way.

So, cast your imaginations back to the moment when cinema is still young and fresh. There are no rules, and few conventions. The legendary "King of Comedy" Mack Sennett (1880-1960) would head out each day with his crew and cast. They would find a nice spot in the Californian sunshine and start making up gags, bits of business. They never had much of an idea of how the improvisations and inventions of one day would fit with those of the next day – that is the kind of logic they made up as they went along.

Soon enough, behind Sennett followed an earnest accountant. He had been sent by the head office of the studio that was financing this madcap adventure in filmmaking. The accountant would trail behind making expenditure notes – "Demolition of a car, 500 dollars," "Payment for a crowd of extras, 300 dollars" – and so on. The accountant would go home each night and put these notes in order – an order of days and of scenes. He would write at the top of each page indications like: "Daytime – car chase scene – garbage dump." Everything arrived at by chance for Sennett & co. duly became a matter of record.

Naturally enough, the studio, via the accountant, then started leaning on Sennett to *foresee* what expenditure he would incur each day. "What scene do you think you'll shoot tomorrow, Mack?" When Sennett started grudgingly responding to these questions and figuring out in advance what he would shoot, rather than just making it up on a whim, the accountant thrust his own ordered pages in front of the director and instructed him: "Lay it out like this – write on the top: Scene 3 – outdoors – love scene – front porch – late afternoon." And then Sennett was encouraged to write a little more by way of explicit scene instructions – so that everyone involved in production (art director, props director, actors, and so on) would know beforehand exactly what they had to do, how much it would cost, and how to plan for it.

The day that Sennett acquiesced to all these demands, according to Godard, marked the historic beginning of that odd form of writing that the film industry calls the *screenplay*. An official document in writing, or (in Godard's terms) an ominous Law engraved in stone. And when that happened, in his view, cinema lost some of its original innocence and metamorphosed into yet another routine in the Society of Control.

Portuguese director Pedro Costa (born 1958) recycles Godard's story of creativity and accounting in his various masterclasses and interviews. But he goes further still, crafting his own, fanciful vision of film history. His origin tale sets out to prove that there is no distinction between fiction and documentary cinema, other than the one we artificially impose with our financing and marketing categories. "What the cinema does really well, what it has as its ultimate function, in the first place isn't artistic or aesthetic." Cinema is a primal *gesture* for Costa, and the "primary function" of the medium is "to make us feel that something isn't right." *Disquiet* – and the communication of that feeling of unease to the spectator – is cinema's essence.

When and where did it all begin? In an imaginary moment: "The cinema, the first time it was seen or filmed, was for showing something that wasn't right." He traces this origin back to still photography, and links the cinematograph indelibly with this "very realist basis" of capturing and reproducing a trace of the world. The technological tool, here, is important: Costa does not liken the cinema to painting a landscape, composing a sonata or writing a poem. A machine must intervene in order to enable the 20th-century process of cinema.

> Somebody took a machine in order to reflect, to think and to question. For me, there is in this gesture, this desire – be it the gesture to make a film or a photograph, or today to make a video – there is in this gesture something very strong, something which says to you: "Don't forget."

This, too, as in Godard's tale, is a moment of innocence – even if it is innocence in distress at what is about to be lost. In Costa's view, when "fiction is born" in cinema, then "things deteriorate, go awry, become complicated." That first gesture, "this first act of love," is gone, compromised, sold out. It becomes an object of pained nostalgia, because (as Costa lyricises) "the first gesture, the first film, the first photograph, the first love, is always the strongest, always the one that we don't forget." In Chapter 26, considering the writings of Jean Epstein, we shall encounter a similarly gloomy account of the birth of fiction as a precipitous Fall from cinema's Eden. The Biblical scenario of sin, shame and drop from grace provides an excellent, indeed inexhaustible template for origin tales.

Elaborating his theory – the inspiration for his own approach and practice as a filmmaker – Costa arrives at a position that is closer to the "artistic or aesthetic" bias he initially put aside. He describes fiction in cinema as "always a door that we want to open or not – it's not a script." A film should not only exist to show us easily recognisable things, to flatter our own sensibilities as in a mirror. There has to be an element of discretion, of the secret or hidden

– intermingled with that sensation of primordial disquiet, even horror.

So, there has to be an ever-present sense that a film can *deny* things to the spectator, not only unveil them. "The spectator can only really *see* a film if something on the screen resists him." He attributes to D.W. Griffith the discovery of this ethical approach, because Griffith "saw that the cinema could show things that everybody knows, that everybody wants to recognise and, at the same time, not show certain things which are very violent, which must be hidden."

Later masters of the art – Robert Bresson, Carl Dreyer, John Ford, Kenji Mizoguchi – will develop what Costa refers to as a "closed door" effect that is fundamental to the cinema that he values. "Starting from here, it's going to be so unbearable that there's not even a film. After this closed door, a film is no longer possible, it's terrible, so don't come in. It's a closed door for you."

The various strands of Costa's reflection – apprehending disquiet and shutting doors – come together when he concludes: "The more I close the doors, the more I'm going to have the spectator against me, perhaps against the film, but at least he will be, I hope, uncomfortable and at war. That is, he will be in the uneasy situation of the world."

Somewhat paradoxically (given his evident anti-spectacular leaning), Costa also appeals to the innocence of the earliest erotic or frankly pornographic films. Because, at least, they functioned, like the best Mack Sennett comedies, without screenplays! "The first films without a script, thus documentary, are vaguely amateur films, vaguely secret, pornographic." They show the raw "gesture of love," without need of any imposed, exterior plot. It would be possible to compile a hefty dossier of filmmakers who (especially in recent decades) have indicated pornography to be, in their minds, the purest, highest or most ideal type of cinema – the roll-call would include Lars von Trier, Gaspar Noé and Australian avant-gardist Ken Shepherd, all of whom made some headway on realising (how well or authentically, you be the judge) their own, ultimate "sex films." But the most eloquent of them all is Philippe Grandrieux (born 1954).

Grandrieux evokes the birth of cinema in a different way to Costa. It does not begin with the pointing of a camera at some beloved object or creature of the world, but in the scientific experiments of *movement analysis* carried out by pioneers including Étienne-Jules Marey (1830-1904), Lucien Bull (1876-1972) and Georges Demenÿ (1850-1917), with its gradual animation or superimposition of successive photographic snapshots. "Chronophotography. Horse, birds, man, woman. It runs, it jumps, it flies and it starts again."

Then the commercialisation of these scientific findings begins, but Grandrieux does not find the results immediately contemptible – for they are still well below the watermark of civilised, bourgeois respectability. Combining management-systems analysts Frederick W. Taylor and Henry Ford with Sigmund Freud and Antonin Artaud, gastronomy with transportation, the Marquis de Sade with techniques of theatrical staging, Grandrieux celebrates the entry of pornography into cinema.

> And immediately, the pornographic use, for cinema is the industry of bodies. Our great-grandmothers suck and are humped in the kitchen. The smell of soup and fucking, that is the smell of the century of the locomotive and the unconscious. […] An assembly of bodies, *mise en scène*, the script of cinema was de Sadean from the beginning.

Just as Costa did, Grandrieux goes on to envision the kind of cinema he is compelled to make. Less severe and controlled than Costa's, it is a cinema of intensities, sensations, perceptual chaos and confusion (see Chapter 15). Now all the arts can be called to the cause, for the conceptual models and raw material they provide for inspiration in the churning, organic ocean of cinema: painting, music, performance, writing, dance, lighting, costume, make-up. Plus, once again, the decisive role of technology, where machines enter into a reciprocal, unpredictable choreography with human bodies.

> [French painter Edward Degas] fabricated, blindly and slowly, cinema. And he invents it just as de Sade did before him. He shows us the way: cinema is made (above all) with the hands, with the skin, with the entire body, by fatigue, by breath, by the pulsations of the blood, the rhythm of the heart, by muscles. Body and sensation, that is the machine, its absolute power, its obsession. That is its becoming. Invented bodies, comical, grotesque, obscene, the improbable bodies of the stars and the monsters, and light, its palpitation, and the beating of the shots, and in us, fear joy, hope, sadness, the obscure deployment of human passions.

Grandrieux's tale of cinema is more libidinal than Costa's. Like Pier Paolo Pasolini (see Chapter 24), he embraces a savage reality of the world, as well as the core animality of humanity. But Grandrieux and Costa do intersect on the matter of fundamental disquiet.

> The future of cinema is to be free and great and strong, to transmit some of that "windy chaos" that we tend to protect ourselves from, as if we desperately wanted to believe that the world is ordered, reasonable, possible, when it's exactly the opposite: chaotic, delirious, untenable, driven by the unstoppable force of desire. Beyond will and morality, the world is what we desire, absolutely. Terribly.

Source: Sergei Eisenstein's *Notes for a General History of Cinema*, written between 1946 and 1948, was compiled in 2016 for Amsterdam University Press by Naum Kleiman and Antonio Somaini. Pedro Costa's Tokyo masterclass of 2004 has been transcribed as "A Closed Door That Leaves Us Guessing" in *Rouge* magazine: http://www.rouge.com.au/10/costa_seminar.html. Philippe Grandrieux's text "About the 'Insane Horizon' of Cinema" (2000) can be found in María Palacios Cruz's English translation at https://www.diagonalthoughts.com/?p=1423.

6
The Famous "Invisible Style" Defence

At least since the 1930s, some directors have – with an entirely genuine sense of conviction – tried to wave away discussion of their creation of film *style* by referring to a long-held ideal of classical art: *invisibility*, that manner of making that passes without undue notice. It is, in a sense, the style that is no style, a *transparent* style that allows the viewer direct and immediate access to and complete involvement in the fictional illusion: the created world, the characters and their story.

From a critical angle, the style that is no style is a literal impossibility: every film has a material form, created from a complex set of decisions. That form or style is perfectly evident on screen, and can be broken down and appreciated via analysis. Certainly, some films highlight their style more than others, but it is always there – because the effort to *hide* or minimise style also constitutes a style! Or, as Jean-Louis Comolli loves to quote from the French circus performer-director Alexis Grüss: "Art is the work effaced by work."

Some directors, however, are wary of an excessively "formalistic" approach to their work, which they feel diverts attention from the content of their themes or subject matter. Ken Loach (born 1936), for example, has always maintained that he prefers people to discuss the socio-political issues highlighted by his films, not the manner in which he made them. As a side result of that belief, he thereby keeps the "trade secrets" of his filming method private. Only his long-time producer, Rebecca O'Brien, has (in conferences for filmmakers) revealed details regarding the enormous number of takes Loach shoots (and how this is incorporated into the budget), his filming strategies, and how he works with actors and non-actors.

More generally, from the viewpoint of a more-or-less classical filmmaker, what has to be avoided at all costs, in practice, is an overly *ostentatious* or obvious style. There must be no sign or trace of the hard work that went into a film's crafting. George Cukor commented on this in 1938.

> In my case, directorial style must largely be the absence of style. [...] The finished picture shows to the layman in the audience no visible "direction," but merely seems to be a smooth and convincing presentation by the players of the subject.

The naïve, "untutored" notion that the "players" (i.e., actors) are the ones who make a film is borne out by a joke that French critic-filmmaker Luc Moullet (born 1937) often cracks: among the rural French communities that he visits, the actors, cinematographers and other technicians are regarded as genuine "workers," while the director is regarded as the person who sits or stands around and does precisely nothing!

The advice proffered by Andre De Toth (1913-2002) (whose name gets spelt many different ways because of his cosmopolitan, international career) is blunter than Cukor's. In the 1997 book-length interview conducted by Anthony Slide, *De Toth on De Toth: Putting the Drama in Front of the Camera*, the director usually waves away with impatience all discussion of filmic style, preferring to speak – rather vaguely – of the absolute need to maintain "realism" at all times. Frequently breaking off from the interviewer's questions to directly address the reader as "Herr Future Director," he dispenses pearls of wisdom like this: "On occasions, Herr Future Director, you may emphasise a point of view, but reality should never be distorted for a thrill."

As strange as it may seem in a contemporary cinema landscape – in which Lynne Ramsay, the Coen brothers or Paul Thomas Anderson make an overt spectacle of their stylistic pyrotechnics, as Hitchcock did before them – we still hear the defence of invisible style. For a truly mindboggling example of this continuing tendency, here is Michael Mann (born 1943) describing the work of both himself and (of all people) Martin Scorsese (born 1942).

> For the working director, there is no conscious form from film to film. We all know what our ambitions are, but in a very healthy way we are all unconscious of a "signature."

This filmmaker, too, as we can see in the interview-heavy 2006 book *Michael Mann* by F.X. Feeney, stresses realism (and, as with Stanley Kubrick, the meticulous research that goes into establishing it) as a prime value. His remarks here reveal another key aspect of the invisible style defence: an aversion to *auteurism*, with its (sometimes lazy) assumption that every true director will or must have a stylistic "signature" that is stamped on each and every film they make. Critics do not come up short on examples to help prove this claim: Max Ophüls' elaborate camera movements, Otto Preminger's wide or "democratic" staging of many characters in a single frame, Robert Bresson's constant insert-shots of hands, Wes Anderson's geometrical vistas… this list proceeds to infinity.

Note Mann's careful equivocation: the filmmakers with whom he chooses to identify are *unconscious* of a signature… therefore, they may have one without realising it. Later in this book, I quote Blake Edwards' statement endorsing such a feeling – that the director needs to be actively *unaware* of what recurs as a signature or thematic obsession in their work, that they need to repress thinking about it in order to function effectively as a creator. Naturally, this amounts to a psychological contortion – and/or a professional pose.

For self-styled "invisible" directors, what's the real problem with auteurism? Its assumption or implication is that every film by a particular filmmaker is always approached in the *same* way, and is treated in the *same* style, no matter its subject, genre or source. A director such as Stephen Frears loudly outright rejects this notion (which he regards as a dangerous and irresponsible one). For him, as for many professional filmmakers, it is always the particular project, already nailed down in the script (on which the director may or may not collaborate), that calls forth the specific style in which it must be made. This was also Sidney Lumet's refrain in his influential 1995 book of practical craft advice, *Making Movies*: "I have no theme," meaning no recurring, central concern that unites all his (very diverse) films.

Every project, every film, is therefore different. A Western will demand one kind of treatment, a romantic comedy, another. Factually based subject matter will require "realism," however that is to be defined. There is a good point to this resistance: on the contemporary festival circuit, we too often see new directors who are wholly identified with their quickly cultivated and cemented stylistic signature (long takes, garish colour scheme, elaborate montage structure, etc.) – to the extent that, if they decide to alter or vary their style, they are suddenly cast out of the fickle pantheon of current hype.

It is wiser, finally, to steer a middle course through these arguments: what Pascal Kané defines as the true, subterranean *subject* of an auteur's work (see Chapter 9) is tied neither to the vagaries of different topics or genres (look, for instance, at the surface variety of Fritz Lang's films), nor to the unchanging regularity of a set style (several of Kané's exemplars, such as Elia Kazan, Roman Polanski or Billy Wilder, have no such discernible signature on the level of camerawork, *mise en scène* or editing procedures).

The book you are reading will not devote further time to the critique of auteurism, which I regard, ultimately, as a fruitless debate. I take the centrality of the director to be axiomatic in all forms of cinema, from narrative to documentary and experimental. One last caveat that is constantly aired needs, however, to be dealt with swiftly here. It is the response to auteurism that claims, triumphantly, that film is properly *collective* work – not the expression of a single, individual sensibility. Of course, it is a plain fact that most (but by no means all) films are made by a team working collaboratively. And some films (for instance in the field of militant political cinema) are signed collectively, or left entirely unsigned. In television, it is the "showrunner" or creative producer who takes the overseeing, auteur role, sometimes as part of an "executive team" – not the director, who functions as a professional-for-hire, fitting into a pre-established series template or format. It is also the case, certainly in the sphere of contemporary Hollywood blockbusters, that some films are made (and obsessively reworked) "by committee," via a complicated chain of command – and it shows.

Some directors like to downplay their own, central contribution and play up the collective, collaborative aspect. Robert Altman (1925-2006) often boasted (especially when he was receiving awards) that he simply gathered great people – actors and technicians – around him and "let them do their thing," while he just stood and watched (recalling Moullet's comical description of his role). He set up the event and let it happen – an almost party-like atmosphere to which his films bear witness, perhaps deceptively. Another example: I once found myself on a typical film festival panel with a young American filmmaker, Jeff Nichols (born 1978), who had just completed his first feature, *Shotgun Stories* (2007). Where Altman feigned modesty, Nichols took the tack of aggression. When I casually invoked the role of the auteur, Nichols mocked me mercilessly.

> Do you think I framed the shots in *Shotgun Stories*? I let the cinematographer make those decisions, he's been doing it for years! Do you think I lit the set? I wouldn't know how to! Do you think I edited the film myself? No, a professional editor did! I was learning everything from these people. You critics understand nothing about how a film is really made by an entire crew of many people, not just one guy!

And the Australian writer-director Bob Ellis (1942-2016), a studied provocateur, once proclaimed at an industry event in Australia – having just dismissed my analysis of sample scenes by various auteurs – that the director is only the "tenth most important person involved in any film" beneath scriptwriter, actors, cinematographer, production designer, music composer, editor, and so forth. Certainly, taking a look at Ellis' own films will confirm the almost complete absence of an integrated *mise en scène*! (For more on what I take *mise en scène* to entail, see Chapter 8).

Integration should indeed be our keyword, not individual creation *ex nihilo* – which is a properly "sublime" idea from the Romantic age, not applicable to all art forms and media. On this front, it is too easy to be shackled by the reigning metaphors we employ. If we compare the film director to a writer facing the white page or a painter before the blank canvas – models of lone creation, an individual with the tools of their medium – we are, of course, going to find the "auteur theory" (as it is misleadingly called) insufficient and even ridiculous to apply to much cinema. If, by contrast, we compare the director to an orchestra conductor or the ringmaster at a circus, we may get closer to a correct image of cinematic creation. Cukor's summary of the situation is apt.

> You will detect through all I have written one theme running continuously – that the art of the director is to hold the delicate balance between giving something to, and taking something from, the people with whom he works. That is, to my mind, the root of the matter; that is why a director must never think of his work as a one-man job; that is why I, as a director, always want to have the best possible help in all departments.

The important point is that, in filmmaking, it is most often the case that the ultimate *decisions* – on camera angle, the colour of a set, the placement of music cues, and so on – are made by the director on the basis of what is presented by all collaborators; that is, after all, a director's job. It is in the *coherence* of the decision making, the overall system, gesture or *gestalt* that is arrived at in, and imparted by, the finished work, that we should locate the director's contribution. Cukor himself said it: "It seems to me from experience that the mood, the psychological pitch, if you like, comes from the director."

Source: *De Toth on De Toth* is published by Faber and Faber. F.X. Feeney's *Michael Mann* is published by Taschen. George Cukor's "The Director" is reprinted in *Hollywood Directors 1914-1940* (Galaxy, 1976), edited by Richard Kozarski, pp. 322-331. It is sometimes the case that texts signed by Old (or even New) Hollywood directors are not composed by them at all, but rather "ghost-written" by assistants or journalists, perhaps on the basis of conversation, perhaps on the basis of sheer guesswork. Cukor's essay, however, seems genuinely to be his own work.

7
Invisible Imaginary Ubiquitous Winged Witness

Alexander Mackendrick (1912-1993) had an unusual and varied cinema career. Following a short but illustrious stint as a director (mainly of comedies) in Britain from the late 1940s to the mid-1950s, he relocated to the USA, making there one of his greatest and most enduring successes, the high-voltage melodrama *Sweet Smell of Success* (1957). However, production difficulties on a range of subsequent projects led him, in 1969, to jump at the opportunity to retire from directing and become a teacher of filmmaking at California Institute of the Arts. This he did energetically for nearly a quarter of a century. His very detailed teaching files (written lectures, notes, diagrams, handouts) provide the basis for the book *On Film-Making*, selected and edited by Paul Cronin. It is among the most precious documents of a filmmaker's thinking that we currently have.

Although CalArts is known, today as in the past, as a bastion of experimental and independent film and video making (its teachers have included Kathryn Bigelow, Bill Viola, Nina Menkes and Thom Andersen), Mackendrick saw his role as imparting a "mastery" of craft, of the "basic mechanics of filmmaking" – defined, in this instance, as narrative filmmaking. He often repeated an old piece of wisdom: you have to know the basic principles before you can presume to bend or break them in the service of a more "modern" vision (one of his lectures is devoted, open-mindedly but critically, to "Modernist Trends").

I need to say a little more on the notion of *craft*, since it is (I have found) a frequently misunderstood or even unfamiliar term in the film worlds of the 21st century. Craft is not the opposite of art; neither does it refer to purely *artisanal*, hands-on, direct production of objects or artefacts (as in, within the English language at least, the popular "crafts" of pottery, knitting, glass-blowing, and so on).

In the sphere of filmmaking, "mastery of craft" (in the sense that Mackendrick intends it) does involve the acquisition of *skills*, the knowledge of, and command over, a loose set of more-or-less established conventions. But filmic craft is not an ironclad book of *rules*. The *principles* of an aesthetic craft can be provisionally enumerated or inventoried (Mackendrick's nearly 25 years of teaching strove toward this goal), but they can never be simply, mechanically memorised and applied by rote. Intuition, inventiveness and playfulness are all part of the skill set of film craft.

Craft is tied to what is *expressive* in cinema – themes, ideas, the poetry of film – and, as Mackendrick certainly believes, is fundamental to these high goals of any art form. But, fundamentally, craft *begins* from the basic, technical questions that every director must face. Questions like: How do I best and most clearly convey this piece of story information? How do I orient the spectator in the organisation and flow of the whole film? How will I position and move the actors? What's the quickest, most economical way (both in aesthetic and budgetary terms) to depict an action? The craft of great directors is very often what we do not (or only dimly) perceive and appreciate; we are too eager to get to the higher realms of philosophy, emotional affect and cultural significance. Craft, however, is singularly important.

Even though he sought to transmit principles of craft rather than lofty ideals of art, Mackendrick did intersect with both Eisenstein and Fellini in one crucial area: nurturing the creative process or, as Mackendrick called it, "incubating the material" and "preserving the spark." There are many practical tips and procedures in his book (especially the chapter "The Solomon Exercise") to help with that process.

Many filmmakers, including Stephen Frears and Martin Scorsese, have extolled the virtues of Mackendrick's generously dispensed craft advice. For example: "The geography of a scene must be immediately apparent to an audience." Seems sensible and obvious enough, but how often this is ignored (sometimes deliberately, sometimes just artlessly) in contemporary action movies! Or let's take a more complex instance of craft difficulty: how does a director handle apparently banal scenes or actions, like a family getting into their car, or packing their bags for a vacation?

Mackendrick outlined the ways in which, once an action is off screen, it can be ruthlessly – in fact, with complete unreality – telescoped, without disturbing the fundamental flow or verisimilitude of the scene. A man starts filling his suitcase; cut away to his partner for a line or two of dialogue; cut back: voilà, the suitcase is zipped and ready to go! Narrative films are made of thousands of such small but telling details. Frears, in his tribute to "Sandy" (as Mackendrick was known to his friends and colleagues), quotes George Devine of the Royal Court theatre: "All problems are technical" Frears adds ruefully: "It has taken me all my life to see the truth of this."

> How do you solve this dramatic problem? How you keep the audience interested while a man is getting dressed? How do you speed up time? How do you cross space? How do you stay as graceful and witty and expressive as you want to? What begins as an artistic question is eventually reduced to a series of practical matters. What do you want to show the audience? Where do you put the camera? What do the actors do and say? [...] Mackendrick is the ideal man to study if you are interested in these kinds of problem.

As a teacher of narrative film technique, Mackendrick focused on the "emotional and dramatic content of any scene" and what he defined as "film grammar" – primarily visual in nature. Like Hitchcock, he believed that dialogue should play a secondary function in cinema, and endorsed François Truffaut's dictum that "dialogue is almost always less effective than visible activity" – as well as less "believable" (by the viewer) and less memorable or retainable in the flow of the movie-watching experience. Andre De Toth substantially agreed with him: "The combination of set-ups, the rhythm of the images and words can give a different emphasis to motion pictures; the silent shadows can speak louder than words."

A key example that Mackendrick used in his classes was from André Cayatte's *The Lovers of Verona* (1949); it is strikingly similar, in certain respects, to the imaginary scene conjured by Jean-Luc Godard that we will encounter in the next chapter. In a glassworks factory, a young woman enters with her much older companion. A secret attraction has formed between the woman and a worker at the factory. Wordlessly, this younger man cuts a heart-shape into the pane of glass that he is standing behind. The older man sees not this detail, but a far more pleasing one: his companion smiling as she looks into a mirror that he has just selected for her as a gift. Finally, "the camera shows us something that he cannot see: she is really smiling into the mirror at the reflection of the young man behind."

For Mackendrick, this scene depends on "quick glimpses of detail, the flicker of reactions on faces and a switch of viewpoint by the camera." We can add that it also fully depends on *mise en scène* or staging: the respective positions of the characters in the space, where their look is directed, the handling of props. Mackendrick concludes from this illustration that the film's scriptwriter, the celebrated poet Jacques Prévert, is "writing for the cinema, and nothing else" – another case of implicitly defining the essential elements of the medium. But Mackendrick is never dogmatic (he is not anti-dialogue *per se*); he refuses to accept filmmaking "rules" as much he avoids general theorising, and states in this particular lecture that "mute action supplies the most basic information, while verbal information adds another, secondary dimension."

Switch of viewpoint brings us to an especially fascinating aspect of Mackendrick's teaching, and his own immaculate art and craft as a filmmaker. He did not conceive the role of the camera in primarily *subjective* terms – i.e., entering and embodying the viewpoint of the fictional characters. This puts him at odds with much teaching in film schools today, where both image *and* sound are marshalled toward subjective effects – allowing spectators to thus "be in the head" of a character (usually a single, central character). It is a salutary effect of historical relativity to remind ourselves that this was *not* always received wisdom in the annals of film craft. For Mackendrick, the camera was, according to his marvellous formulation, the "invisible imaginary ubiquitous winged witness."

> At each particular moment of any given scene, the position of the camera, as a point in time and space, implies a specific point of view. It is from this spot that the audience views the story.

So point-of-view exists, strictly speaking, *outside* the fiction, never *inside*; it is, above all, the viewpoint of the invisible or implied narrator, the storyteller. We can be fully *involved* in a screen story without being (as the contemporary lingo says) *immersed* in it – a critical distance (through, for example, irony), a constantly reflective process, is possible.

> Far from being passive, [the camera] is an active participant in the imaginary events being portrayed. It is the embodiment of the audience's curiosity, a creature whose attitude to persons and events is coloured by feeling: sympathetic on occasion, alienated at other times.

This accords well with Hitchcock's intuition of the potentially distracted spectator who needs a shot of dope to stay with the film!

"The camera always takes what could be construed as a psychological attitude to what it is filming." For Mackendrick, this process is not static but dynamic, ever-shifting. Materially, it involves directorial skill in establishing a play of *size* and *scale* in the passage from one shot to the next – another point of crossover between Mackendrick's advice and Godard's, as we shall see: *mise en scène* on the set already implies a specific relationship of the images in post-production editing.

Mackendrick goes on to define three standard attitudes adopted by the camera-as-witness. The first is *disinterest* (which doesn't mean lack of interest): an objective and neutral attitude. Things are, as it were, established and noted, perhaps for later use in the story. The second attitude is what he describes as *balanced sympathy* alternating between two or more characters in a scene. The third attitude is a strong sense of *empathy* with one particular character whose point-of-view is rendered subjectively (the "modern mainstream" style), while other, less significant viewpoints are shown merely in cutaways. "Within any scene," Mackendrick insists, "there can be several shifts of sympathy and attitude" – indeed, as we see in his own work, the greater the number and complexity of such shifts (which he calls *peripeteia*), the richer the film (and its drama) becomes.

Along these lines, Mackendrick traces three interrelated factors that determine our loose, malleable "identification" with one character over another: relative *screen size* as given by the placement of the camera; the *eye-line*, referring to the degree to which a gaze off screen is given either narrowly or widely to the lens; and the *timing of interactions* in the editing plan – which character is "held" longer on screen. This amounts to a remarkably supple set of tools for analysing film scenes, whether from the vantage point of a critic or a practitioner. It allows us to detect, for example, how Hitchcock "cinematised" even the talkiest of his scenes.

"Direction is a matter of emphasis. In telling a story, the task of the director is to emphasise what is significant by under-emphasising what is less so." Once again, this is advice that one is unlikely to hear in many contemporary film schools. Mackendrick suggests we proceed through *understatement* rather than the *overstatement* of an effect – truly untimely wisdom in an age where every important point or moment in a film is "ramped up," variously or all at once, with sound effects, visual underlining through ostentatious camera angles, quick editing and emphatic, actorly gestures. What would it mean to *de-emphasise* a detail? Classical film craft can furnish us with many examples, once we know to look out for them. Mackendrick's lessons alert us to this.

Source: "The Pre-Verbal Language of Cinema" and "The Invisible Imaginary Ubiquitous Winged Witness" are two chapters in Mackendrick's *On Film-Making* (Faber and Faber, 2004), edited by Paul Cronin. Stephen Frears' tribute to Mackendrick appears on pp. 66-69 in *Projections 4½* (Faber and Faber, 1995), edited by John Boorman and Walter Donohue in association with *Positif* magazine. This special issue of the *Projections* series is an invaluable source of many filmmakers' thinking.

8
Chance and Destiny

In the second half of this book, we shall survey how some filmmakers responded to what we might call one of the primary *temptations* of film theory: the attempt to define a sole or major *essence* of cinema as a medium. Jean-Luc Godard, however, is different. From his very beginnings in the 1950s as a critic, he resisted this "essentialising" gesture. A natural lover of paradox, of multiplicity, of the inversion and reversibility of concepts, he sought generative ideas for cinema that were flexible, mixed, impure. If he begins from a duality – defining one pole by one principle and the opposite pole by an opposite principle – he usually switches it around in a witty and provocative way. He routinely does this with the "received" ideas of other people, too. It's the way Godard thinks and creates, the way he moves forward in his work.

In 1956, in his short but potent text "Montage, mon beau souci" or "Editing, My Fine Care" (only four paragraphs set over two pages, scarcely a thousand words), Godard set out to distinguish his own sensibility from the cult (somewhat attributable to André Bazin) that asserted the supreme value of *photography* – the photographic trace or imprint of the world on celluloid – as the essence of cinema, as distinct from and superior to the *manipulation* introduced by post-production editing, an emphasis long associated with the "constructivist" ethos of Sergei Eisenstein. (As we shall see in Part Two, Tarkovsky, the anti-Eisensteinian, returned to the valuing of photography over editing.)

Godard set out to rescue and value the role of editing within fiction cinema. The original publication context of this piece is lost to anyone who doesn't consult it in a *Cahiers du cinéma* issue of more than 65 years ago; it sits in a dossier titled "À propos du montage," between Henri Colpi's forgotten "Degradation of an Art: Editing" (a litany of the aesthetic and technical obstacles in film history standing in the way of creative editing), and Bazin's oft-reprinted classic "Forbidden Montage," a quasi-manifesto of his by-then highly elaborated theoretical position. (Bazin was also, at the time, one of the three chief editors of the magazine).

Yet, in the same gesture, Godard wished to oppose those – especially producers in the film industry – who lazily assumed that editing is what not only fundamentally coheres a film, but also *saves* it from being a fragmented wreck, editing as literally a "be-all and end-all" of cinema. Godard was, in short, against all grand, totalising ideas: the twin peak-positions that cinema was either primarily *mise en scène* (what was arranged before the camera) or primarily *montage*, taken either in the classical/industrial sense of assembly and continuity editing, or the more assertive methods and theories of Soviet montage.

In Godard's view, any model of cinema aesthetics that separated *mise en scène* from editing was "hardly any longer true" in relation to the silent films of F.W. Murnau (1889-1931) or Charles Chaplin (1889-1977), and it became "irretrievably untrue with sound film." Situating his commentary in his present moment (as critics very often do), it's clear at the outset that Godard wants to particularly defend, via his polemic, two recent, contentious releases: Jean Renoir's *Eléna et les hommes* (1956) and Orson Welles' *Mr Arkadin* (1955), with Alfred Hitchcock's self-remake of *The Man Who Knew Too Much* (1956) later serving as the "best proof" of his thesis.

If there are any good films merely "saved in the editing" then, according to Godard, it's because they managed to "transform chance into destiny." In other words, they took filmed material that was, at various levels, unplanned, rough, undisciplined, unsystematic, and gave it the appearance of a logical, pre-planned form. Godard, for his part, does not want to eliminate the spontaneity of the chance factor in filmmaking (Renoir's famous advice that "one must leave a door open on the set through which chance can enter"), the aspect of improvisation and in-the-moment invention. But he does desire the special alchemy that comes from the *foreseeing* of effects (on all levels) and the mutual *interplay* of direction and editing.

In order to film, one must at least have a montage concept already in mind, even if it is not set down in all details in advance. As he puts it, "To speak of directing is automatically to speak, yet and again, of editing" – or at any rate, this constitutes the ideal state of things in a particular realm of cinema.

In the mid-1950s, Godard (26 years old in December 1956) was still mainly absorbed in classical cinema of various shades, from Renoir and Ophüls to Hitchcock and – at the very brink of modernism – the increasingly baroque cinema of Welles. So he focuses on dramatic meaning in film, the emotions and psychology of characters within the scenes of a fictional narrative. The core of Godard's proposal concerning the interdependence of *mise en scène* and montage is the following, superb formulation: "If to direct is a glance, to edit is a beating of the heart. To anticipate is the characteristic of both. But what one seeks to foresee in space, the other seeks in time."

At the outset, then, Godard wields a conventional distinction, still often reiterated today in much filmmaking training: space is the domain of the image (the visual dimension), while time is the substance and material of the editing process. As we shall see, Godard later merrily undoes and complicates this very distinction. But the crucial aspect to stress here, which Godard proposed in a novel way, is the dynamic idea of *foreseeing* or anticipation.

Similar to how Mackendrick deploys his example from *The Lovers of Verona*, Godard poses to us an imaginary scene.

> Suppose you see an attractive girl in the street. You hesitate to follow her. A quarter of a second. How to convey this hesitation? The question "How to approach her?" will be answered for you by the *mise en scène*. But in order to make explicit this other question, "Am I going to love her?," you will have to grant importance to the quarter of a second during which both arise.

It is thus the gesture of editing to weigh and balance, to underline and even deform, that fraction of a second. Perhaps it will be a matter of going beyond strict verisimilitude – by lengthening the fraction of filmed time, for instance, or repeating it. Examples of scenes quite close to the one evoked by Godard can be found in Michael Powell and Emeric Pressburger's *I Know Where I'm Going!* (1945) and Martin Scorsese's *Casino* (1995). Godard then extends his general meditation on the craft of editing.

> It may be, therefore, that it will be for the editing rather than the *mise en scène* to express both exactly and clearly the life of an idea or its sudden emergence in the course of the general narration. When? Without playing on words, each time that the *situation* calls for it; whether in the middle of a scene, when a shock effect demands to take the place of an arabesque; or each time between one scene and another when the inner continuity of the film enjoins with a change of shot the superimposition of the description of a character upon that of the plot.

Godard is determined here to bring out the expressive role of editing – how it may end up eliminating and substituting for certain filmed effects (such as an "arabesque" camera movement). We can also detect the birth of a properly modernist notion here in Godard's thinking: the *superimposition* of character description over plot calls up a model of layers and levels – sometimes harmonious, sometimes in conflict – upon which the Nouvelle Vague, and many similarly radical film movements in the 1960s and beyond, will be based. The ideas of fragmentation, heterogeneity, multiplicity, "interval" (see the discussion of Dziga Vertov in Chapter 22) are embryonic here. In 1956, however, Godard is still devoted to the hopeful *fusion* of levels and procedures: "When editing effects surpass those of *mise en scène* in efficacy, the beauty of the latter is doubled."

Godard goes on to discuss the issue of "knowing how long one can make a scene" as another instance of *mise en scène*/montage interrelation, and the "appeal of the brief shot." The key tool in this discussion picks up an element from his imaginary scene: the *regard* (look, glance or gaze) of an actor in a scene. Note here a not-insignificant detail omitted from all translations and reprints of the article: the accompaniment in the layout of two images paired side by side, of Buster Keaton (in *Spite Marriage*, 1929) and Welles (in *Mr Arkadin*), and a caption (supplied either by Godard or the *Cahiers* editors) stating that these actors share "equivalent facial hair" (both are wearing bushy, artificial beards) and exhibit "the same forceful look fixed on the camera lens" – it's just like an inspired montage moment from Godard's subsequent *Histoire(s) du cinéma* (1988-1998) series!

Godard develops his idea of the *regard* as a "key piece" in the editor's game, with special reference to emotion or affect.

> Cutting on a look is almost the definition of editing, its supreme ambition as well as its submission to *mise en scène*. It indeed brings out the soul under the mind, the passion behind the machination, making heart prevail over intelligence by destroying the notion of space in favour of that of time.

Notice the subtle shift here that prefigures Godard's own aggressive montage strategies to come: immediately after invoking the properly Romantic ideals of soul, passion and heart, he eulogises the creative role of destruction! Again, a budding modernist sensibility looms.

Looking to the analogies that Godard uses to describe the inseparability of *mise en scène* and montage throughout his essay, the first main one is thoroughly familiar, used by many filmmakers: a musical analogy. "It would be like trying to separate rhythm from melody." You will have also noted the equally familiar, anthropomorphic appeal of the comparisons Godard makes: the camera "glances" with its eye, while editing is equated to heartbeat. The evocation of the *regard* as the editor's "key piece" is a clever chess metaphor – and indeed, throughout his life (he died in 2022), Godard regularly drew his metaphors from every kind of sporting activity (tennis, especially).

The second major analogy is less usual, but previews many of Godard's future formulations: an appeal to the domain of the sciences, in this case mathematics. When editing effects "double" the charm of directorial effects, "its charm will consist in disclosing the unforeseen by an operation analogous to that in mathematics which makes an unknown entity evident." Godard evidently prefers this type of quasi-scientific formula to the common evocation of ineffable "magic" in filmmaking (compare this to Jacques Rozier's account of a Jean Renoir scene in Chapter 10). Indeed, in this very same *Cahiers* dossier, Colpi (himself a noted editor-turned-director) sternly warns us "not to look for exact laws governing cinematic cadence," since "scientific rigour or mathematical calculation fail in the face of sensation: we *feel* rhythm, it is a matter of impression." Colpi speaks not of magic in his intervention, but certainly implies the prime role of creative *intuition* guided by practical experience.

Godard's texts are usually littered with a vast array of references constituting his particular cultural horizon; here, that process begins with the title, an appropriation of *Beauté, mon beau souci*, a 1920 novel that belongs to a lightly autobiographical trilogy by a romantic dandy little cited today, Valery-Nicolas Larbaud (1881-1957). However, "Montage, mon beau souci" is relatively sparse on this allusive level, beyond its filmic touchstones (ten directors and seven films cited – plus one then-current editor, Marguerite Renoir, cited negatively for her "too mechanical" tendency). At a striking moment, he gives a model example of film editing *from a novel*, Balzac's *A Shady Affair* (1841), and he does so without distinguishing the media of cinema and literature.

> When Peyrade and Corentin break open the door to the Saint-Cygne *salon*, their first notice is of Laurence: "We'll get you, my girl" – "I shan't tell you a thing." Both the proud young woman and Fouché's spies guessed at first glance that this was their most deadly enemy. For this terrible exchange of looks, a simple shot/reverse shot, by its very restraint, would render the scene more powerfully than any premeditated track or pan.

Here, Godard has effectively, in his mind, dramatised – or cinematised – the description (and dialogue) of Balzac's prose. More than a canny "adaptation" from page to screen, this is an amazing multimedia transposition! Godard seizes on Balzac as a filmmaker before his time (and medium).

Ultimately, Godard's essay is a theory of expressive creation. Foreseeing the editing in the shooting does not equate with what the French call basic *découpage* (the breakdown of a scene into a shot list) or the English-language term *coverage* (shooting the details of a scene from many angles). Godard stresses that "one improvises, one invents in front of the Moviola just as one does on the set." His example prefigures a technique he will himself use, for instance in *Vivre sa vie* (1962): "Cutting a movement of the camera in quarters can reveal itself more effective than keeping it as it has been filmed."

I have mentioned the lively, generative role of paradox in Godard's thinking as expressed both in his texts and his films – sometimes dismissed as mere word play or mind-game sophistry. I do not agree with this negative judgement. Here is a Godardian paradox in action. In passing, he casually defines "one of the aims of *mise en scène*" as "giving the impression of duration through movement" and "of a close shot through a long shot." Those initially separated realms of space and time have just been confused: images now convey a temporal dimension (duration) through physical action (movement). They also literally leap through space, by appealing to a mental and emotional experience on the part of the spectator: *mise en scène* makes us "see" or feel or sense a close-up magnified within what is literally a distant long shot. For movement-as-duration, we might recall the ghostly movements of the phantom in Murnau's *Nosferatu* (1922), and for close-up-in-long shot, the far away details of the young lovers during their island idyll in Ingmar Bergman's *Summer with Monika* (1953 – an enduring favourite of Godard's).

Then Godard flips his terms: if that's what *mise en scène* aims for, then editing aims for "the opposite"; in other words, duration registered in our minds as movement (through the tension of stillness, for example, in Tsai Ming-liang's films), and the suggestion of a long shot projected from a close-up! The actor's *regard* – off screen, into infinity – may once again count as the "key piece" in this final, somersaulting twist of the concept.

Source: Godard's French original appears in *Cahiers du cinéma*, no. 65, December 1956, pp. 30-31. For the English quotations, I have combined and reworked phrases from two separate translations: Nell Cox's 1961 rendition "Montage, Mon Beau Souci" reprinted in Toby Mussman's *Jean-Luc Godard* (New York: Dell, 1968), pp. 47-49, and Tom Milne's "Montage My Fine Care" in *Godard on Godard* (New York: Da Capo, 1972), pp. 39-41. A good Spanish translation, Laia Colell Aparicio's "Montaje, mi gran inquietad," appears in *Cahiers du cinéma España*, no. 13, June 2008, pp. 68-69.

9
A Genealogy of Inspiration

Some film critics, when they become filmmakers, essentially give up criticism. They may write occasional, fond appreciations of filmmakers present and past (as François Truffaut did and Víctor Erice still does), they may post comments about their viewing on social media and revise their previous publications (as Paul Schrader does), they may – as Godard testified – continue their critique in a different form, on screen. Some filmmakers get the opportunity to make (generally positive) essay-films about their contemporaries and/or collaborators: Luc Moullet's *Catherine Breillat, la première fois* (2012), part of the long-running *Cinéastes, de notre temps* TV series, and Elaine May's *Mike Nichols* (2016) in the *American Masters* documentary series. In America, it appears that several generations of cinephile-minded directors (Tim Hunter, Allan Arkush, Amy Jones, Jonathan Kaplan, Katt Shea, Mary Lambert, John Sayles) have, since 2007, gravitated to Joe Dante's online *Trailers from Hell* project as a fitting outlet for their undying enthusiasms.

Many directors (including Miguel Gomes, Claude Chabrol and Kent Jones) give up criticism – in particular, the negative reviewing of any contemporary cinema – altogether, once they have "crossed over." There is too much at stake, professionally, it seems, to take the risk of criticising (even attacking) one's peers. That is a perfectly understandable position. When ageing filmmakers, to maintain their connection with the industry, do accept the invitation to a regular reviewing gig (as occurred with Nelly Kaplan and Paul Mazursky), their reports tend to be soft, whimsical, anecdotal, wryly humorous, rather than truly critical of anybody or anything.

Among critics-turned-filmmakers, the surrealist Robert Benayoun (who did continue writing and publishing alongside his directing until his death in 1996) gave this vexed relation between the two vocations a new twist: "It is only when I make films that I am truly lucid about cinema."

Luis Buñuel, Michelangelo Antonioni and other great directors who began as critics (but later expressed great antipathy toward theory and critique alike) would have no doubt agreed.

An arresting variation on all these scenarios is provided by Pascal Kané (1946-2020). A quick glance over his biography would suggest that he followed the usual, predictable path: a critic at *Cahiers du cinéma* when young, from the mid-1960s on, followed by a transition, beginning with *Dora and the Magic Lantern* (co-scripted by Raúl Ruiz) in 1977, into directing fiction and documentary for film and television. However, although he published relatively few texts after the early 1980s, Kané publicly returned, at regular intervals, to his particular vision of the traffic between criticism and filmmaking. For him, they were intimately linked in a special, generative way. He eventually structured a 2015 book of his collected writings around this theme: *Savoir dire pour vouloir faire*, subtitled "Criticism, an origin for creation."

That main part of Kané's book title is hard to translate elegantly, but easy to explain. Everyday French distinguishes between *savoir faire* – "know-how" in English, practical knowledge, acquired skill – from *vouloir dire*, a wish to say something, to speak and make a point. In the company of the celebrated critic Serge Daney (to whom Kané devoted a 1993 documentary portrait, *Le cinéphile et le village*), a play of words and ideas was born: "learning how to say" (*savoir dire*) leads to the "desire to make" (*vouloir faire*). Criticism does not merely *precede* the stage of creation, but truly *prepares* the path for it, and not just in a professional, networking sense.

The fruit of Kané's lifelong reflection on these matters is concentrated in the final, epilogue chapter of his book, a careful revision made in 2014 of a lecture first given at the Cinémathèque française in 1995 – "Genealogy of Inspiration" – a title which, in its ultimate version, is preceded by the question that motivates the entirety of *Savoir dire pour vouloir faire*: "What's the use of criticism?" That may sound like a cynical question, but Kané gives a positive answer.

Kané, addressing himself primarily to an audience of prospective filmmakers, is drawn to the elusive topic of artistic *inspiration*. Once decried for political reasons (such a mystified, bourgeois notion!), Kané came to see it as a "rich and complex" subject. Where does a great, inspired idea come from, how does it form in our minds? Nobody really knows, despite the best efforts of the human sciences. Kané is certain of this much, however: he considers the properly Romantic idea of "divine inspiration," ideas falling from the skies and magically popping up in our heads, as utter nonsense.

No, if inspiration is real, it must possess roots, origins, a *genealogy* within us and our experiences. And the chosen focus of his own genealogy will be cinema – the major "formative" films he saw and loved, and particularly those he was moved to write about in his period as a working critic (the rest of his book offers a selection of these texts dating from 1969, when he produced a structuralist study of Roman Polanski, to the early 1980s).

You may be thinking: this is pretty common and even banal stuff, filmmakers testifying to the films they loved, the favourites and classics that shaped and influenced them as creators. We see that on TV arts programs every week. The British book series *Projections*, which ran in seven volumes from 1992 to 1997 under the guidance of director John Boorman and script editor Walter Donohue (with a "best of" selection in 2006), published literally hundreds of pages (many of them good) devoted to this idea. So what's different about Kané's account?

Two things matter here. The first is the specific way in which Kané views the act of criticism – analysis, interpretation – itself. The second, following on from that, is how he portrays the mechanism or process of inspiration.

> When we speak of what we love, we speak about a whole lot more! We speak of what we have been and also, without always recognising it, of what we are. That is, what we try to make…

Kané begins his auto-investigation by determining that his fondest and most enduring cine-love has been for classical Hollywood films – and, in them, especially their *form* (or forms in the plural, for each auteur inflects the general form), their way of relating cinematic style (for which he uses the shorthand term *mise en scène*) to story.

> I've always had a predilection for the forms of classic Hollywood cinema. Why those? Because they are the narrative forms that know best, I believe, how to visually concretise, via *mise en scène*, the themes of their auteurs. Theme – i.e., the more or less unconscious subject of an auteur – only exists fully for me, as the arrangement of images within a narrative mode, at certain moments of cinema, and particularly Hollywood cinema of the classic era. Before, in the silent era, themes were more explicitly visual; more recently, in Hollywood and elsewhere, they become more and more spoken aloud (and less and less inscribed in *mise en scène*).

We must avoid a potential confusion here, because Kané does not intend *theme* in the plain, literary sense that many of us learn (boringly) in school. The category of theme, for Kané, is different from the explicit, conscious *subject* of a film (e.g., the horrors of war), or even its evident *motor* (e.g., comparison of rich and poor classes on board the Titanic). What those schoolteachers of our childhood called a theme, Kané considers a mere subject. Nor is a theme a simple pattern (motif), or a striking, isolated moment (what Roland Barthes designated as a *punctum* in photography or a "third meaning" in film). A true, profound theme has a secretive dimension, spreading in a subterranean fashion and animating an entire film, and then (as far as possible) *all* the films of an auteur – and, crucially for Kané, it is at least partly ("more or less") unconscious on the part of the creator who shapes it on screen, as well as for the responsive spectator who receives it into their deepest being and psyche.

> So there's that great, loose term: *mise en scène*. Those sets, lighting, words, faces, bodies, costumes, camera movements... In short, all the mixed signifiers that have been ordered by the magic of a *mise en scène*. Now, the *mise en scène* is transformed by something – and certainly not by "know-how." No, what deeply resonates in itself is something on the order of an *invisible thematic* – and the *mise en scène* is at its service.

How does film criticism grasp and deal with these invisible themes of cinema? Not very well, usually, according to Kané. For him, most film reviews and analyses trade only in what is superficial, whereas "to disengage a thematic in a work is indeed to uncover a sort of second discourse."

> How many [critics] have truly practised thematic criticism? How many take the risk of developing the conception of the world implicit in a film? (I know of one who has done this magisterially, and has even more or less founded a school upon it – namely, Jean Douchet.) What's most interesting to say about an auteur is, in my opinion, said by very few critics. They prefer paraphrase, commentary (what Barthes called "cosmetic" criticism), or perhaps some judgement of timeless value.

Against such superficiality and "timeless value," Kané poses something like the inner, driving necessity of the work, the large-scale pattern or scenario it forms across the entire œuvre of an auteur. He gives the major example of Billy Wilder (1906-2002).

> The typical Wilder character is somebody really ordinary, with nothing exceptional. He resigns himself to that until, suddenly, he wants to change, he wants to raise himself to the level of an exceptional person, the master. Which is to say, he starts dreaming of attaining *jouissance*. But, of course, he never gets there. However, he takes to suffering over this, because he believes that, to achieve his goal, he must suffer. And, in a characteristic reversal, he ends up loving his suffering; he imagines that the more he suffers, the more certain it becomes that he will achieve *jouissance*, and that it will be intense. [...]
>
> Cinematically, in terms of shots, all this is translated in the following way: Wilder's privileged inspiration-objects are *beds* and *offices*. That's all there is in his films, beginning with *Sunset Boulevard* (1950), which already constitutes a matrix. The former is supposedly the place of *jouissance*, and the latter the place of suffering. Whereas, in fact, nothing happens at all as programmed: beds become places of suffering [...] and offices are places of ecstasy.

What is the connection between this superior style of criticism (according to Kané) and the initiation into the life of a creative artist? Again, unconscious processes are at play: the deep *attraction* of a critic to a film (or filmmaker's œuvre) has nothing "objective" about it; an emotional and psychological drama is already forming.

> These works in which you recognise yourself to the point of wanting to make them "speak" are, in fact, your mirrors. You

> think you are "objectively" disengaging a theme from a work, but meanwhile what you don't see, and what you will perhaps understand only much later, is that this theme, if you have discerned it from a particular angle, appears like that because, quite clearly, *it matters to you*. And there are many other angles, many other themes in the work in question, about which you absolutely could not care less – because they don't matter to you.

Criticism, for Kané, is thus a form of *preliminary elaboration* of the styles and themes that will later be groped toward in the material work of filmmaking.

> A filmmaker's own themes, those upon which his or her inspiration rests, were first encountered, without knowing it, in the work of other filmmakers. Forcibly blind as to this unconscious inspiration, he will always owe a debt to others, in order for this inspiration to be set in motion. [...]

> I believe that the thematic content of works is constituted in the contact with other creations, and that the labour of elaboration that we feel necessary upon viewing certain works (elaboration which often remains implicit, half-formed) is the first step toward genuine artistic creation. If criticism is necessary, it's because it triggers (or should trigger) this journey.

Gradually, every artist comes to figure out, half consciously and half unconsciously, the themes and forms that, in the deepest sense, appeal to them and spark the energy and commitment necessary to make and complete a film. The informed subjectivity of the artist takes over, as in a relay, from the perhaps deluded objectivity of the critic. In retrospect, critique is a creative, or at least pre-creative act; it lays the groundwork of one's own obsessions, one's truths.

> In the realm of art, everybody must construct their own truth; there is no objective view of works. And the first step of creation is all the "small truths" that you build for yourself. At first, you think they are "foreign" truths, the property of others, and you have merely detected them. And then you realise, when you embark on the work of writing a script and "stumble" upon these small truths as if by chance, that they are also your own.

Source: Pascal Kané's *Savoir dire pour vouloir faire* was published by Éditions Yellow Now (Belgium) in 2015. The original, looser, transcribed version of his 1995 "Genealogy of Inspiration" lecture appears in *La Mise en scène* (Éditions DeBoeck Université, 2000), edited by Jacques Aumont, pp. 167-175.

10
Magical, Secret Ingredient

In 1993, Jacques Rozier (1926-2023) was asked by an interlocutor from *Cahiers du cinema* to re-watch a scene of *French Cancan* (1955) by Jean Renoir (1894-1979) on VHS and comment on it. The film has a special significance in Rozier's professional life: as a young man, he was an assistant on the set. But he doesn't speak about anything he saw or heard during the shoot, beyond observing that Renoir "never knew what he was going to do when he arrived on set. He was the first, privileged spectator of the actors."

Rather, Rozier talks about a particular scene that, when he re-saw it many years later, completely captivated him. It was the "magic" of this scene that he wished to break down into its component parts and understand, using the tool of video rewind and freeze-frame. "I wanted to look at it closely on video, so as to grasp the reasons for the emotion I felt, to figure out exactly how it had been done." We will often encounter filmmakers who speak this way about studying the work of their peers. Rozier takes a craft approach.

> I simply want to speak of a certain "bag of tricks," like a cooking recipe. Renoir himself, in his writings, always evoked cinema or painting in terms of know-how (his own, his father's, his actors'...), rarely in theoretical terms.

Nonetheless, what Rozier uncovers in his commentary is not a matter of simple or obvious filmmaking know-how – where to put the camera to correctly capture the detail, how to best mix the levels of the soundtrack, how to guide the actors, and so on. Rozier is on the trail of a *secret*, an element that brings the scene together, but one that could also possibly be missed by a casual viewer.

In order to reveal this "concentrated, explosive moment that offers proof of Renoir's immense talent" near the end of *French Cancan*, Rozier sets the scene and sums up the plot.

> It's almost the end of the film. The singer Esther (Anna Amendola, dubbed by Cora Vaucaire, one of the last surviving "realist" singers) is about to make her appearance performing "The Hill's Lament," composed by Van Parys for the film, with lyrics by Renoir. At this point in the story, Henri (Jean Gabin) is in an established relationship with Nini (Françoise Arnoul), while also nurturing Esther's career. We know that Esther is about to make her entrance into the Moulin Rouge show, in her debut performance... not on the stage but in the room, in the midst of the audience.

Rozier notes that, when Esther enters the room, "suddenly, there's a change in the sound atmosphere, which has been hitherto comprised of applause. [...] A blast of fresh air enters with the music. All Renoir is already there." Rozier is absolutely right: the interplay between inside and outside, the transitions between speech and song, the use of glass and windows as a bittersweet expression of the longing for freedom: it's all here, every signature of Renoir, encapsulated in this scene. As Esther enters, a change of shot scale (wide shot) accompanies the change in sound ambience. The scene is built upon a song but, as Rozier recognises, "the music maintains the emotion, but this emotion is not only musical."

There is also, in the plan of the scene, an elaborate bit of *mise en scène* business on stage, behind the curtain, that Rozier admires.

> We find Henri and Nini – who has caught on that, for a while now, her star has been fading, and so she is prone to jealousy. She is the one we must see first; she crosses the stage, and a pan shot moving left takes her to a spot behind the curtain. She parts it slightly, in order to observe the crowd. She will soon dance in the following number. She walks slowly, visibly disappointed. Meanwhile, Henri too has taken up a position on the stage, in a background we see only after Nini has finished her stroll. Renoir has used two stagehands, carrying a piece of the set, to hide him (he can be glimpsed for only a fraction of a second). Each character is alone. So Nini gazes upon her rival, gleaning that Henri's feelings of love for Esther are growing. The camera returns to Nini, who now seems sadder.

But where is the secret element located – the element that, for Rozier, incites his deepest emotion? "Something else arises, something different, inexplicable, inexpressible," and Rozier locates it in "the presence of Gaston Modot (uncredited, as Henri's valet) in the room." Let me insist: you may need to look closely, or look again, to see this scene exactly as Rozier sees it, through his eyes. Here is how he describes the gradual inclusion of Modot in the scene, following the vignette behind the curtain.

> We go back to the room. Esther executes a move, thus uncovering the characters we noticed behind her before. And, at a precise moment, we clearly observe two characters in the frame: Esther and the extremely strong presence of Modot. He's quite tall, very stiff, with thinning white hair: it's the portrait of a good-looking, older man. He gazes upon this woman as

> if she were Woman, a model for Auguste
> Renoir. A mysterious current is therefore
> created between him and her.

A question arises for Rozier, and for any of us who now look at the scene: did Renoir intend, in the scene and in the image, this comparison between Esther and Modot? How did this "moment" become "precise"? Did Renoir foresee it? How spontaneous was the director's "discovery" of this magic element before his eyes, hidden within the panoply of the scene? Rozier muses on this.

> To my mind, it is impossible that Renoir
> captured this by chance, involuntarily.
> That's the magic of cinema: Renoir became
> captivated, within this shot, by the deep,
> internal feeling of Modot in relation to this
> woman. That's what he hooked onto.

We find here an interpretive and appreciative position close to Kané's formulation: an auteur's true *theme* is not the nominal *subject* of the particular story they are treating, but emerges at a deeper level of the realisation of the work. Here is how Rozier perceives and spells out the theme of this scene of *French Cancan*, and hence of the film as a whole (perhaps Renoir's entire oeuvre as a whole!).

> The passing time of age, compared to
> this woman's Eternity – it's devastating.
> On one side, the Renoir who deals with
> emotion (jealousy and love); on the other,
> Renoir the pantheist.

At any rate, Rozier's reception of this fragment by Renoir accords well with Kané's idea that a budding filmmaker recognises part of his or her own identity in what they see and relate to in other people's films.

> These are the kinds of moments, at once very simple and very complex, that give you the desire to make cinema.

Indeed, we will easily find the trace of everything that Rozier has described and evoked in Renoir recreated in his own films, such as the whimsical but masterly *Maine Océan* (1986), with its extended, seemingly spontaneous but meticulously staged musical improvisations.

Source: "*French Cancan*" by Jacques Rozier, interviewed and transcribed by Jacques Morice, from the *Cahiers du cinéma* special issue *100 Films pour une vidéothèque* (1993), p. 61. My complete English translation is at http://www.screeningthepast.com/issue-46-classics-re-runs/jacques-rozier-on-french-cancan.

11
Nailing Down the Parameters of Cinécriture

Doing my duty on a film festival jury in Las Palmas in 2008 allowed me to spend some precious (as well as volatile) time in the company of Chantal Akerman (1950-2015). During that week, she told her fellow jurors many juicy stories about the films she had made, the people with whom she had collaborated, the many projects in film and installation art she was developing (some of which she was subsequently able to realise) – and, most crucially for me, how, in general terms, she approached any project and worked on it.

In terms of her temperament and personality, Akerman could swing wildly from displays of gregarious charity and affection to gestures of cold, impatient dismissal. The latter mood overtook her whenever she decided that her interlocutors (whether an individual or a group) were simply unable to comprehend something that was so obvious to her it needed no elaboration or justification. Sometimes, though, if she figured she could influence somebody's thinking, she would persist in spelling out her filmmaking "method." And this was especially rewarding when coming from such a great artist who wrote a lot, often in a highly literary and personal style, but explicitly "theorised" little.

It was on one of those days in Las Palmas when she was hesitating between walking away to smoke another cigarette or sticking with her discourse that Akerman outlined something which, once you are primed to see and notice it, is evident everywhere in all her works. She explained that almost the very first step in a filmmaking or art project – once a basic subject or source (such as a novel or play to be adapted) had been fixed on – was to set its *parameters*.

This process involved making a set of decisions that would more or less determine, in advance, the tone, texture, rhythm, even the running time of the work. And it would also eliminate, from the outset, what she regarded as fruitless and wasteful (i.e., costly) experimentation, such as trying out different ways of capturing a scene on the set or location. (Aside: when I asked Thai director Apichatpong

Weerasethakul [born 1970] whether he worked in this same, parametric way – as seemed to be the case from the highly rigorous, stylised evidence on screen – he laughed and replied that no, he plans nothing in advance and shoots many takes of everything in many different styles, leaving it to the editing stage to discover a film's best, final form. The complete opposite to Akerman, it seems!)

What did Akerman mean by parameters? It indicated a set of formal or stylistic choices. These were some types of examples she mentioned. Deciding the basic camera strategies: static or moving shots? If the camera moves, what kind of motion will it be – inward, outward, lateral? Questions of rhythm: fast, slow, torpid, agitated, calm, reflective, immersive? How much of the film will happen indoors, and how much outdoors (see her musical *Golden Eighties* [1986] for a stunning example of this parameter)? Design of colour: what is the central palette informing the sets, the costumes, the hairstyles? A harmonious fusion of colours, or a discordant clash? (Recall how Alain Resnais [1922-2014] would sometimes deliberately keep the various production design departments separate from each other, in order to finally achieve unforeseen conflicts between clothes and walls.) What kind of music track, specifically commissioned and composed or borrowed from elsewhere, how often used, in what balance or mix with other parts of the sound design, such as voices, atmospheres and silences? How much of the action will be seen on screen, and how much placed off screen? (Akerman had an aversion to showing explicit violence, for instance, even if it was at the core of the plot – she found this "pornographic.") How is the ensemble of actors going to function, not only in terms of acting styles, but also physically and physiologically, in terms of differences in their height, shape, vocal tone?

It was apparent, at the end of this impromptu speech (which I have reconstructed from memory and my notebook), that there was no element of audiovisual media which Akerman did *not* deeply consider before filming the first take of any new project. And, furthermore, all these stylistic elements carried a strong *ethical* component for her. In the extensive "Pajama Interview" of 2011 (so titled because she conducted it in her pajamas!), Akerman outlined her predilection for "filming things frontally" in order to achieve a *face-to-face* relationship between the spectator and the screen images. Her idea of the frontal face relation is inspired by her reading of the Jewish philosopher Emmanuel Levinas (1906-1995), who equally influenced the Dardenne brothers (see Luc Dardenne's fascinating *On the Back of Our Images, Volume 1: 1991-2005*). Citing Levinas' notion that coming "face-to-face with the Other" initiates a "sense of responsibility," Akerman evokes the force of frontal close-ups.

> [A close-up is] material and it moves, even when it seems fixed. And when you avoid low angles and subjective shots, you avoid fetishism. When you film frontally, you put two souls face-to-face equally, you carve out a real place for the viewer. So it's not God-like. You contemplate something that's fixed. Not an eyelid batting, not a beat skipping.

Not an eyelid batting or a beat skipping could almost be Akerman's rewrite of Godard (whose *Pierrot le fou* [1965] wielded a huge impact on her) and his *if to direct is a glance, to edit is a beating of the heart*. Although, when we watch the most rapturously lyrical passages of her *Nuit et jour* (1991), we might want to combine both formulae! At any rate, we must take Akerman very seriously when she defines her "idea of ethics" within such cinematic parameters. "It's why I want equality, always, between the image and the spectator. Or the passage from one unconscious toward the other" (see Grandrieux's similar musing in Chapter 15: "This movement leaving from itself to go toward the other, then returning from the other back to the self").

Two addenda to this lesson in cinema. First, Akerman made no distinction, in her working method, between fiction and documentary; it was not as if she staged and filmed narrative in a highly stylised, artificial way, and then shot her documentaries "wild" and spontaneously. No, even if reality was not always "directable" or amenable to her *mise en scène*, the camera strategy was always figured out in advance, and that gave her and the usually small crew a definite line to follow in projects including *From the East* (1993) and *South* (1999). Second: even if it's easy for a fan to spot the "signature style" of Akerman from film to film in certain, recurring devices (such as the lateral tracking shot following a person walking), the parameters are never exactly the same; they are open to variation, alteration, surprise. It's the specific combination and the balance of the parameters that is always unique.

To describe her art installations, Akerman would regularly use the French word *dispositif*. Not in a theoretical way (as it is often deployed today), but as a "practical aesthetic" means of describing the format, layout or set-up of a piece in a space, and the parametric decision-making that necessarily accompanied it: how many screens, how big, how far apart, what level of illumination in the room, what level of sound (or mix of multiple sounds) and silence, what would be the narrative (or non-narrative) path enabled for the wandering gallery viewer by this spatial configuration? As spectators or analysts, we are fully authorised to consider her films and videos, also, as particular *dispositifs*, in the sense that they arrange their parameters in an unfolding (and this time more fixed and circumscribed) time and space.

In film history, the forerunner to Akerman's mindset in relation to stylistic parameters and formal *dispositifs* is the cherished notion of *cinécriture* or "cine-writing" coined by Agnès Varda (1928-2019). Like Akerman, Varda was not temperamentally given to theorising; both filmmakers produced books for a *Cahiers du cinéma* series that are more like elaborate collage scrapbooks than explanatory texts. However, Varda was determined to present to the public, from around the mid-1960s onwards, her way of working, and she was still musing on the method of *cinécriture* in her final film-essay, *Varda by Agnès* (2019).

The term is sometimes misunderstood and misused; it refers neither to the scriptwriting process, nor to what critic-filmmaker Alexandre Astruc (1923-2016) in the late 1940s called the *caméra-stylo* or camera-pen – so it doesn't mean camera-writing as in spontaneously tracing movements or framing shots with the camera, the way (for example) Jonas Mekas (1922-2019) did. (Already in Astruc's formulation, it meant more than simply this, but reductive, literal-minded clichés have a way of enduring…) Since Varda never published any sort of manifesto on *cinécriture*, we are forced, just this once, to refer to somebody else's accurate summary of what the idea amounts to. Here is Bérénice Reynaud's definition.

> …the singularity of composition that [Varda] strives to achieve at every level of production: screenplay, shooting script, casting, location, position and movement of camera, rhythm.

Varda herself has amplified the idea in an analogical comparison – familiar from much filmmaker thinking, as we shall see later with Pasolini – between cinematic language and literary language.

> The cutting, the movement, the points-of-view, the rhythm of filmmaking and editing have been felt and considered in the way a writer chooses the depth of meaning and sentences, the type of words, number of adverbs, paragraphs, asides, chapters – which advance the story or break its flow.

There are several observations worth making about the idea of *cinécriture*. On the one hand, it strongly resembles the parameter/*dispositif* approach expressed and practised by Akerman, which it slightly anticipated in film history – and, in fact, by the time we reach the 1980s, we find in Varda's career highly formalised, parametric films (such as *Vagabond*, 1985) that seem to overlap with Akerman's in their form and manner, as well as many manifestations of installation art (sometimes more "interactive" than Akerman's preferred mode), a path that Varda increasingly took.

On the other hand, it might also be observed that what Varda defines as *cinécriture* is what any decent director, in almost any production situation, does or tries to do: to set a coherent style and ensure that all the elements, as they fall into place, fit the overall schema. Neither Cukor nor Mackendrick would have disagreed with that, in broad terms. It's what "preserving the core idea," as we have seen, is all about.

However, the important difference here is that both Akerman and Varda belong to a particular stream of art (rather than strictly "commercial") cinema that relates to the traditions of the "cinema of poetry" (Pasolini's mid-1960s term, to be explored in Part Two) and a level of *overt* and systematic stylisation that tends, at its extreme, to an invocation of avant-garde experimentation. Even if only temporarily or intermittently, the complex movement of the filmic forms takes prominence over narrative illusion (which is partly what Varda means when she talks of "breaking the flow" of a story) – and this is something that classical filmmakers (or TV showrunners of today) can never countenance. It is a different *economy* or relation of style to content than we find in mainstream, storytelling cinema.

Already with *Le Bonheur* in 1965, Varda was posing *against* the narrative a dizzying series of stylistic spectacles involving explicit rhymes and symmetries (two heroines who look alike and take the same place, successively, in the hero's life), extraordinarily vivid use of a patterned colour scheme (far outstripping the facile "symbolism" routinely attributed to colours), and an aggressive, Vertov-like *kino-eye* editing (the brief frames of close-up sunflowers alternating with blurred shots of human figures in motion during the opening credits). And, once again, there are some boldly ethical implications to these stylistic provocations…

Source: The two books expressly created by these filmmakers for publication by *Cahiers du cinéma* remain the richest source for exploring their respective methods and practices: *Varda par Agnès* (1994) and *Chantal Akerman. Autoportrait en cineaste* (2004). The text in the latter is reprinted in the massive, 3-volume *Œuvre écrite et parlée* (L'Arachnéen, 2024). Neither memoir has yet been translated into English. Akerman's "Pajama Interview" can be found in English at http://lolajournal.com/2/pajama.html. The English translation of Luc Dardenne's *On the Back of Our Images, Volume 1: 1991-2005* is published by Featherproof Books.

12
Cool, Clear Water

> You have to make believe that you are going one way and then not go there. Create stopping points. Destabilise the framing in an unpretentious manner. Avoid images that are easily translated into one word. Disrespect the narrative structure of familiar spaces: home, bedroom, garden, car. Try to use sound to weaken the relationship between an image and its referent. Betray expectations. Manage those betrayals. It's all easy, but you have to train yourself.
>
> Lucrecia Martel, 2019 interview

At the Rotterdam Festival in 2018, Argentinian Lucrecia Martel (born 1966) spoke to her Masterclass audience about not having had a university training in film – and being proud of that. "I decided to train myself," she declared.

> I wanted to move away from the training you receive at cinema school. Training programs are essential for filmmakers but, in the end, they can also limit them; it can submerge them into a bubble from which they have to break free in order to make cinema.

The metaphoric imagery of the bubble or the box is central to Martel's thought and, as we will see, it has two aspects, negative and positive. Here, she is referring to the bad kind of socio-cultural box: the one that imprisons you, or blinds you. "Freeing perception" is a major motif in her oft-repeated discourse since the 2000s – although she has not yet committed her reflections to the page in an essay or book, she has given numerous in-depth interviews, appears frequently at film festivals, and many of her lectures in Spanish can be found online.

Freeing perception – renegotiating how we see and hear things through cinema – is the shortcut to enlarging our social attitudes, and our contact with others different from us. This, at any rate, is her hope and dream, and it is one shared by many filmmakers; it's one of the primary ways of making a longed-for connection between film and reality, rather than languishing in a despair that they are two, autonomous tracks that never meet.

It was hard to decide in which part of this book to place Martel's thinking. Although she reveals the ways in which she generates her own ideas for how to treat narratives and scenes – i.e., her personal poetics – she is also committed to sharing her generative method as part of a more general, theoretical reflection: on the structures and meanings of narrative, on the role of sound, on our understanding of the categories of time and event. In the merry list of hints offered above, Martel might be thought of as sharing the type of "bag of tricks" or "cooking recipe" that Rozier (Chapter 10) invoked in relation to Renoir. But, at the same time, her reflections open onto a wider field. Feel free to reshuffle the chapters (Maya Deren anagram-style) according to your own intuition!

So, we've had the bad box of training and education. And something else, another national, contextual box against which Martel strongly reacted when she began her filmmaking career in the late 1980s: the *cine costumbrista* of Argentina, a genre of naturalism fixed on daily habits, manners and "social issues," schematically presented. Martel's good box, or more exactly glass jar, is the one that she seemingly carries with her to every part of the world where she will talk to a crowd. That, and a mobile phone with a screen of pure light, constitute the tools for her demonstration of What Cinema Is. She first places the phone with the screen beaming its illumination down into the space of the jar. With the room lights down, she evokes the scene for us. (I am here transcribing a simultaneous translation from Rotterdam of her speech, with all due allowance for its necessary spontaneity and paraphrase.)

> I have this concept, this system called *submersion*. The concept is called diving, submersion or immersion. The first experience we can have as children of this immersion experience is when we dive into a swimming pool; we immerse ourselves into the swimming pool. But now with any mobile phone, you can take your own phone to represent the light surface of the pool. If we look at this box and we see it as a swimming pool, and we try to dive in with as much air as we can in our lungs, we will experience the childhood experience, which is the experience of diving, of submerging oneself – *immersion*.

Let us pause here to clarify that Martel does not mean immersion in its currently popular sense – the spectator becoming completely lost in the imaginary plot, characters and world of a film. (Later in her talk, Martel mocks 3D as the paltry, "industrial" path to cinematic image-immersion.) Immersion in a film for Martel is a little like *fascination* as defined by Pascal Kané: it is an *experience*, perhaps a very emotional and involving one, but foremost an experience of the forms, materials, and shifting positions that a film proposes to us. Narrative, and all it entails, will only be one element in this total experience. Now, what is the nature of this experience happening within the water of the pool?

> If we are at this point of the pool, at the bottom, if we dive right to the bottom, we see that water is an elastic, flexible space, so that if anything falls into the water in which I am submerged, I will feel the vibrations of the water. My body will feel the presence of something: someone that dives into the pool, the sound that comes from the surface, we will hear this, I will

> hear this in my ears but I will also feel the
> vibrations generated in the water.

Vibration is an important concept for Martel, and it is more than a metaphor – a vibration is what we take in and feel in our bodies. It is also a specific way of describing the impact of an *event* in a story, or in the world – the event is there, something located in an amorphous space (the water), and perceived by us in our "now," even if it is literally an echo, or on a delay: this is a little like the complex "eternal present moment" that the young Godard of the 1950s evoked in his appreciation of Ingmar Bergman's films. But I am getting ahead of Martel's demonstration here; let us return to the scene of the pool – and its metamorphic flip into something else.

> If we have this pool and if we turn it around, it is a cinema room, right? So the spectator is submerged in a field of air, and sound is what enables cinema to be 3D. We cannot have three dimensions that are stronger than sound. Sound changes the air. Sound creates movement in the air, the waves of sound move along the room around the space, and they generate different types of *pressure* around the spectators.

Sound is a more primary component than image in Martel's view of cinema. In Spanish, she has borrowed the Baroque term *phonurgia* (intermingling sonics with wonder, and echoing "dramaturgy") to describe her approach to both scripting and *mise en scène* with sound always leading the way and setting the stylistic and formal parameters (as discussed in the previous chapter). This is both a sketch of her own way of working – she talks of how economically she shoots a scene, since she has already defined the elements of its soundscape – and a strong proposition concerning the *sensorium* of cinema and its proper economy, somewhat akin to the ideas of Robert Bresson (but taken even further than he did). It is justified in an oft-used comparison between the sensorial, bodily states of seeing and listening: "You can close your eyes and stop watching the film… but you still hear the sounds."

> What does this mean? It means that the element in which the spectators are immersed is *sound*, in the end. […] It is quite possible for us to perceive *volume* – deep sound creates very strong waves of sound, and you can perceive this on the surface of your skin. So this is where spectators are submerged.

Referring again to her glowing jar, Martel does her level best to diminish the role of the image.

> The surface of light that we can see on the mobile phone is a small cut in a much larger universe, a huge universe. The space of cinema is infinite, it's huge. The surface of the screen is finite; it has its limits, it's flat. So sound goes beyond the image in the end, it submerges, it takes over the space.

To the concepts of vibration/sensation and the primary role of sound, Martel adds an important reflection on the characteristics of narrative and time, which she again compares to the volume of water.

> Cinema tends to think about linear timelines. Linear timelines that have been very useful, that have been very productive in masterpieces – but they're not useful for everyone! And so, if we look at timelines: a timeline is very associated with a perspective. If we think of future and past, we draw a line with an arrow, and we think of cause and consequence, of beginning

> and end. This is, of course, very useful. But sometimes we forget the fact that this is an invention. Time has no direction…

We shall again encounter in the following chapter this notion that time and space are not entirely natural, that the conventional way we imagine their workings can be changed. According to Martel, we must strive – in whatever speculative, experimental way we can – to "somehow realise that the way we think, the way we organise perception, is based on a general idea." Martel herself has a background in science; she notes that "some scientists say that there is no timeline," while acknowledging cheekily that this stance "may irritate the more scientific among us, because it doesn't have a lot of scientific evidence." Nonetheless, she presses on with her mission to redefine these properties.

> I like to think of time as volume. This volume, this box, is time. If time were contained in this volume, all of the particles that are usually organised in a timeline, with cause and consequence and so forth – if it was all found within this container, if all of these particles of events were found within this volume and we had to build a narrative based on this time, it wouldn't be so easy to find meaning in time. We wouldn't be able to find cause and consequence – or we would have to reflect a lot more in order to trace a relation between cause and effect. So we would have to think with more depth.

Ultimately, Martel's aim is political – a politics achieved through the material, poetic forms of cinema. Near the end of her Masterclass, she states: "I think it's important to know that the first thing in cinema is to challenge ourselves first, because if we don't challenge our own perception, we won't be able to see anything." Her aim is to sow *doubt*.

Whenever you manage, through cinema, to cast doubt on the assumed nature of things, you might be approaching something really interesting. This is not obligatory, but it's one of the highest aims to which language may aspire. And when you have done that once, there's no way back. Because once you become aware of what makes no sense, never again can reality manage to completely hide its quality of disguise.

Source: Lucrecia Martel's 2018 Rotterdam Masterclass/interview can be found with simultaneous English translation at https://www.youtube.com/watch?v=TKO0tBMIvZI&feature=emb_title and in the original Spanish at https://www.youtube.com/watch?v=Z_zdESWSTxw. I have quoted mainly from points between the 90 to 105-minute marks. Of her many illuminating interviews, I especially recommend the 2019 discussion with Silvina López Medin that follows up on her lecture at The Museum of Modern Art in New York: https://post.moma.org/to-cast-doubt-on-the-assumed-nature-of-things-an-interview-with-lucrecia-martel.

13
The Power of Negation

Although I have concentrated, so far, on the positive and productive aspects of craft, poetics and artistic goal-setting in cinema, it is just as important to recognise the reverse of this picture: all the calls and campaigns, throughout film history, to negate or destroy this medium, to jam its mechanism, to drag it back to the default mark of zero. There are always good reasons to do so! And the anger of such negation can bring with it a liberating, punk energy. In a paradoxical but very real way, destructiveness is also creative in cinema.

Isidore Isou militantly argued in the early 1950s for almost total erasure of the cinema's past. Jean-Luc Godard, in the company of comrades including Jean-Pierre Gorin (born 1943), moved in the uncompromisingly radical direction of anti-cinema (certainly anti-commercial cinema) post-1968, leaving behind both the Hollywood classicism of the 1950s and the Pop Art Modernism of the early-to-mid-1960s. Yvonne Rainer advocated, from a feminist perspective, the necessary desecration of a predominantly patriarchal, narrative language of film. These are only three of the many efforts to effectively destroy cinema.

We will hear more about some of these anarchistic exemplars in Part Two of this book. For now, as a hinge-point between ideas of cinema and ideas about cinema, let's listen in to Kijū (short form of Yoshishige) Yoshida (1933-2022) from Japan.

"Whatever you put after *anti-*, as long as *anti-* is there, it fits my films." In 1960s Japan, Yoshida was one of the most eloquent exponents of the *anti-film* or *anti-cinema* movement. His thought intersected with other filmmakers in the Japanese context of that time, including Masao Adachi, Toshio Matsumoto and Nagisa Oshima. Some Japanese directors – another, more contemporary example is Shinji Aoyama – exhibit an intellectual, theoretical ambition, and express themselves in this way in essays and books, very differently to the type of professional reticence once associated with past national masters such as Kenji Mizoguchi, Mikio Naruse or Yasujiro Ozu. Yoshida even wrote a text in 1971 blatantly titled "My Theory of Film" – to which he added the subtitle: "A Logic of Self-Negation." For one must negate not only the cinema, but also oneself!

In a surprising turn later in his life, Yoshida decided to look back, more charitably than he had as a young artist, upon the work of Ozu, whom he had briefly known personally near the end of the latter's life. Where once he had rejected Ozu's serene, apparently conservative classicism, Yoshida now found much to value. But guess what? His book is titled *Ozu's Anti-Cinema* (1998)! It offers a remarkable example of a "re-reading against the grain" of canonical film work, a re-evaluation and redemption of it by tearing it out of its original context, disturbing the typical framework of its reception and interpretation, and claiming it for a totally different tradition – in this case, the paradoxical tradition of anti-cinema.

Yoshida's negatory-at-all-costs drive is both aesthetic and political, a combination we will often find in anti-cinema manifestos. He especially pits himself against certain conventions in narrative cinema, effectively rejecting the ideas (embraced, as we have seen, by some filmmakers) of any kind of grammar or syntax of film language, any basic, craft procedures. In 2009, Yoshida offered this example.

> When you finish filming and go to the editing room, when you cut, you have to have a reason to cut. The clumsiest way is when somebody gets angry and hits a table with his hand, and you cut at this moment and go to another shot. It's such a clichéd technique that people who are used to seeing films just automatically accept it without any resistance.

Later we shall encounter Raúl Ruiz's in-depth thoughts on the connection and disconnection between film shots. Yoshida's theory is more directly reactive: if there's a typical or set way to do something, don't do it! Resist or retard or eliminate that cut altogether; find a completely unconventional, surprising way to render the scene. Involved in this attitude is a concern for the spectator: to reawaken him or her through shocks, deliberate frustrations, the unexpected.

Like his contemporaries, Yoshida experimented relentlessly with pulling apart the standard relations of image and sound synchrony, and with introducing black frames to break the illusionistic flow of a *découpage* of shots. Violent metaphors – breaking, tearing, dismembering – take the place of Godard's mid-1950s language of the glance and the heartbeat.

A major part of many avant-garde movements in aesthetics (John Cage's music, for example) has been the dominant role accorded to *chance* or the accidental – indeed, the innovative filmmaker-theorist Noël Burch (born 1932) named a chapter of his influential 1969 book *Praxis du cinéma* (in English, *Theory of Film Practice*) precisely "Chance and its Functions." According to the youthful, early text of Godard that we looked at, chance must be married to *destiny*, and that is, in fact, an underlying motto of the entire, early 1960s Nouvelle Vague to which he belonged in France. There should be an element of risk, of chance, of spontaneity (this is what the Nouvelle Vague members loved, and were inspired by, in the work of Jean Renoir) but, once discovered and captured, this chance element needs to be integrated, shaped, worked into the form-content ensemble of the whole film.

Yoshida, for his part, rejects such an organic, flowing, *resolved* aesthetic approach to the function that can be played by chance. He seeks to preserve the roughness of the accident.

> My task is how to replace that kind of ordinary cinematic experience that people have in the theatre with something unusual. For that, you need accidents. Because when I calculate certain things or prepare certain things, the audience can always tell.

Another strategy that Yoshida explored and theorised in the 1960s is what, a decade or so later, the critic-turned-filmmaker Pascal Bonitzer (born 1946) would call *deframing*.

> I also went beyond the normal rules for setting up the camera and framing a scene. The common rule is that when you make a close-up, the focus of the shot should be at the centre of the frame, so that for most people it's easy to look at, it's comfortable. Which also means that as part of the set of rules of cinema, the person at the centre is often unconsciously defined as the protagonist.

Notice here this constant movement, in Yoshida's thought, between the process of filmmaking and its theorised effect on the spectator: for the filmmaker, framing a close-up and choosing a central character is surely a conscious process; but for the spectator, watching and receiving this close-up is the *unconscious* internalisation of an ideology, a set of values embedded in socially constructed narrative. Yoshida's response is to upset this unspoken contract between film and spectator – by militant deframing.

> So I very often only film only half the face of the actor. It's a kind of resistance, telling the audience: "Don't trust so blindly what you see on the screen. Please try to define by yourselves what is really important to you as the audience, in what you see within this frame." That kind of feeling became stronger and stronger for me.

This desired freedom of the spectator is often insisted on by Yoshida. "A film is ultimately not about what I tell the audience to see, but about what the audience sees and discovers for themselves."

Like many filmmakers working within a sphere we could loosely define as *experimental narrative* – neither completely abstract nor using conventional storytelling – Yoshida is committed to a double-sided action. There must be some illusion, some people, some plot in order for it all to be broken, redefined, reassembled in a new way both on the screen and in the spectator's mind. The viewer, here, is theorised as somebody ensnared by the film in a life-and-death, cognitive struggle, and willing to grapple with it: by the end of a movie, can an individual or mass consciousness be altered, reformed, radicalised or revolutionised? Dziga Vertov was (as we shall see) preoccupied with exactly the same question, as was Godard during the 1970s, when his already political cinema practice increasingly intersected with TV formats, technologies (videotape) and broadcast opportunities (see his and Anne-Marie Miéville's 1975 feature *Numéro deux* for a reflection on this heady period).

The Belgian surrealist Louis Scutenaire (1905-1987) once expressed his love for certain popular, animated cartoons of the 1930s in this way: "My taste for Popeye the Sailor, in the cartoons by Max Fleischer, owes much to the liberties he takes with those cherished beliefs of humanity: space and time." What a truly wonderful, cinematic idea: that humanity's deepest and most illusory beliefs are not God, love or society, but space and time! And that, therefore, we need to create a permanent anti-cinema waging war against space and time however and wherever we can, even (or especially) in cartoons for children. This resonates with the thought and work of Lucrecia Martel (who has also worked in animation). Let the last word in the first part of this book belong to Yoshida, flying to the most extreme, philosophical point of his own theory of film practice.

> I myself was the kind of viewer who believes that cinema can exist as a means of communication without following the commonly accepted rules of time and space.

Source: Kijū Yoshida's book *Ozu's Anti-Cinema* was published in English translation by University of Michigan in 2003. His essay "My Theory of Film" appears translated in the December 2010 issue of academic journal *Review of Japanese Culture and Society*. Most of the quotations that I cite derive from a 2009 interview by Chris Fujiwara, "No Wasted Moments: The Anti-Cinema of Kijū Yoshida" at http://www.movingimagesource.us/articles/no-wasted-moments-20090402. Pascal Bonitzer's 1985 book *Deframings* has been translated into Spanish as *Desencuadres. Cine y pintura* (Argentina: Cegal, 2007).

Interlude
Statements of Intention

14
Chantal Akerman: *Almayer's Folly*

This section of the book, poised between Parts One (Ideas of Cinema) and Two (Ideas About Cinema), is devoted to a loose and often publicly invisible genre of written document: the Statement of Intention (sometimes also known as a Vision Statement) composed by a director. They are used in film production circumstances in many countries. Beyond this professional role, I recommend anyone embarking on any kind of creative, artistic project to formulate a Statement of Intention – if even purely privately, for oneself. It can clarify many things, and is especially helpful when it comes to the struggle I have described as "preserving the core."

Statements of Intention should not be confused with treatments or synopses – those are different sorts of documents (often key to production processes) that are focused on communicating the purely narrative part of a project. In the Statements we will be looking at, however, plot is almost secondary to the central intent. Rather, the director seeks to express a desired constellation – the goal they are aiming for – of mood, atmosphere and emotion; both how that constellation will be formed on the screen, and how it is meant to affect its future spectators.

The Statement of Intention is, above all, a privileged place or moment in the creative process where the filmmaker figures out, at some level, what their project is, what it represents, what it is really all about for them. It's the site where (in Pascal Kané's terms) a director searches for their theme (rather than their surface subject), and attempts to, in some way, identify, marshal and orient the sources of their inspiration.

The aspect of a filmmaker clarifying their private thoughts is present in most such Statements. At the same time, such a document – typically only a few pages long – can serve other functions: as something to show producers (actual or potential); as a guide to the heads of the various production departments (cinematography, set and costume design, sound); as a way to establish a close rapport with the assistant director; and so on. These texts often disappear or go into an inaccessible archive once a work has been completed; sometimes all that's needed is a polite request to the filmmaker in order for them to be dug out of the pile of whatever pages were generated before, during and after the shoot (this is how, for example, I managed to see Chantal Akerman's document discussed in this chapter, and the special example of Raúl Ruiz's imaginary "tales" that he used to send to his central actors to help prepare them).

In some cases, it is the director's main assistant, serving as a "sounding board" and close collaborator – such as Charles Bitsch for Godard in the 1960s or Claire Denis in her apprenticeship years working with Jacques Rivette in the 1970s – who preserves these documents until, perhaps many years later, a researcher comes along asking to see them. More rarely, directors sometimes return to their initial Statements and re-present them as articles for publication (as is the case with Australian-born John Hillcoat, whose text on *The Proposition* I present in this section of the book). Across the expanse of world cinema and its history, Statements of Intention constitute a largely untapped goldmine!

We cannot show a particular dimension of some Statements of Intention here: a form of scrapbook, sometimes referred to more grandly as an Image Book or, in industrial-corporate parlance, a "lookbook," where the director collects and presents all manner of images, gathered from anywhere and everywhere (news photos, screenshots from other films, reproductions of paintings, personal drawings, etc.). Such pictorial materials may stand alone or be interwoven with written text of different kinds (notes, quotations, key words). This type of document usually appears once funding is in place and pre-production begins. Leos Carax, Kelly Reichardt, Todd Haynes and Pedro Costa are only a few of the filmmakers who proceed in this way. For a stunning example of Costa's elaborate procedure in this regard, see the supplemental material provided on the Second Run DVD edition of *Casa de Lava* (1994), where the pages of his image-notebook are set to music.

We begin looking at samples of Statements of Intention with Chantal Akerman's prospectus for what would turn out to be her final narrative feature, *Almayer's Folly* (2011). The adaptation of Joseph Conrad's 1895 debut novel necessitated a long and elaborate screenwriting process; as was often the case in her career, Akerman tried out various scenarists and, through successive rejection of their proposed versions, came to more completely define her *own* sense of how the film should be made, and what parameters should be set for it (as we saw in Chapter 11) – on the final result, she receives the sole screenplay credit, while previous collaborators discarded along the way are discreetly thanked at the end.

Akerman began her December 2008 "Synopsis and Statement of Intent" – set out poetically, in short paragraphs, some only a single sentence long – with this telling reflection.

> The fall of a European in Malaya. That is what Joseph Conrad wanted to write about when he started his first book, *Almayer's Folly*.
>
> And he did write about that but about much more besides.

So the deep, underlying theme of the material – according to Akerman, unknown to Conrad himself when he began writing – is what attracts and inspires her as a filmmaker. If you compare film and novel, you will see how completely *abstracted* and elliptical her adaptation ultimately became.

> The action unfolds in Malaya, not far from Borneo in the 1950s when Malaya was still under the control of the English.
>
> In a little isolated village far from anywhere.
>
> On a wide river and the river will play a very important role in this story that is simple yet deals with passion and dream, racism and money.

> Yearning for independence and cowardice, but above all the love of a father for his daughter which, when he loses her to another man who is not even white, will go as far as madness and his complete downfall.

Note (as we shall also see in relation to Philippe Grandrieux) the emphasis on *place* or location ("the river will play a very important role") and the identification, underneath the peripeiteia of the story, of its key themes: "passion and dream, racism and money." In Conrad, she found a framework in which these themes were fully *inscribed* – embodied and lived out by characters. It is a veritable principle of melodrama, a genre in cinema that Akerman loved, even as she applied a highly modernist sensibility to it.

Above all, Akerman attests to her indifference to certain realistic specifics of the novel: "As time went by and the detail – the book is filled with it – faded, I realised just how universal it was." Even the political context of history in Conrad's story has been sifted and shifted, all the better to bring out a "whole collective dimension" of racial prejudice and cultural intermixing that is "even more powerfully relevant for us today."

Akerman's evocation of the film in her mind is richly cinematic, complete with sudden changes in mood and atmosphere that are tied to no specific plot event.

> I would like to treat this story with simplicity, a father, a mother, a girl, a young man in love with her; and with sensuality, thanks to the setting.
>
> The vegetation is lush, the overwhelming heat of the sun, the humidity heavy in the air, the richness of colours in the sky and on the earth, the wildness of the water endangering those who venture into it. Sudden calm. Mist that lifts, dugouts

sliding across the water. Birds flying over
the water. Nearby jungle.

As for Akerman's cinephilic horizon of reference, it comes down to a single, classic film, *Tabu: A Story of the South Seas* (1931), made by F.W. Murnau and Robert Flaherty (the latter doesn't get a mention in the Statement). Her citation is a fanciful time-travel shuttle: while she travels backward in time, Murnau gets to travel forward: "There's something in this story that reminds one of Murnau's *Tabu*. And I like pondering how Murnau would make this film if he were in the 1950s like me." One filmmaker's dream picks up from another's…

Source: Chantal Akerman's "*Almayer's Folly*: Synopsis and Statement of Intent" is translated into English at http://lolajournal.com/2/almayer.html. Between 2003 and 2016, both the online publication *LOLA* and its forerunner *Rouge* (www.rouge.com.au) published many texts by filmmakers, including Víctor Erice, Keja and Robert Kramer, Pedro Costa, Raúl Ruiz, Jayce Salloum, Stephen Dwoskin, Hou Hsiao-hsien, Yvette Bíró, José Luis Guerin and Mark Rappaport. Other Statements of Intent by Akerman can be found in her *Œuvre écrite et parlée* (L'Arachnéen, 2024).

15
Philippe Grandrieux: *Sombre*

What is involved in a Statement of Intention? This type of document has no set form or convention, so it can include many, diverse things, according to the desire of the filmmaker in question.

For Philippe Grandrieux (born 1954), for example, in his "Notes of Intention" written in July 1996 before the shooting of *Sombre* (1998), *place* or location – in this case, the Rhône-Alpes region of France – is deemed a crucial factor to elucidate.

> I need these landscapes, their earthy colour, the soil blackened by coal, the often cloudy sky: I need them so that the film can find its unspoken, unexplained material – the means by which the images touch us.

What is the nature of this "material" Grandrieux evokes? It is a complex, compound sensation linked to an idea of childhood.

> I come from the centre of France, a small town. The hills and woods of this story belong to my childhood. And if I wanted to go shoot down there [...] it was not to "flatter" any biographical urge, but so that the film could be as close as possible to what it recounts: this murky, blind, inconsolable state of childhood.

Moreover, certain background script elements of the project – "the Tour de France, parties, 14 July" – ensure that "the aspect of childhood will be ever present." And although there are many kids (and manifestations of children's culture) visible in the film, Grandrieux's idea of childhood is broader than simply biological age. It is more like the brute, polymorphously perverse bedrock foundation of every human being, a churning, uncontrollable ocean of drives, sensations and impressions, both a "dawning" or opening to life and a constant malaise that never goes away. This is a theme to which Grandrieux frequently returns in his highly poetic, reflective writings.

Grandrieux organises his statement about *Sombre* under five headings: Landscape, Light, Actors, Frame and Story; there is a short consideration of each. It is rare for a filmmaker to describe his or her preparatory work doing "test shots" for camera lenses and film stock within the chosen location, but this is precisely a pre-production phase that Grandrieux highlights.

> What seemed (at the Louvre in front of [Nicolas] Poussin's works) to be able to belong only to painting – we saw it down there, in the sky that was clear blue and tenderly, menacingly grey, this child's-sky circling the horizon, in this up-close faded green, which we measured: sky 11, field 8 – and with these gestures of cinema, the film was already happening [*au travail*], as much as it will be in its shooting, editing or mixing, because it happens every time that one thinks about it, right there and then, every time that it *matters* for us.

Like any filmmaker eager to unite sheerly material elements (landscape, cinematography, etc.), first with a central theme of a project, then with the more amorphous emotion or mood underlying it, Grandrieux here is concerned to evoke how – by what means – the film to be made will come alive within himself and his collaborators. Hence his stress on all the phases at which the film *happens*, when an overall vision of it is *felt*.

The shoot itself is an intense phase of the process for Grandrieux. Sixteen years later, in another (and generally rarer) kind of filmmaker document – a production diary –

he would write of the difficult experience of making *Malgré la nuit* (ultimately released mid 2016).

> The film is here, in these faces, these voices [...] There's a truth in the rushes, a terrible truth. It's right there. That's what has hooked onto the weight of things, the heaviness of the camera, each person's fatigue, everyone's agony, the fear that animates us.

This is Grandrieux's veritable ethos: the film has to be found in the materials assembled for it; like the sculptor faced with a block of stone, the final work is hidden inside that material, and nowhere else. Grandrieux even allows, at this level, for a certain vacillation or discrepancy between what the project may have started as (as originally envisaged in the screenplay) and what it becomes as the actors incarnate it, and the director responds to their "live" presence – in Grandrieux's view, there is no such thing as a "miscasting" error (all people have soul, all bodies are interesting), only an inability on the director's part to seize what is present and available for creation. Bruno Dumont (born 1958), too, in the period of making *Twentynine Palms* (2003), has spoken, in a related way, of simply "accepting," as a director, the gap that may arise between a character as scripted and the actor who may perform the dictated actions and lines without ever "fitting" the role. (In Dumont's case – very different to Grandrieux in this regard – he even credits his active *dislike* of and non-rapport with his actors as part of his general working method!) At the outset of making *Sombre*, Grandrieux sets out his intuitive method.

> The film is a whole, it's a movement, and this question of movement is very important. [...] The relation with the actor (whether professional or not) is above all a relation with alterity. I want my directing of the actors to be the *mise en scène* of

> this relation. The film, the fiction in all of this would then be the "documentary" in which we would see this movement leaving from itself to go toward the other, then returning from the other back to the self: there is no relation other than a reciprocal one.

The act of cinematographic framing (Grandrieux generally serves as his own camera operator) is an intimate and integral part of what he calls this *movement* of feeling and experiencing the film as it is being made and taking shape.

> I've always framed my own films, in order to have a direct, immediate, intuitive relation with what's there, with presence, it's a sensation, first of all a sensation, an emotion, a movement of the soul, that's what framing is, to let myself be carried away by what I feel, it's to forget myself… The presence of the other, of what is in front of me, and then the oblivion of the light, eyes tight shut at times… and yet it hits the mark, it frames, I don't know how to explain it better… it's movement and it goes from one face to another, it's a rhythm, a means of moving brusquely or, on the contrary, hesitating, of going beyond what is there, then to come back, to bring into focus or to remain blurred, to be too close, a way to follow the action and then to distance myself from it and allow it to finish outside of the frame, to go back there when nothing is happening anymore, just before the cut, this is the materiality of the frame, its incarnation, it's the cutting-up of the Real, that's what is mine.

It is significant that only in the fifth and final section of his "Notes of Intention" does Grandrieux raise the nature of *Sombre*'s narrative – we can sense that he deliberately does not wish to put the storyline "up front," hence shaping and determining all further remarks as secondary to or merely expressive of it. This may well be because it is a very "charged" plot, potentially loaded with the expectations that viewers bring to certain genres: in this case, a male serial killer story that also involves rape, and a disquieting brand of subjection or even submission on the part of its central female characters (Claire, played by Elina Löwensohn, and her sister Christine, played by Géraldine Voillat).

But the narrative line is not primary for Grandrieux (this is true in all his work), and certainly not the type of traditional "explanation" or "psychology" of narrative that he explicitly refuses.

> So it's the movement, making it circulate, between the light, the landscape, the frame, the bodies, the actors, the grain of their voices, making all that cohere, tie into the story, a love story, about a love which is a grace, which touches Claire and makes her feel this explosion which we are, held in her, leading her to a new life, and it's Jean [Marc Barbé] who takes her there, the fact of passing from one side of the river to the other, he who can be nothing but the *passeur*, condemned by his murderous drive and unable to live among others, he who is night… It's inexplicable, it's beyond psychology, it could be a fairy tale.

Source: Philippe Grandrieux's "*Sombre*, notes d'intention" is included as a bonus on the French DVD edition of the film from Diaphana, and in the anthology *Jeune, dure et pure! Une histoire du cinéma avant-garde et expérimental en France* (Cinémathèque française/Mazzotta, 2000) edited by Nicole Brenez and Christian Lebrat, p. 547. My complete English translation of this Statement of Intention is at http://www.screeningthepast.com/issue-46-classics-re-runs/sombre-notes-of-intention.

16
Jean-Luc Godard: *Vivre sa vie*

Jean-Luc Godard has produced many kinds of statements of intention, and increasingly did so as his productions became more and more independent. His self-documentation archives (especially since the start of the 1980s), as well as those kept by some of his collaborators, are impressive, and have already provided the basis for several hefty publications, including Alain Bergala's *Godard au travail: Les années 60* (2007) and the Pompidou Centre catalogue *Documents* (2006).

Back in the 1960s, in the first, narrative period of his filmmaking, such statements took the form of often freewheeling *script treatments* – a tentative plot synopsis (even when the plot had not yet been entirely decided) filled out with diverse observations and notations. These would sometimes be provided to a producer; at other times, they would be furnished to Godard's main assistant (Charles Bitsch or Suzanne Schiffman) so that a largely fake script draft, purely to reassure others involved in the process, could be quickly assembled.

There is no doubt, however, that whatever the impetus behind these various documents – and however ephemerally he may have regarded them during the 1960-1967 period – they have always allowed Godard an opportunity to think through the basis for his film or video projects. He clearly enjoyed writing them!

The *scénario* treatment for *Vivre sa vie* (1962) is exemplary. At the point of writing it, the details were still floating in Godard's mind.

> This is a story of Nana [played by Anna Karina]... My story is going to follow her for a period of five to six months, perhaps less, perhaps more: I don't exactly know yet... The film will consist of approximately 20 episodes concerning

> Nana's most important experiences during these six months... The few episodes in her life which I'm going to film are very likely of little interest to others, but most important to Nana.

One already detects Godard's sense of humour here: the character's "most important experiences" will be, provocatively, "of little interest to others," meaning not the other characters, but the film's eventual viewers! Godard is deliberately downplaying the most sensational element in his scenario: Nana is a woman, suffering financial hardship, who by steps falls into a life of prostitution (a sociological photo-study of a prostitute's daily life provided one of the film's major sources, unacknowledged in his Statement).

On the contrary, Godard is endeavouring to push to an extreme the "mundane everyday life" aspect of Italian neo-realism as seen in a film such as Vittorio De Sica's *Umberto D.* (1952), anticipating the beginnings, ten or twelve years later, of what we now call the *slow cinema* movement in Chantal Akerman, Sohrab Shahid-Saless and Wim Wenders. He was even slightly ahead of Andy Warhol's first, silent "screen test" films in his fix on finding a form of cinematic "portraiture" to capture an image of Nana – and of Karina herself, who was, at that time, his wife. In an interview at the moment of its release, Godard stated that the film in some conceptual and imagistic way "follows on" from *À bout de souffle* (1960): "I knew that *Vivre sa vie* was to start with a girl seen from behind – I did not know why. It was the only idea I had." What can be termed the *matrixial image* of a project – the matrix from which everything else is generated – can begin from something this fuzzy!

From the start of his career, there was an almost perverse formalist will driving Godard – perverse in the sense that certain stylistic parameters seem to take precedence in his mind over the details (to be decided later) of the narrative content. His use of numbers indicates this tendency: five or six months, twenty episodes. He would often announce a formula on the order of: eight sequences of ten minutes, or maybe ten sequences of eight minutes… playing on the arbitrary nature of such parameters.

With Godard, more than probably any other filmmaker, the scenario-statement exhibits a long list of references that establish a project's basis in his cinephile culture. The horizon of reference becomes a working tool here. Also fairly unique, in this regard, is the manner in which Godard posits not only the films and filmmakers he wishes to emulate (or whose possibilities he wishes to develop), but also those he wishes to avoid emulating! Notice also in the following evocation how completely, for *Vivre sa vie*, he mixes inspirations from both fiction and documentary cinema.

> It's not a question of spying on her (François Reichenbach), trapping her (Robert Bresson), or of surprising her (Jean Rouch), but simply following her; nothing more than to be good and just (Roberto Rossellini).

Rossellini was certainly one of the most central influences on Godard in this early 1960s period – partly for the way that, in films including *Viaggio in Italia* (1954), he had interwoven movie stars (Ingrid Bergman and George Sanders) with the *temps morts* of a mundane narrative itinerary, and employed a quasi-documentary reportage style of shooting to surprise the actors and catch them in unusual and unglamorous behaviours. The Master was, however, unhappy with the results of this blend in *Vivre sa vie*: the story goes that Rossellini nearly ran the car he was driving off the road as he castigated his disciple for veering into "Antonionism"!

A more specific film reference from 1955 provided Godard with one of the major motifs in *Vivre sa vie*.

> Indeed, Nana, as in the song in Max Ophüls' *Lola Montès*, is gracious, which means that she has grace and will be able to safeguard

> her soul while selling her body. *Vivre sa vie* will prove [Michel de] Montaigne's saying that you can lend yourself to others, while giving yourself to yourself.

The precise, corresponding line from a song scene in *Lola Montès* that has come to resonate in Godard's recollection here is: "You give your body and you keep your soul." But, with this reference, Godard hits upon an overlap (a true device of Godardian montage) that allows him to cross to one of his favourite domains: philosophy. The philosopher Brice Parain would eventually be cast in a crucial interview/conversation scene of the film. Here is how Godard conceived this thematic idea in the scenario.

> Basically, I would like to show what modern philosophy calls existentialism as opposed to essence. However, thanks to cinema, which can demonstrate that the two are not really in opposition to each other at all, I want to prove that existentialism presupposes essence, and vice versa, and that this in itself is something quite beautiful.

Existence (the visible acts and choices of life) presupposes essence (inner soul), *and vice versa*! Godard's fierce love of reversible paradoxes is in full evidence, once again. (It pops up elsewhere in the scenario: "Since the film is rather sad, Nana, in line with Renoir's beloved law of contrast, is often happy.") But, in his view, it is the medium of cinema that allows this dizzy interchange of existence and essence, outer and inner life. That, already, implies a theory of cinema.

Source: The scenario of *Vivre sa vie* is translated in *Jean-Luc Godard: A Critical Anthology* (E.P. Dutton & Co., 1968) edited by Toby Mussman, pp. 77-80. Bergala's *Godard au travail* (Cahiers du cinéma, 2006) gives a detailed account, based on many rare archival documents, of the film's making.

17
John Hillcoat: The Proposition

When John Hillcoat (born 1960) sent me his Statement (titled "Notes on Style") concerning the Australian/UK production *The Proposition* (2005) – a strikingly stylised "outback Western" – he commented to me that, looking back on his words, he felt proud he had managed to retain so much of his initial intention in the final product. That's a sign he had managed to preserve its core – something he has not always been so fortunate to control to this extent, and in such detail, on all his various projects around the world.

Until this film in his career, Hillcoat had managed to make only two previous narrative features, one per decade: *Ghosts… of the Civil Dead* (1988) that, like *The Proposition*, involved a collaboration with writer-musician Nick Cave; and the Sirk-like melodrama *To Have and to Hold* (1996). Alongside these three projects, he has pursued his craft in music video, and in television (the 2017 *Black Mirror* episode "Crocodile"), the digital Machinima format (*Red Dead Redemption* in 2010, another unusual Western), and the mini-feature *Corazón* (2018). One can sense from his Statement how much was riding on the success of *The Proposition* for his future filmmaking prospects, and how deeply he was invested in ensuring it would work as a coherent whole.

Hillcoat's statement is unusually long and detailed, as if he wanted to leave absolutely nothing to chance (an enormous difference from our next example, Jacques Rivette). All the levels are enumerated: production design, cinematographic "look," costume, soundtrack, and so on.

The project began in Hillcoat's days as a student in Swinburne film school in Melbourne in the early 1980s, when he made his first, short attempt at an "Australian Western" – i.e., a merging of conventions from the Hollywood genre (and thus its hopefully global or "universal" market appeal) with the natural, often harsh landscape of Australia, and aspects of its "pioneer" history, especially the conflict between British settlers and indigenous Aborigines.

Many directors, including Glauber Rocha in Brazil, Wisit Sasanatieng in Thailand and Takashi Miike in Japan, have been drawn to the project of nationally "customising" the Western genre, often in ironic, eccentric or critical ways.

Although Hillcoat is a cinephile well acquainted with the Westerns of John Ford, Budd Boetticher, Samuel Fuller and (in a more modern vein) Monte Hellman, Sergio Leone or Sam Peckinpah, at the outset of the Statement he makes only one allusion to a popular classic of the genre, Henry Hathaway's original version of *True Grit* (1969) – the Coen brothers' remake of that property did not come along until five years after *The Proposition*.

> For many years I have wanted to make an Australian Western. In 1994, after an extensive trip [...] I was convinced by the dynamic power of its rugged landscape and its brutal history that an Australian Western, a drama set within its isolated frontiers in the late 1800s with the "true grit" of the genre, had yet to be achieved.

Australian cinema has a reputation (both good and bad!) for specialising in historical or "costume" dramas, such as Gillian Armstrong's *My Brilliant Career* (1979). Hillcoat carefully distances himself from this "purely factual" legacy, without criticising it outright, by recourse to a heightened idea of *myth* and mythic storytelling.

> Many Australian productions evolved from actual events that covered history in a purely factual way, without effectively conjuring the potential mythic potency of this period. Nick Cave's narrative contains some time-honoured ingredients of the "Wild West," and offers up a classic morality tale.

Hillcoat is alluding here not only to such familiar Western narrative ingredients as a revenge quest, but also the mythic/classic "morality tale" of brothers in mortal conflict. There is no doubt that this near-Biblical element, and its inherent intensity, derive from Cave's input. (Amusingly, in a public discussion I led in Melbourne with Hillcoat, Cave and lead actor Guy Pearce at the film's premiere, the singer boasted that he had read none of the mountain of historical research the director gave him; he worked purely from his imagination, plus a few photos.) Hillcoat also answers, in this Statement, the predictable objection that the Western is, in the 21st century, a thoroughly "dead" (and thus commercially unpopular) genre.

> The legendary power of the genre could be reinvented but in a specifically Australian context. In the necessity to reinvent genre, established myths are demolished, only to reform new ones. History and genre have always needed a new angle in order to be revitalised.

When Hillcoat speaks of "demolishing established myths," it's clear that he is quietly addressing the problem of the sometimes racist legacy of the American Western, especially as it pertains to indigenous peoples (in a later "Director's Statement" for the film's press kit, he celebrates "a deeply rewarding and genuine collaboration with the film's indigenous community"). But it is not necessarily a matter, for him, of turning instead to a modest register of realism in order to reset the historical record (as some other "factually based" Australian films have attempted). Instead, a new, heightened myth of indigenous rebellion – and white, settler degeneracy – must be brought alive ("revitalised") in its place.

Pursuing the generic connection with the Western, the Statement stresses that *The Proposition* will go further than the typical American examples, old or new. Here he appeals to both the reality and romantic mythology of the Australian "bushranger" or outlaw – for, since its very earliest days, Australia has cultivated a strain of "bushranger Western," most popularly around the historic figure of Ned Kelly.

> The Australian frontier, as depicted in *The Proposition*, is even more extreme and dangerous than that of the American Wild West. The land was even more inhospitable and the outlawed bushrangers even more desperate and dangerous. […] Photographs of the time and place show us the Victorians' stubborn refusal to yield up to the truth.

A major section of Hillcoat's Statement addresses the screen depiction of violence. He first advances a cinephilic argument sensitive to the evolving history of the Western genre.

> There was a clear brutality in all struggles to "civilise" the new frontiers of the 19th century. The grubby ruthlessness highlighted in many of Peckinpah and Leone's characters made their Westerns more believable, more visceral and engaging, as they were potent revisions of a sanitised past. This raw ferocity from the era helps create a "heightened realism," intensifying reality by highlighting all those messy truths that are glossed over and sentimentalised – the appalling evidence of our base human nature right down to the unshaven, sweaty, fly-ridden surface details.

Hillcoat – perhaps rightly, given the cultural "temperature" at the moment he embarked on this project – takes pains to *justify* the violent content of the film.

> There will be a conscientious and penetrative approach to violence within *The Proposition*. It runs thematically through the narrative, the central characters, and the very nature of frontier life. The majority of specific incidents take place off screen and often focus upon the aftermath, the actual consequences of violent actions. The few incidents that do take place on screen will be unglamorous and, like in real life, abrupt, messy, and quick.

Turning to matters of style, Hillcoat appeals to *realism* (as many contemporary filmmakers do), but what he calls an "invigorated" realism, based on surprise and the overturning of staid conventions (especially in the historical, period or costume film). Certain clichés need to be avoided, such as "helicopter shots or other such contemporary devices" – here the outdoor action will be "only ever seen from horse height or mountain peaks." Realism is not the absence of style or its invisibility for Hillcoat – quite the opposite.

> The nature of the characters and the material within the film calls for a bold, sparse style. Specific stylistic devices will help create an invigorated realism. I believe that part of the magic of great period films comes about when one's expectations are challenged by special attention paid to certain historical details. These crucial principles ground in reality the broader artistic license of the narrative, making it all the more immediate and credible. [...] For example, in period films, guns always seem to go off with a weak, dull, flabby "pop," with very little recoil. In reality, when those black powder guns were fired, they give an intensely violent "crack," very

> powerful, much more so than modern firearms.

Hillcoat thus aims to balance the realism of minutely researched historical recreation with the requirements (or parameters) of his chosen film style.

> It is by concentrating and distilling details in behaviour, production design, lighting and sound that the whole piece will come to life. Through meticulous research, we will create the illusion of ultra-reality, which will add credence to the other deliberately stylised elements – the creation of our own dramatic world. Our bushrangers will not resemble the typical bushy-bearded, floppy-hatted image so often portrayed, but will rather have more stylish outfits from the times.

Hillcoat details his vision of an aesthetic based on contrasts: "darkened interiors" will provide a "polar contrast" to "exteriors under a limitless sky"; "face-scapes will be juxtaposed with landscapes, close-ups with panoramic wides." Pace or rhythm is polarised between "frenetic bursts of action" and "abrupt stillness." These contrasts add up to a large-scale structure of mounting tension: a constant low-level of irritating sounds (buzzing flies and hot winds) "intensify" the mood and "build up the atmospheric pressure" (again, we recall Martel's swimming pool).

Natural sources of lighting – fire, candles, kerosene lamps – are highlighted (Benoît Delhomme, who has worked with everyone from Tran Anh Hung and Tsai Ming-liang to Julian Schnabel and Anthony Minghella, handled the cinematography); even the view through windows will be "blown out with intense white sunlight." This integrated form is tied closely to the script's dramatic content.

> The key to the style of the film will lie in the dynamic use of contrasts. It is already thematically in place within the script with the tensions between the brothers, between love and hate; the underlying class war between the poor Irish outlaws and the wealthy English ruling class; between "Civilisation" and the Wild; between dark, claustrophobic interiors and vast, barren exteriors.

In counterpoint to all that has preceded it in the statement, Hillcoat finally stresses a *lyrical*, even Romantic side to *The Proposition*. "There will be a sense of the inevitability of change with the advent of unstoppable progress." This is intended to give "the sense of a mournful elegy, of things coming to an end" – another echo of Peckinpah and Leone (or indeed, beyond the Western, Visconti) – except with the pointed inclusion of not only the white and British "pioneer age," but also "the systematic elimination of the indigenous peoples to which the film bears witness."

A last note from this rich Statement. Hillcoat evokes the "underlying cyclical structure" of the narrative that will be underlined in the deliberate use of "many scripted sunsets," which he describes poetically as "the annihilation of one day in order to create another." This points to a fascinating, general topic surely shared among virtually all filmmakers. The creative, expressive treatment of *night and day* – and the gradual or sudden transitions between them – is something essential to cinema but rarely talked about in print, as if it constituted one of those "trade secrets" filmmakers keep close to their chests.

It is an intense matter of both film craft – since, if handled badly, it registers on the spectator's psyche – and art. Jean-Claude Carrière's superb book *The Secret Language of Film* (1995) provides the major exception to this seeming rule of industrial silence; I recommend taking a good look at the chapter "Time Dissected." I have a feeling John Hillcoat had already done so.

Source: John Hillcoat's "*The Proposition*: Notes on Style" is in issue 45 of the online journal *Screening the Past* (http://www.screeningthepast.com/issue-45-classics-re-runs/the-proposition-notes-on-style). It also exists in a French translation, "Notes sur le style" in *Positif*, no. 586 (December 2009), pp. 31-33. The 2005 press kit for the film, containing a much shorter "Director's Statement," is at http://static.thecia.com.au/reviews/p/proposition-production-notes.pdf.

18
Jacques Rivette: *Daughters of Fire*

There is a large difference – both in Statements of Intention and in cinema history – between those filmmakers who set out, essentially, to make the film they already have in their heads, meticulously planned and prepared (the Hitchcock, Fritz Lang or Brian De Palma model); and those who set out to explore a loose set of given elements, leaving themselves open to surprise, discovery and chance.

This latter tradition, of those who "find the film in the making," is the province of directors including Jean Renoir, Rita Azevedo Gomes, Jacques Rozier, and Jacques Rivette. (Godard, as we have seen in his 1956 essay, preferred a path *between* "chance and destiny," and this would also be true of John Cassavetes or Elaine May.) Certain genres or modes of film favour this second approach – documentary, obviously (since perhaps little in the reality captured can be foreseen or manipulated), but also narrative formats such as the road movie (Monte Hellman's *Two-Lane Blacktop* from 1971 offers a prime example), where the script may be little more than a geographic itinerary, a vehicle or two, a bunch of actors, and a sketch of character types and their possible relationships.

Where the first "family" of control-oriented directors may use improvisation in extremely circumscribed ways (to encourage the best performance from an actor, for instance) – or not at all! – the second family tend to place enormous trust in the improvisatory process, and commit themselves to working with and reshaping, in post-production, whatever results "in the moment."

When it comes to Statements of Intention specifically, we are facing the difference between a project that needs to be *realised* or executed in a very specific way – Hitchcock may never have written any such Statement, but he did meticulous preparatory work with storyboarding – versus a project of which perhaps little can be "predicted." This latter type of Statement thus faces a particular challenge in wishing to persuade a producer or a national film commission that such a project is worth investing in. (All over the world, documentary filmmakers, especially those who seek TV funding, are now burdened with the onerous demand to indicate the "story" they will tell before even turning on their cameras.)

It is hard to imagine any official film commission anywhere on the planet today that would advance money to Jacques Rivette on the basis of his short Statement of Intention for a proposed series – not one but four feature films, to be shot back-to-back – first titled *Daughters of Fire*, and later *Scenes from Parallel Life*. It was obviously a propitious moment for Rivette: he had just enjoyed a relatively popular success with *Céline and Julie Go Boating* in 1974, and his standing among audiences, critics and institutions as an innovative but accessible auteur was at its height (a status he was not, alas, to enjoy for much longer).

Note, however, that Rivette rarely referred to himself as the sole creator of his films; he not only regarded but also involved key members of his team (both on and off camera) as close collaborators – writers (such as Eduardo de Gregorio or Christine Laurent) were always on-set to provide new lines and scenes; actors (such as Bulle Ogier and Jeanne Balibar) brought in their own costumes or wrote their own songs; and so on. Hence the plural "we" form of address that Rivette uses in his Statement is not just a polite formality, but a reality.

The 1974 prospectus "For the Shooting of *Daughters of Fire*" begins by asking: "Why four films at the same time?"

> In the first place because (since the filmmaker does not enjoy the same status in relation to his characters as the Balzacian novelist does) it is the only way of being able to establish a specific "circulation" between these films with certain characters and certain décors reappearing from one to another under different lights, contradictory or complementary.

> But mainly to see "what happens" if four stories, whose respective genres would theoretically make them very different from each other, are filmed in one burst: how the reciprocal influences from the four productions would function, the interactions between the casts, their attitudes, their relationships – and what might be modified (accentuated, influenced, transformed) by this interplay.

Mainly to see what happens! As we shall see later, Rivette's personal theory of film embraced chance as *risk* – the possibility of losing one's way during a shoot, or of failing to bring anything together in the editing room. Improvisation was an integral part of this highwire game, a role it had already played in the epic, 13-hour *Out 1* (1971).

As it happened, the complete *Daughters of Fire* project did eventually fall apart due to the director's ill health, brought on by nervous exhaustion. He shot the second and third instalments in the cycle as envisaged (the films subsequently released as *Duelle* and *Noroît* in 1976); the first (a love story starring Leslie Caron and Albert Finney) was abandoned after only a few days, and the fourth (a musical) was dropped altogether, forcing Rivette to patch together, in difficult conditions, another semi-improvised project (*Merry-Go-Round*, ultimately released 1981) to fulfil his and his producer's contractual obligations.

Many years later, in 2003, at the prompting of his former assistant Claire Denis (who had kept her script notes from the shoot), the abandoned romance film was reworked as *The Story of Marie and Julien*, but with different actors and no explicit connection with the *Daughters of Fire* cycle. As has often been noted (especially by the director himself), *Marie and Julien* became Rivette's "phantom film," the one that haunted and stuck with him until he could eventually resolve the possibility of its production.

But let us return to *Daughters of Fire* in its full-blown *virtuality* as an imagined, yet-to-be-made project. Once he began work on it in earnest, some details of the original prospectus changed: neither the same characters nor the actors playing them "circulate" like novelistic figures in *Duelle* and *Noroît*. But the broad *parameters* stayed in place: four stories in starkly different genres (romance, magical-mystery horror-fantasy, quasi-pirate Jacobean tragedy, and musical), all featuring central female characters who are mythic phantom spirits (the daughters of fire), and all "timed" to unfold during particular phases of the moon. Rivette's method resembles Godard's for *Vivre sa vie*.

> First, starting from the basic principle of each of the fictions, the building of not so much a traditional scenario as a canvas: a construction, a framework of some fifteen block-sequences. Evolving parallel in time, the four stories are all divided into three main sections, three acts, corresponding to the three lunar phases (from new moon to full, return of the new moon, then finally full moon again – therefore with the same number of transitions from darkness to light) which circumscribe the forty days of Carnival.

Alongside these given (if already surreal!) parameters of narrative and genre – providing a basic *canvas*, as he makes explicit, not dominating the theme – Rivette envisages a particular method of *cinécriture* (Rivette alludes to Varda's term) centred on the principal elements of the shoot: actors, settings, *mise en scène*. Above all, Rivette seeks something new – in particular, a new type of acting performance.

> During shooting, each unit (each block-sequence) will be subjected to a method designed to break down not only conventional dramatic techniques but also the more recent conventions of improvisation with all the prolixities and

> clichés it entails (hesitations, provocations, etc....), and to establish an écriture based on actions, movements, attitudes, the actor's "gestural," in other words. The ambition of these films is to discover a new approach to acting in the cinema, where speech, reduced to essential phrases, to precise formulas, would play a role of "poetic" punctuation. Not a return to the silent cinema, neither pantomime nor choreography: something else, where the movement of bodies, their counterpoint, their inscription within the screen space, would be the basis of the *mise en scène*.

Rivette adds one further, very novel element into his *mise en scène* program: live music, improvised by players who are watching (and even interacting with) the scene as it is shot. Think of the challenge this sets for the sound recording, editing and mixing team, especially if there is the slightest deviation from a "block-sequence" rendered in a single, unbroken, completely usable take! (Traditionally, music is never played back, let alone performed live in professional shooting situations, not even for dance party or related scenes: a low-level pulse takes the place of a soundtrack element that will be carefully constituted later.) Rivette, of course, welcomed whatever radical bumps and detours this *parti pris* could introduce (entirely evident in the two completed instalments).

> In order to enable us to make a definitive crossing of this frontier which separates traditional acting from the kind we are looking for: the constant presence during shooting of musicians (different instruments and styles of music according to each film) who would improvise during the filming of sequences, their improvisation dependent on the actors'

> playing, the latter also being modified by the musicians' own inventions (recorded in direct sound along with the dialogue and the "stage noises" properly speaking).

In a 1969 workshop-seminar on montage, Rivette went so far as to remark: "At its extreme, film is the rejection of film, its contradiction (its 'anti-film')." Kijū Yoshida would be proud! There was a destructive (or deconstructive), negatory impulse built into the plan for *Daughters of Fire*. Rivette hoped to stage, across the series, a *progressive dissolution* of coherence, meaning, and stylistic systems, a movement from stately modernism into chaos and excess – the endpoint we see in *Noroît*. Did Rivette's unfinished master plan inspire the Argentinian makers of *La flor* (2018), I wonder, which stages a comparable dissolution of narrative across genres and homages to past cinematic forms, this time with the same ensemble-cast across the entire 14 hours?

> The interaction of our four films will thus be doubled by the progressive accentuation, from one film to the next, of these principles of *mise en scène*: from the first film (*Marie and Julien*), where they will function as an element of dislocation and strangeness within a dramatic construct still following the rules of romantic fiction – by way of the horror/fantasy film [i.e., *Duelle*] and the musical – to the fourth film (*The Revenger* [retitled *Noroît*]), where the various aspects are to be driven to paroxysm.

Rivette's Statement concludes by summing up the project in the following, almost content-less, purely formalistic way.

> To create one's own space through the movements of one's body; to occupy and traverse the spaces of the décors and the

camera's field; to move and act within (and in relation to) the simultaneous musical space: these are the three parameters on which our actors are going to attempt to base their work.

Source: Jacques Rivette's "For the Shooting of *Les Filles du Feu*" appears in English translation in *Rivette: Texts and Interviews* (British Film Institute, 1977), pp. 89-90, and at http://www.dvdbeaver.com/rivette/ok/lesfillesdufeu.html, while the French original is included in Hélène Frappat, *Jacques Rivette, secret compris* (Cahiers du cinéma, 2001). For a lively exchange between Rivette and Frappat, see Chapter 32. The rich 1969 workshop-seminar "Montage," conducted by Rivette, Jean Narboni and Sylvie Pierre, appears in *Rivette: Texts and Interviews*, pp. 69-88, and at http://www.dvdbeaver.com/rivette/ok/montage.html.

Part Two
Ideas About Cinema

19
Pure and Impure Vocation

"Film theory" can be a frightening term; it needs to be demystified. In the simplest sense, it refers to *general* reflections on the cinema as a medium – not accounts or reviews of particular films (that's film criticism); and not the application of templates or methodologies to a film or group of films (that's film analysis).

So, the discussion of (say) Martin Scorsese's style of camera movement is not an example of film theorising; and nor is the (correct) claim that films can express the ideology of imperialist or totalitarian societies. Let me be clear on this: there is no hierarchy of value between film theory, criticism and analysis. None is more important or valuable than the other; each has their purpose and their target; each one asks a particular kind of question and seeks to answer it.

Film criticism asks: how does this movie in front of me work, what is its logic, its meaning, its affect, its value? Film analysis (often overlapping with sociology and cultural studies) asks: where does this film "come from," what conditions it, in what broad social contexts can we understand it? Study of *mise en scène*, style and form belong to film criticism; study of genre, psychoanalytic or political frameworks belongs to film analysis. Of course, there are always overlaps, and one doesn't need to police the boundaries of these territories too tightly. But it is good to have a working sense of the differences in approach, and of which one we are using (consciously or not!) in any situation of film talk.

What is the driving question of film theory? It is the question of what defines cinema as a medium, a definition that has two aspects. First, what is *essential* to film (we have explored this a little already in Chapter 4)? Second, what is *specific* to film, what is that makes cinema a medium or form distinct from all other arts? It is frequently the case that responses to these sub-questions will overlap: if I claim, for instance, that camera movement is essential to cinema – that films without such movement are "not true films" – I may simultaneously be claiming that movement is what cinema does that no other art form can do, at least not in the same way. We will often encounter filmmakers' pronouncements that intermingle essence and specificity.

In a way, every filmmaker has their personal sense of what is essential to cinema – a sense that drives their own work and determines their decisions. For Chantal Akerman, for instance, her strong, ethical belief that certain violent acts are "pornographic" and should not be shown on-screen leads her to an aesthetic practice based on an elaborate use of, and investment in, off-screen space and temporal ellipsis. For another type of filmmaker – Quentin Tarantino, say – the exact opposite would be true: the belief in a very "literal" aesthetic of what Pasolini calls "monstration" (showing) leads to the rigorous inclusion of violent spectacle on screen! All traditions of "gore" in cinema (e.g., the Italian *giallo* genre) proceed from this same, underlying assumption, just as the opposite, "Bressonian" tradition (to which Akerman belongs) proceeds from a reverse set of values.

The plane of cinematic specificity is more special and, in fact, rarer. Some filmmakers are simply not terribly interested in trying to stake out what makes cinema a unique medium or art form. It may figure as a momentary illumination along the path of their work – such as when Stanley Kubrick recalled the value of encountering the Russian book *Film Technique and Film Acting* by Vsevolod Pudovkin (1893-1953), originally two separate volumes written in 1929 and 1933, respectively, in its 1954 English translation.

> The most instructive book on film aesthetics I came across was Pudovkin's *Film Technique*, which simply explained that editing was the aspect of the film art form which was completely unique, and which separated it from all other art forms. The ability to show a simple action like a man cutting wheat from a number of angles in a brief moment, to be able to

> see it in a special way not possible except through film – that this is what it was all about. This is obvious, of course, but it cannot be too strongly stressed.

Kubrick's friend Joe Turkel, who appeared in three of his films from the mid-1950s to *The Shining* in 1980, recalls that "every time I saw Stanley in his chair, there was a copy of V.I. Pudovkin's *Film Technique and Film Acting* in the side pocket, and it wasn't unusual to see Stanley reading it on a set." That's devotion to a film theory!

It is just as often the case that filmmakers reject any specificity claim and take an entirely different position – that film is not a specific art form unto itself, but the happy, profuse amalgamation of all previously existing art forms: theatre, literary fiction, music, painting, sculpture, architecture, and so on. This is a claim for the broad *impurity* of cinema as a medium, rather than a *purity* that can specify and justify it in the pantheon of the arts.

Naturally, such a broad claim can be broken down into many possible inflections. If I say that cinema belongs to the lineage of the circus, the weekly *feuilleton* novel, and rock'n'roll music, that is something very different, in cultural and aesthetic terms, to saying that it belongs to the lineage of the *tableau vivant*, the code of pictorial perspective in Renaissance art, and experimental *musique concrète*!

We can find many diverse examples of this type of "impure" rhetoric in the declarations of filmmakers. Baz Luhrmann (born 1962) revels in the collage-like collision of the arts (citing Shakespeare, 20th-century modernist art, pop music, and so on) in his invocation of Red Curtain Cinema, with its "three rules": set the film in a heightened, creative world (such as the theatre, or an artistic "movement" like Cubism or hip hop); use a "recognisable story shape" deriving from popular fiction or ancient myths and fairy tales; and allow the audience to "participate" by letting them know that the stylistic, narrational devices used (dance, poetry, singing, etc.) are heightened, artificial and deliberately unreal.

In a completely different and decidedly less populist vein, Peter Greenaway (born 1942), for his 1995 essay "Just Place, Preferably Architectural Place," provides the densest horizon of reference I have ever encountered – literally hundreds of architectural monuments and films cited across seven pages – in order to evoke the back-and-forth interplay of real places in the world and the imaginary places conjured by cinema.

> Are you going to find an audience who want to watch a film solely about place? There aren't going to be any people in this hypothetical film – no actors, no extras, no crowds – but just the marks they have made, preferably the marks they made a long time ago. Maybe there could be just a few [Giorgio de] Chirico shadows on a wall in the middle distance. But the film would be full of quotations, like those impressive *capriccios* which, avoiding the inconvenience of the unobtainable vantage-point and the uncooperative weather, could put your favourite building in a location of your choosing, could mix up chronologies and styles, could build a Utopian city of immaculate perspectives like della Francesca's Ideal Town. Make your ideal city.

The impure-cinema line of reasoning seeks every kind of crossover, transfer, transmutation, mixture and echo between the various arts as brought together (or brought into conflict) by film – what we today call *intermediality*. Eisenstein began his theorising in a pure vein and gradually became more and more intermedial, long before the term was coined. In this approach, the other arts have not only preceded and influenced film; the traces of their aesthetic structures are literally *in* film.

Intermedial speculation is qualitatively different to the once (and sometimes still) popular trope of *analogy* in filmmakers' thinking: "Cinema is *like* music, like poetry, like painting." The great experimental filmmaker Stephen Dwoskin's book *Film Is... The International Free Cinema* (1975), and indeed virtually all his public statements about the art of film, follow this analogical model. Pudovkin, in his time, offered a typical example of the linguistic analogy that Agnès Varda later used for her own, broader goal of defining *cinécriture*. This is from the introduction to *Film Technique*.

> To make clear my point and to bring home unmistakably to my readers the meaning of editing and its full potentialities, I shall use the analogy of another art form – literature. To the poet or writer separate words are as raw material. They have the widest and most variable meanings which only begin to become precise through their position in the sentence. To that extent to which the word is an integral part of the composed phrase, to that extent is its effect and meaning variable until it is fixed in position, in the arranged artistic form. To the film director each shot of the finished film subserves the same purpose as the word to the poet. Hesitating, selecting, rejecting, and taking up again, he stands before the separate takes, and only by conscious artistic composition at this stage are gradually pieced together the "phrases of editing," the incidents and sequences, from which emerges, step by step, the finished creation, the film. The expression that the film is "shot" is entirely false, and should disappear from the language. The film is not shot, but built, built up from

the separate strips of celluloid that are its raw material.

Let us return to pure theory – an activity that has certainly attracted, and continues to attract, a long line of filmmakers of every kind. To recapitulate, a film theory seeks what is essential and specific to the medium. In the quest to define an essence, attention will sometimes be paid to circumscribing the *limit* of this medium (a motif we shall encounter in Hollis Frampton and Abigail Child) – the point beyond which it cannot (or should not!) go. Once essence and specificity are in place, the *vocation* of cinema can be defined: what it does best, what it should aim to do, what it should not waste time doing. A vocation is an obligation that can either be fulfilled or betrayed – remember that, long ago, the coming of sound to movies was taken as one such betrayal of a fundamental artistic vocation.

Implicit in all these operations, almost always, is a forcible exclusion: what cinema is *not*, and should never be. To that extent, an "enemy" or Other gets defined. To some filmmakers, the enemy is conventional theatre; to others, it is classical narrative; it can be the "male gaze" of the cinematic institution as it has historically developed in patriarchal society; or "spectacle" construed as something hypnotic, seductive, mind-numbing and passivity-inducing (as in the bluntly titled 2009 book *Cinema Against Spectacle* by critic-filmmaker Jean-Louis Comolli, born 1941). And spectacle, in the 1960s, tended to be a code word for "advertising" (both on screens and in the streets); later, it became code for "mainstream television"; today, it is more likely to signify "Internet"! Again, we may have to become historical detectives to ferret out the precise sense of an implied opposition.

A crucial premise of this book is that "all film theories are born equal." We may not find one or other theory congenial to our own sensibility or way of thinking; that's OK, that's human. But I believe we must grant each theory its space of exploration and experimentation. Filmmakers are influenced by many things: childhood experiences, family, education, social and religious background, encounters with charismatic people, travel, reading, the experience of powerful artworks. It is impossible to know from where that inspiration which touches the core of our ever-evolving selves derives (as Pascal Kané noted).

Lucrecia Martel, for example, speaks of the experience of "primitive" medicine from her region of Argentina that saved her traumatised self in her early youth after a serious car accident – and how that treatment gave her a palpable idea of "energies gathered on the surface of the ground" which informs her veritable theory and practice of film today. When she tries to tell that story in public, audiences sometimes react defensively, with laughter, as if no "rational" theory could proceed from such folk-mysticism. Her response is to simply assert: "I would not be here, alive today, without it." Where each filmmaker locates not only their most inspiring ideas but also the most powerful material *energies* of the film medium is a highly personal matter – one finds it in the image, another in the human voice, yet another in the landscape – and we must be willing to entertain or, better, *inhabit* all of them.

A film theory, whatever its veneer of rational and scholarly "objectivity," will always spring from the *temperament* of the person driven to propose it. In some quarters, this is a controversial claim to make: doesn't (or shouldn't) the activity of theorising spring from a position of philosophical "disinterest" and detachment? The scholar Brian Henderson, who worked closely alongside Frampton, Steina and Woody Vasulka, Paul Sharits and other experimental film/video artists at SUNY Buffalo in the 1970s and '80s, reminds us that "*theoria* in the classical Western sense" presumes to be "an essential analysis of an unlimited object," i.e., the object in its totality. But he swiftly came to question the assumption that a detached apprehension of the totality of cinema is even possible, since many film theories exclude so much of the total cinematic field (including unquestionably significant areas like experimental work, or animation).

The great Bengali filmmaker Ritwik Ghatak (1925-1976) – who, at one point, wondered whether "perhaps one should not theorise" at all! – stressed that theory is *partial*, in both English senses of that word: it is a fragment of the totality of cinema, grasped from a particular angle; and it is motivated, inevitably, by the "personal obsessions" of the theorist, which Ghatak compared to the animating obsessions of any artist. Ghatak was speaking predominantly of theorists who were not filmmakers, such as Siegfried Kracauer, whose work he disliked; I don't share his negativity on that point.

However, when the theorist is *also* a filmmaker – as Ghatak was – those personal obsessions can become their, and our, heuristic tools. This is because the temperament or sensibility of the thinking filmmaker quickly leads to *convictions*, which then express themselves in a set of argued *values*. However we may choose to ultimately judge any particular instance of film theory, we should begin by facing up to the fact that it is – whether it knows this or not – a fully creative, inventive act.

Source: Vsevolod Pudovkin's two books, joined together as *Film Technique and Film Acting*, were published in English by Grove Press in 1957. The quote from Kubrick is in Gelmis' interview (see next chapter). Peter Greenaway's essay on film and architecture is in *Projections 4½* (see Chapter 7), pp. 74-80. Lucrecia Martel's story is told in her 2018 Rotterdam Masterclass (see Chapter 12). Brian Henderson's major work is *A Critique of Film Theory* (Dutton, 1980). Daniel Fairfax's English translation of Jean-Louis Comolli's *Cinema Against Spectacle: Technique and Ideology Revisited* appeared, with extra material, from Amsterdam University Press in 2015. Ritwik Ghatak's remarkable essays are collected (in English) in *Rows and Rows of Fences: Ritwik Ghatak on Cinema* (Seagull Books, 2000). Dwoskin's *Film Is* was published by Overlook Books.

20
Do It and Show It, That's All

Some – perhaps many – filmmakers resist talking about their work in theoretical terms. There are, I believe, complicated and varied reasons for this.

For some, it is simply an alien activity, something to which they have never (or barely) been exposed, and to which they are not attracted. In their minds, they work on individual film projects, one after the other, all of them different – so thinking about "the cinema in general" has nothing to do with any of that. Stanley Kubrick, for example, confessed in the late 1960s to having read Eisenstein's books in translation in the 1950s, but "to this day I still don't really understand them"; Vsevolod Pudovkin's *Film Technique*, on the other hand, gave him some practical understanding of editing ("Pudovkin gives many clear examples of how good film editing enhances a scene, and I would recommend his book to anyone seriously interested in film technique").

In testy interviews, Kira Muratova (1934-2018) defied the demand to put into unambiguous, concrete words a medium of image and sound that is not, in the first place, based on verbalisation. Like Godard, she cultivated wily paradox and the confusion of neatly defined and opposed terms. In 2013, recalling her youthful experience of an official Bertolt Brecht production held in Moscow, she bristled at the interviewer's mention of the Brechtian theory of "estrangement" or alienation.

> I never think in such categories. But I really liked Brecht's play. He wrote the content of the following act onto the curtain. That was beautiful, so modern. What beautiful ideas! Then the next act started and I completely forgot what had been written on the curtain and I was so empathetic. He, however, thought that I would watch from a distance and without emotion. But I didn't watch emotionlessly.

> I was empathetic, even though Brecht was hoping that I would watch unmoved. Those are beautiful ideas. This is art, too. His theories are like a frame to the art. Estrangement. Not-estrangement. All this is meaningless. I want this and that and something else, too. I want people to look at this little brooch, this little bracelet, emotionless or ardently, to just look at it for a long time and not turn away from it. That means I want emotion, and estrangement, and everything else.

Michelangelo Antonioni, at the time of *The Passenger*'s release in 1975, was equally dismissive of overly abstract interview questions. "We should also not talk theoretically about film. We need to do it, to show it, and that's all."

Some filmmakers (such as Stephen Frears, born 1941) seem to be "naturally" anti-intellectual, possibly on the basis of a class identification, actual or fanciful, with average workers rather than the educated, elite, upper-middle-class. Others like to stress the role of intuition rather than cerebral speculation in their creative process, and mock over-intellectualised interpretations of their work (Luis Buñuel: "Sometimes I weep with laughter when I read certain articles in *Cahiers du cinéma*"). Philippe Grandrieux has great respect for and familiarity with the writings of many philosophers (such as Gilles Deleuze), but fears that reading too much theoretical commentary on his own work will interfere with his spontaneous, instinctual invention. Likewise, Philippe Garrel (born 1948) is hardly an anti-intellectual – he likes to quote Freud's *Civilisation and its Discontents* when introducing his work at festivals – but he is at pains to point out that many decisions made during a film shoot are eminently practical and pragmatic (how to film in a public thoroughfare?), not primarily conceptual in nature. He is not among those directors who openly discuss their stylistic "parameters"!

From the ranks of American directors who began their careers in the "classical" studio system, we find very few who have ever gone on record talking about any kind of film theory. (Abraham Polonsky [1910-1999] is among the exceptions.) Sidney Lumet (1924-2011) declared that he wrote his manual of practical craft advice, *Making Movies* (1995), because he was "so tired of theories" – and he was so averse to any generalisation about the film medium that he swore "the word *cinema* won't pass my throat"!

By the early 1990s, Blake Edwards (maker of *The Party*, *10* and the *Pink Panther* films) had been the subject of much high-level critical commentary – including several books that he was aware of, but could not recall the authors' names! At this time, near the end of his directorial life, he reacted to the probing questions of an Australian interviewer in the following, immortal way.

> It's hard to respond to your ideas and questions, because while I recognise what you are saying, I don't recognise it so strongly that I can really address myself to it without a lot of thought. It's so fucking hard trying to.

American directors, from Billy Wilder to Abel Ferrara (born 1951), may have good "professional" or industrial reasons to reject theory-talk: they don't want to sound pretentious, and they don't want to endanger any future chances of getting work. Josef von Sternberg once said: "Actually, it is advisable in our craft to conceal all knowledge"! Along a similar line, certain Americans, such as James Gray (born 1969) or Joe Dante (born 1946), are more likely to express themselves intellectually to non-American (and non-English speaking) journalists or critics: in Gray's case, he appears far more at ease discussing the influence on his work of Louis Althusser and the notion of "ideological state apparatuses" with *Positif* critics than with *Hollywood Reporter* journalists!

One of the most surprising anti-theory declarations of recent years has come from Claire Denis (born 1946), who, like Kubrick, reads widely in many fields in order to research her projects (such as the space-travel-based *High Life* [2018]), and has frequently taught courses that "examine contemporary filmmaking as an exploration into multi-ethnic and cross-cultural environments, with the cool passion and distanced engagement of an anthropologist" at the European Graduate School in Switzerland. But Denis expressed no such passion or engagement in relation to film theory, especially when focused on her own work.

> If there are theories about me, I'd rather not know. Astrophysics – now that's fascinating. String theory, worm holes, the expanding universe, the Big Bang versus the Big Bounce – those are the kind of theories that make you feel like living and understanding the mystery of the world. Film theory is just a pain in the ass.

Some filmmakers, even if absorbed by theoretical thought and conceptual art practice in their youth, tend later in their careers to downplay or distance themselves from that past, again perhaps for "professional" reasons. "Oscar winner" Kathryn Bigelow (born 1951) is currently a prime example, as was Wes Craven (1939-2015), a former humanities professor who become a celebrated auteur of horror cinema. When I had the (nerve-wracking) opportunity to ask Craven in 1988, at the height of his success with the *Nightmare on Elm Street* franchise, his opinion of the academic studies carried out on his work, he eyed me suspiciously, as if I had transformed in an instant from a dutiful "entertainment reporter" to an alien interloper from the lost world of his former life. But, after taking a deep breath, this is what he told me (note the complicated, ambivalent way his thoughts keep shifting: "on the other hand…").

> I'm suspicious of any extreme, to the extent that I wouldn't want to be just *there*, in one place. Back when I was teaching humanities, it always fascinated me about Shakespeare, and the scholars that wrote about him, how much he provided for the groundlings [i.e., ordinary spectators]. I don't mean to say this in a patronising way, but you must be aware that a large part of your support comes from people that are not looking at it as an intellectual exercise. On the other hand, as an adult and as an artist you should be putting your own highest intelligence into it as well. So that, in an ideal piece, whatever it is, it should be accessible on any level. I think Mozart is like that. You can study Mozart at genius level for the rest of your life and you'll never quite plumb what he did. I think it should be the same way with a horror movie. I could write a book about what I feel about *A Nightmare on Elm Street* as a study in consciousness and responsibility. On the other hand, it should grab people by the throats and slam them against the wall. On the other hand, it should stand up for 20 or 50 years by intelligent analysis. So that's just my approach, I try to do an entire thing.

On the other hand, there are filmmakers entirely unashamed of their training in film theory: Todd Haynes (born 1961), Kelly Reichardt (born 1964), Jean-François Richet (an Eisenstein specialist, born 1966), and others who straddle, over many years, the worlds of theory (as teachers as well as writers) and film production projects, such as Laura Mulvey (born 1941) and Peter Wollen (1938-2019). In New Zealand in 1984, a group of women filmmakers – Gaylene Preston, Merata Mira, Anne Maxwell, Alison Maclean and

Jane Campion among them – published in-depth articles on feminist film theory in the magazine *Alternative Cinema*, drawing from Mulvey, Claire Johnston and other influential commentators; some of them have stuck to that position. Avant-garde artist figures such as Hollis Frampton and Abigail Child generally encounter few problems existing simultaneously in the two worlds of theory and practice.

It takes a particular type of temperament for someone to want to formulate a coherent book (or series of books) from their unique vision of cinema. We are speaking here of something qualitatively different than simply "collected essays and reviews" (as has occurred for Rohmer, Buñuel, Rivette, Wim Wenders, Olivier Assayas, Rainer Werner Fassbinder, and Paul Schrader); or the interviews assembled and published by University Press of Mississippi in their *Conversations with Filmmakers* series (covering everybody from Fred Schepisi to Kasi Lemmons via Resnais, Magarethe von Trotta and Charles Burnett). Some filmmakers choose to "talk theory" only in extended, book-length interviews, as is the case in Enzo Ungari's *Bertolucci by Bertolucci* (1987). Nor am I referring to the type of musing, sometimes whimsical "art book" that Peter Greenaway, for instance, chooses to create for the publisher Dis Voir in France, often based on future, imagined or unfilmed projects. Rather, I mean the type of book – often intended as a personal legacy or testament – that is explicitly presented by a filmmaker as a grand statement, the summing up of his or her holistic perspective on cinema.

Eisenstein envisaged many such volumes of his weighty reflections, in various, ever-shifting constellations of material (theoretical, historical, analytical, autobiographical…) – leading to his Utopian plan for a *spherical book* that (like Maya Deren's *Anagram*) could cross-reference itself, be read in different orders, and remain perpetually open to the re-categorisation of its parts, hence allowing different meanings to arise: a striking prophecy of many projects within today's "digital humanities," and the Internet in general. Raúl Ruiz's published diaries (in two large volumes) frequently testify to his fervent drive to compose a "theory book" to stand beside his filmic œuvre: in the event, he assembled it "on the run" between his many assignments, using his university lecturing gigs as the pretext to concretise his complicated reflections in the *Poetics of Cinema* series (the overall "plan" for this project tended to morph over the years he poured his writing into it). Eugène Green has taken a more "classical" and gradual path to the composition of his theoretical work, across a series of books including *Présences, essai sur la Nature du cinéma* (2003) and *Poétique du cinématographe* (2009).

For the remaining pages of Part Two, we turn to those filmmakers unafraid of the "temptation to theorise." As in Part One, the sources are diverse: books, essays, masterclasses, a manifesto or two. Sometimes, the theory has already been fully laid out for us by its creator; at other times, we will need to tease it out a little more from the poetic outline of its suggestion.

Source: The interview with Stanley Kubrick is quoted from Joseph Gelmis' invaluable *The Film Director as Superstar* (Penguin, 1970). My 1988 Wes Craven interview will appear in 2025 on my website www.adrianmartinfilmcritic.com. Claire Denis' remarks derive from an interview with Jonathan Romney in *The Guardian* (22 April 2018). The Kira Muratova interview cited is "I Am a Part of Chaos" by Isa Willinger, translated at http://www.isawillinger.de/Interview.htm. Sidney Lumet's *Making Movies* has been translated into many languages, including the Spanish edition *Así se hacen las películas* (Rialp, 2016), the Catalán *Com es fan les pel·lícules* (Viena, 2019) and the French *Faire un film* (Capricci, 2016). Abraham Polonsky's outline of his highly distinctive approach to film style in the classic *Force of Evil* (1948) can be found in *Interviews with Film Directors* (Avon, 1969), edited by Andrew Sarris. I discuss it in my book *Mise en scène and Film Style* (Palgrave, 2014).

21
Plunging Down into the Unreally Real

One of the most extraordinary meetings of creative minds took place at Cinema 16 in New York on 28 October 1953. Five respected authorities on film and/or poetry gathered on a panel (masterminded by Amos Vogel, author of the 1974 classic *Film as a Subversive Art*) to discuss the relationship between the two media: filmmakers Maya Deren (1917-1961) and Willard Maas (1906-1971), arts critic Parker Tyler (1904-1974), poet Dylan Thomas (1914-1953) and playwright Arthur Miller (1915-2005). The gender imbalance (four men to one woman) is no doubt more egregiously visible to us now than it was to the audience of 1953. But no one, even then, could have missed the abuse unfairly heaped on Deren during that memorable (and, fortunately for us, well-documented) session.

First, let's backtrack and fill in some context in relation to Deren. In 1953, it had been ten years since her first major film *Meshes of the Afternoon*, co-made with Czech-born avant-gardist and theorist Alexander Hammid; and seven years since her ambitious, holistic, imaginatively conceived work of film theory, *An Anagram of Ideas on Art, Form and Film*. She had achieved the milestone of that book and three other notable films while still in her 20s; beyond her prodigious involvement in writing and the arts, she would also go on to complete important ethnographical research in Haiti. Thomas (who was dead two months after the Cinema 16 panel took place) and Arthur Miller were not much older than her; Maas and Tyler hailed from a previous generation.

Deren's *Anagram* is a major work of film theory crammed into fewer than 50 pages, and an endlessly readable one – partly because she designed its discrete sections to be read in multiple orders and combinations, according to the metaphoric logic of an anagram (set out as a diagram on its opening page), thus adding up to diverse kinds of meanings along the guide-tracks of particular topics. The formal virtuosity and coherence of it is truly vertiginous. These days, we tend to think of an anagram as mere wordplay, like an acrostic. Deren would have been well aware of its more ancient, mystico-religious use. But her book creates not so much an occult secret as what we might describe as a *structure for thinking*. It is arranged as three horizontal themes conjoining four, overlapping terms: the Nature of Forms, the Forms of Art, and the Art of Film. Then, on the vertical axis, there are three further terms added to Nature – Man, Discovery, and Invention – conjugated through five descriptors: State, Character, Mechanics, Methods, and Instrument. Whew! So, a typical section title is: "2C. Film resulting from the Mechanics of Nature and the Methods of Man."

Like Epstein, Isou or Frampton, Deren aimed for no less than a total system of knowledge bridging philosophy, science and aesthetics, a system in which cinema would find its appropriately defined place. The *Anagram* strongly contrasts forms created by humans (especially art) with forms of or in nature. Whereas natural forms are fecund and profuse, the forms of art are economical. For Deren, art's "true vocation" is neither expression nor impression, and it should not be harnessed to experiments in conveying "subjective consciousness" as in Romanticism or Surrealism (this is important to remember when coming across the many accounts that describe her films as surrealist). Rather, her model is what she considers the impersonal and abstract art of tribal ritual. On virtually all these points, Deren's world-view can be contrasted with Pasolini's.

The historical moment of Deren's theory, its field, is significant. She makes many explicit references to World War II and its aftermath (she is extremely critical of the "American values" revealed in this period). Like Vertov, she appeals to the then "new physics" and the theory of relativity. She asserts that, on the technological plane, art should be informed by the inventions of the aircraft, telephone and radio – that it should "aspire to science," and be rigorous in its forms, without itself being a science. She opposes *discovery* in science to *invention* in art; Eisenstein and Epstein could have debated her on that one, since I believe they yoked film to both principles equally, and

Godard took up their refrain in the 1980s (the camera-eye can help solve the universe's puzzles…).

Deren's position, however, is clear, and can be summed up as follows. The *instrument* of cinema is the camera plus editing (not either one privileged separately). It is therefore both a "space art" and a "time art," inseparably. The instrument has the power to *invent* (not uncover) a new reality. This is a matter of medium-specificity: it is something "which only film can achieve and which could not be accomplished by the exercise of any other instrument." Furthermore, "there is no such thing as documentary film" – a bold statement! – for everything leans to, if not fiction, then at least artifice, construction. And, finally, the "delicate manipulation between the really real and the unreally real" is "one of the major principles of film form." A book could be written pondering just those two words: cinema as the realm of the *unreally real* – another of the ways that film practitioners and theorists have tried to resolve the seemingly opposed poles of concrete reality and its artistic, poetic manipulation.

Now the scene is set for us to attend to the substance of Deren's proposal on that film-and-poetry panel of 1953. She begins by defining poetry and its difference from other expressive forms – not to establish "formulae and rigidities," but as "a preparation, an approach" aimed at the potential audience for a properly poetic film. It is "a matter of giving a clue to the frame of mind which you bring" to any particular type of film.

> In other words, what are you going to be watching as this unrolls? What are you going to be listening for? If you're watching for what happens, you might not get the point of some of the retardations because they're concerned with *how* it happens. Now poetry, to my mind, consists not of assonance, or rhythm, or rhyme, or any of these other qualities which we associate as being characteristic of poetry. Poetry, to

> my mind, is an approach to experience, in the sense that a poet is looking at the same experience that a dramatist may be looking at. It comes out differently because they are looking at it from a different point of view, and because they are concerned with different elements in it.

Deren remarks that, since certain characteristics of poetry (such as rhyme, colour and emotion) also appear in other literary forms, we can easily be misled or confused in trying to forge this crucial distinction between poetry and non-poetry. She therefore turns to the level of artistic *structure*, and makes what will become one of the most famous *moves* in the history of cinema aesthetics.

> The distinction of poetry is its construction (what I mean by "a poetic structure"), and the poetic construct arises from the fact, if you will, that it is a *vertical* investigation of a situation, in that it probes the ramifications of the moment, and is concerned with its qualities and its depth, so that you have poetry concerned in a sense not with what is occurring, but with what it feels like or what it means. A poem, to my mind, creates visible or auditory forms for something which is invisible, which is the feeling, or the emotion, or the metaphysical content of the movement.

The "vertical attack" by a poet (in any medium) upon an action is distinguished from "the *horizontal* attack of a drama, which is concerned with the development, let's say, within a very small situation from feeling to feeling." She refers to both levels of structure, both modes of attack, as *movements*. As has often been pointed out, Deren's remarks here anticipated both Pasolini's distinction cinema of poetry/cinema of prose, and the semiotic couplet of *metaphor* and *metonymy*. Narrative linearity is a step-by-step, cause-and-effect unfolding, a chained (metonymic) movement of events through time; while the verticality of poetry offers a stilling of plot matched with a lyrical expansion, a "plunging down" (as Deren described it) into rich, multi-layered moments, a plumbing of metaphoric association. Her cannily chosen example is Shakespeare.

> A Shakespearean work… combines the two movements. In Shakespeare you have the drama moving forward on a horizontal plane of development, of one circumstance – one action – leading to another, and this delineates the character. Every once and a while, however, he arrives at a point of action where he wants to illuminate the meaning to this moment of drama, and at that moment he builds a pyramid or investigates it vertically, if you will, so that you have a horizontal development with periodic vertical investigations which are the poems, which are the monologues. Now if you consider it this way, then you can think of any kind of combination being possible.

For Deren, the problem is how to *prolong* the poetic mode across an entire film – "because it is difficult to maintain such intensity for a long period of time." Short films thus fare better in this quest, while narrative features tend to concentrate their poetic passages in "opening passages" that establish the mood of a place, and in dream sequences – "they occur at a moment when the intensification is carried out not by action but by the illumination of that moment."

Who could argue with any of this? You may well ask! Today, Deren's analytical model seems so sensible, even obvious, accepted knowledge: we could not deal very well with filmmakers ranging from Jean Vigo and Germaine Dulac to David Lynch and Jane Campion without recourse to some working idea of cinematic poetry and its relation to the narrative line. Deren, however, met some tough-guy resistance. Dylan Thomas, for his part, launched in with a declaration that he did not understand "Miss Deren," and proceeded to make sexual innuendo from the terms horizontal and vertical (he's "all for" it, which gets a predictable laugh from the crowd). Having established his credentials as an anti-intellectual ("I haven't a theory to my back"), he complacently mocks avant-garde art (theatre, specifically). He dimly recalls some moments from old films that he liked, that could be construed as poetic. But "I don't know" is his refrain. Basically, he disavows any interest in the topic under discussion: "I'm not at all sure that I want such a thing, myself, as a poetic film… I'm not quite sure that I want a new kind of film at all." He even holds forth as a typical representative of the mass audience: "I'd rather see horizontal films, myself. I like stories. You know, I like to see something going on." This last statement was greeted by "laughter and applause."

If Arthur Miller's behaviour toward Deren is no less bullish ("to hell with that 'vertical' and 'horizontal': it doesn't mean anything"), his position is more interesting, in retrospect, than it might at first seem. In an intuitive and embryonic way, he takes an approach keyed to the technological apparatus of cinema, rather than the artistic singularity of particular films. "I think that it would be profitable to speak about the special nature of any film, of the fact of images unwinding off a machine" – a discussion that he feels should *precede* "on a methodical basis, an aesthetic."

> It seems to me that if we looked at the physiology of the film, so to speak, and the psychology of the film, the way it actually turns off the machine, we begin to get the whole question of style and the whole question of aesthetics changing when one sees it that way.

Miller adds: "We don't understand the psychological meaning of images – any images – coming off a machine." It's almost Isidore Isou speaking! Miller also stresses the often-ignored phenomenology, the "technical, physiological" factors as he calls them, of size and scale in cinema: "You're looking at an image many, many times larger than yourself, and that changes everything." Deren dismisses this machine-talk from a film artist's perspective: "He obviously hasn't made a film because first you have to put it in the machine, and that's awfully hard. It does begin before the machine."

Otherwise, Miller plumbs some fairly banal generalities and homilies, pitched to a broad, humanist perspective: we must "refer to the age we live in," and "the structure of the film is the structure of the man's mind who made it." Like Thomas, he reverts to a pose of populist anti-intellectualism: "It seems to me that if it's a movie, it's a movie." He's even nostalgic for the silent days: "I was against, as a whole, the idea of spoken pictures, anyway." History was against him on that point.

It pains me to report that Parker Tyler (who rates among my all-time film critic heroes) doesn't acquit himself much better than Thomas or Miller. "Miss Deren, who is a professional artist in the poetic film, started out by using a rather complex, a rather difficult, technical vocabulary in order to describe her theory of what she does." That, in fact, captures in a nutshell how filmmakers' thinking is so often re-described and denigrated throughout cinema history: she's just talking about herself, justifying her own work! In fact, although Deren was comradely enough to refer to Maas' films, she scarcely mentions her own creations in the context of this panel. Her proposal was clearly of a general, theoretical nature.

Deren's final word to her critics was sharp, even turning the polite "Miss or Mister" form of address against them.

> I wish mainly to say that I'm a little bit flabbergasted at the fact that people who have handled words with such dexterity as Mr Thomas and Mr Miller, and Mr Tyler,

should have difficulty with such a simple idea as the vertical and the horizontal. These seem to me the most elementary movements in the world and really quite fundamental.

Source: Both an audio recording and a written transcript of the 1953 Cinema 16 panel on "Poetry and the Film" (combining material from two sessions) can be accessed at http://ubu-mirror.ch/papers/poetry_film_symposium.html. *An Anagram of Ideas on Art, Form and Film* was initially published by Alicat Book Shop Press in 1946, and has subsequently been reprinted, in facsimile form, in *Maya Deren and the American Avant-Garde* (University of California Press, 2001) edited by Bill Nichols, pp. 267-322; and also in *Essential Deren: Collected Writings on Film by Maya Deren* (Documentext, 2005) edited by Bruce McPherson, pp. 35-109. A collection in Spanish translation is *El universo dereniano: Textos fundamentales de la cineaste Maya Deren* (Ediciones de la UCLM, 2015), edited by Carolina Martínez. Lastly, a sadly unfinished archival project of enormous interest is *The Legend of Maya Deren: A Documentary Biography and Collected Works* (Anthology Film Archives) begun in the 1970s by VeVe Clark, Millicent Hodson, Francine Bailey and Catrina Neiman, which got as far as the first (published in two parts) of three volumes and the year 1947 in Deren's life.

22
Stepping Off a Fast Train

In 1969, after the release of his milestone *Faces* the previous year, John Cassavetes (1929-1989) was confronted with a rather rude question – one that often comes around again in our era of so-called slow cinema. "When you're dealing with the tempo of reality, don't you risk boredom by imitating its dull pauses?" Cassavetes' response was complex and ingenious.

> I didn't find *Faces* boring in any sense. As a matter of fact, I found it extremely fast-moving. Sometimes when it slowed down from extreme speed it was like stepping off a fast train. I think that, more than the picture slowing down, or reality slowing down, what happens in our picture is that you're getting so many vibrations from people and you're seeing people behave so honestly, when they stop you get irritated. It's more than boredom. It's antagonism.

This is an explanation worthy of Godard (who was a big Cassavetes fan). *Slowness*, in an almost scientific way, cannot be gauged; it is the result of a speed *differential*, a sudden and massive alteration in speed. Moreover, the effect of this differential only exists insofar as it is *experienced*, embodied, processed by the spectator. (And this spectator may well become "antagonistic" from a sense of frustration – a reminder of Pedro Costa's wish in Chapter 5 to put his audience "at war" with his work.) We "step off the fast train" of a passage in the film and are disoriented, dizzy on our new, fixed spot of the platform; our entire perceptual system needs to "gear down."

This fascinating explanation rests on an equally fascinating *a priori* assumption: that the typical scenes in *Faces* of people laughing, dancing, flirting, drinking and talking are, in themselves "fast-moving," full of dense information coming in from all angles, all sides, all aspects of the event. If you are reminded now of Lucrecia Martel's swimming pool, I would not be surprised.

Dziga Vertov (1896-1954), born Denis Kaufman, did not live to see a film directed by Cassavetes, but I believe he would have appreciated the metaphor of the fast train and its physiological effect on the spectator. Not only because his own films (such as *Man with a Movie Camera*, 1929) are filled with dynamic images of locomotion as signs of the modern, industrialised and mechanised world; more profoundly, because Cassavetes perfectly described what has proved to be among the most difficult-to-define concepts in the film theory bequeathed to us by Vertov and his comrades: that of the *interval* in editing.

The interval is a fundamental part of Vertov's conception of montage – a conception that (in ways I won't go into here) differs, in some important respects, from that of his contemporary, Eisenstein, as well as from Artavazd Pelechian's later theory (first conceived in 1971, definitively formulated in 1988) of "montage-at-a-distance." Vertov and Eisenstein were, in their heyday, somewhat competitive, and took many opportunities to critique each other's approach. Where they certainly met, however (and where Pelechian would also concur), was in the centrality placed on editing as the shaper of meaning, energy and form in cinema. Vertov began from a different point in the cinematic continuum than Eisenstein: in documentary newsreel rather than in fiction and its carefully staged *mise en scène*. His "raw material," gathered at the editing table, was therefore particular.

Vertov, it should be noted, did not work alone, and was less of a self-styled Romantic visionary or *auteur* than Eisenstein. Historical research has increasingly come to value the input of his collaborators, particularly his wife, editor Elizaveta Svilova (1900-1975) – a re-vision reflected in the superb films of Australian Karen Pearlman (*After the Facts*, 2018, and *I Want to Make a Film About Women*, 2019), herself a professional editor, teacher, and the writer of an important textbook on editing (*Cutting Rhythms: Shaping the Film Edit*, second edition 2016). This collaborative and collective aspect also bears upon the occasional writings and pronouncements of Vertov, many of which (especially in the revolutionary pitch of the 1920s) take the form and tone of a manifesto. More than just about any other filmmakers, Vertov & co. are *against* many things!

Before we return to the specific Vertovian conception of the interval, let us look at some of the general precepts of these writings. The 1922 manifesto "We" sets itself up in opposition to the then prevalent trend of "theatrical films" – i.e., the "absurdity" of the "psychological Russo-German film-drama." Fiction, almost *in toto*, falls under grave suspicion here.

The "We" manifesto also criticises Hollywood production, and not only for the upfront, Soviet vs. American ideological reasons we might surmise. Rather, it is judged that the "rapid shot changes and close-ups" in USA films are "good but disorderly, not based on a precise study of movement." The *study of movement* chimes in with a constant theme in Vertov's writings: the need to marry cinema, its power and its vision, to the "precision of the machine" in a new society. Indeed, in the full flush of Constructivist rhetoric, a machine-aesthetic is vaunted over merely "clumsy" humanity. Subsequent political history has cast a dark shadow over the extremity of such fanatical rhetoric about "shaping a new human"; nonetheless, we must yet again endeavour to return to the inspiring, truly Utopian moment of its initial enunciation.

Vertov was also a theorist of cinematic specificity. "We protest against the mixing of the arts which many call synthesis" – it is interesting to note that this argument was already in the air in 1922. "Synthesis should come at the height of each art's achievement, not before": an intriguing viewpoint on a medium's evolutionary arc. But, at the origin (or near-origin) of cinema, Vertov rejects the recourse to analogy with the other arts: "Turn your back on music," he sternly warns, speaking not literally (we are still in the silent era, after all) but figuratively – the *forms* of music should not be used as a model or guide for cinema, and especially cinema-as-montage.

The form of cinema, for Vertov, is to be found by exploring an equation: "the three dimensions [i.e., width, breadth and height] + time." Or: space and time, the most familiar couplet in film theory. For Vertov (as for the avowedly esoteric art theory of Pierre Klossowski), movement within the frame is what binds the four dimensions, by literally crossing them; movement indicates the existence of the four dimensions by activating them all. "Cinema's unstrung nerves" – what a metaphor! – "need a rigorous system of precise movement." Here is where things begin to get complicated.

> The metre, tempo and type of movement, as well as its precise location with respect to the axes of a shot's co-ordinates and perhaps to the axes of universal co-ordinates [i.e., the four dimensions] should be studied and taken into account. [Cinema is] the art of organising the necessary movements of objects in space as a rhythmical artistic whole, in harmony with the properties of the material and the internal rhythm of each object.

We can note here a fantasia of *technical measurement* that has overtaken various societies at various moments in 20th-century history – with such programs of measurement often linked to the "forensic" audiovisual recording allowed by film. "Radical necessity, precision and speed are the three components of movement worth filming and screening," writes Vertov. "The geometrical extraction of movement through an exciting succession of images is what's required of montage." Let us note, in passing, something odd and (from one angle) potentially flawed about Vertov's working definition here: he assumes that each shot-unit contains a *single* movement or rhythm. Yet the art of *mise en scène* – which was not Vertov's foremost concern – proves that this assumption is quite false; several or many rhythms can be modulated or combined in the same shot (as in the films of

Ophüls, Akerman or Welles). It simply did not suit Vertov's theory to consider or imagine this possibility; his more-or-less documentary-derived footage was indeed, for the most part, composed of singular, individual, unchanging movements.

Vertov and his comrades believed (or fervently hoped) – and *Man with a Movie Camera* stands as the magnificent monument to this belief – that cinema, through the force of montage, could "educate" the eye and its power of perception, thus helping to evolve the brain for a new type of individual in society. That's a lot to ask of an 80-minute movie! Yet, on the serious side, many filmmakers have wished for just such a revolutionary effect on consciousness wielded by cinema. If only!

Let us now go directly – or as directly as we can manage – to the Vertovian concept of the interval. In ordinary language, and in particular fields, the term enjoys multiple meanings, all somewhat (and confusingly) interrelated. In music, it refers to the step or the difference between one note and another. In everyday English, an "interval of time" refers to a self-contained portion or segment. A temporal interval can also be a block that functions as a divider: interval and intermission are interchangeable words in theatrical presentations. Spatially, interval refers to distance: the gap between things.

In Vertov's theory of editing, interval refers above all to the *change*, *break* or *difference* between movements – each contained within a shot-unit that is devoted to it – and their speed. We pass from one movement at a particular speed (one shot) to another (the next shot) that is different, and we as spectators *feel* that difference: like stepping off a fast train, or a sudden acceleration, or a variation/modulation in the overall mood. The theory is hard to grasp or concretise, precisely because it is about an invisible, *in-between* coefficient that is, nonetheless, present in every editing cut: the change from one shot-unit to the next. Vertov himself defines interval as the *transition* from one movement to another. An invisible, but felt, transition! Intervals are "the material, the elements of the art of movement – not the movements themselves. It is the intervals that draw the movement to a kinetic resolution."

Deploying the analogies, at once linguistic and musical, that have so often inhabited the annals of film theory, Vertov reaches for the idea of the *phrase* as a structuring principle in montage. "The organisation of movement is the organisation of its elements, its intervals, into phrases. In each phrase there is a rise, a high point, and a falling-off of movement." So: from the shot to the phrase, and then onto the larger form of the *composition*: "A composition is made of phrases, just as a phrase is made of intervals of movement." Vertov dreamed of establishing a "film scale" akin to the musical scale, and thus being able to tabulate a montage on the page using "graphic symbols of movement" – something with which many filmmakers, editors and graphic designers have experimented, even if only for a specific job at hand. By the 1950s – when opportunities for his and Svilova's film work had been greatly scaled down – Vertov more modestly (and moderately) used the famous analogy of "writing in filmshots" (cine-writing!), with shots, sequences and segments as letters, words and sentences…

Interval is very close to another, related word, *interstice*. It is, as it were, the "touching of the edges" or of the borders of every shot that matters for Vertov. We may not even see this interval clearly when physically handling frames on the editing table – unless our sensory apparatus is as well trained as Svilova's! – but, when running through or projecting the montage, we see, experience and feel the necessary *relation* between shots, and the degree of success or failure of their "kinetic resolution." Today, digital editing can get us to that moment of material testing, demonstrating and proving even quicker. It will often be a surprise – even a revelation – for us to see how, practically, two movements "click" together, or trigger a modulation, in editing.

It is this precise process of *animating* the edits that *Man with a Movie Camera* reveals to us in one of its most celebrated sequences, passing from film strip to single frame to edited sequence. Pearlman's modern re-vision of this work assimilates such montage practice to a sensorial "thinking" with "facts" (i.e., images or shots). We can begin to appreciate now the enormous challenge – for both the craft and art of film – of "organising the necessary movements of objects in space as a rhythmical artistic whole, in harmony with the properties of the material and the internal rhythm of each object."

At its frenzied peak, the Vertovian program for montage is truly Utopian, and in line with the programmatic plan for a new society: "Cinema is, as well, the art of inventing movements in space in response to the demands of science." He saw the medium as a way of realising "that which cannot be realised in life." Cinema is "drawings" and "blueprints in motion," even "the theory of relativity on screen." The subsequent path of history under Stalin let down Vertov and his comrades, with their initially constructivist vision for cinema, badly. Still, in his 1953 "On Editing," Vertov could extoll the shots in a montage as forming a "collective body, thereby releasing surplus energy." And he called upon the grandest metaphor, the evolutionary path from cosmic dust to nebula to humankind, to hold montage to its best discoveries.

> We have no intention of reverting to the time when only primitive formations existed in nature. We strive on, surmounting the obstacles others are ever ready to place before us.

In the long view, Vertov was right: wherever you are, montage remains one of the best games in town. He said it best: "Hurrah for dynamic geometry, the race of points, lines, planes, volumes"!

Source: Dziga Vertov's essays, composed individually or in collaboration, are collected in *Kino-Eye: The Writings of Dziga Vertov* (University of California Press, 1984), edited by Annette Michelson; and *Lines of Resistance: Dziga Vertov and the Twenties* (Pordenone Film Festival, 2004), edited by Yuri Tsivian. Artavazd Pelechian's "Montage-at-a-Distance, or: A Theory of Distance" can be found in Julia Vassilieva's translation at http://www.lolajournal.com/6/distance.html. The Cassavetes interview is in Gelmis (Chapter 20).

23
Time Imprinted

Andrei Tarkovsky (1932-1986) offers himself to us (his hopeful disciples) as the purest theorist in cinema history. He committed himself to a basic drive – we might even call it the greatest temptation – of film theory: to postulate and define an essence of cinema as a medium, and to include or exclude everything else in strict accordance with that essence. Where some of the chosen case studies in this book are about filmmakers who changed or varied their theoretical ideas with the passing years, Tarkovsky held absolutely firm to his own system. Only – as we shall see – at the very end of his famous book *Sculpting in Time* (1985) did he allow himself to express any kind of reservation to his meticulously assembled model of thinking.

As much as Deren, Stan Brakhage (with whom he had an odd and unsettling film festival encounter) or Ruiz, Tarkovsky has suffered the after-life fate of his theories being regarded (even if respectfully) as simple explanations or justifications of what he himself had put into his films – their style, form and meaning. He often referred, in fact, to the recurring situation that prompted him to eventually write his book: facing audiences, interviewers and various interlocutors who simply did not understand his films, and sought some illumination. Yet his writing goes beyond this immediate, functional aim.

With Tarkovsky, we see the gradual confluence of several factors – his often beleaguered career as a filmmaker, his years as lecturer at a film school in Moscow (1977-1981), and his imminent death in Paris – bringing together, almost by force, the "ultimate statement" on cinema that he assembled, from various notes and fragments, in *Sculpting in Time*. How different this is to, for instance, Robert Bresson, who chose to leave his written "testament" – no less certain and dogmatic, in some respects, than Tarkovsky's – in the form of a collection (spanning 24 years) of clipped, free-floating, sometimes gnomic aphorisms: *Notes on the Cinematograph* (1975). Bresson's accumulated notes up to 1964 were, in fact, as has recently been revealed, partly chosen and ordered by his friend, the philosopher Roger Munier (1923-2010), who in 1963 had written the intense tract *Against the Image* – a book influential, in its day, on the young Raúl Ruiz. Tarkovsky, even on his sick bed, took a far greater, hands-on role in the assembly and publication of his "legacy" book.

The meaning of Tarkovsky's title is a little lost or reshaped in its English translation (and in several other language versions, too, including Spanish). *Sculpting* with time evokes a human, artistic act – time seized and worked through the medium of film. The Russian title, however, is more properly rendered as *Imprinted Time*. That signals a more impersonal, mechanical process: the camera that imprints time (and light) onto a strip of film. Naturally, Tarkovsky believed in both things at once: the photochemical properties of the medium, and the intervention of the artist. But the first and all-important premise, for him, is to grasp what it is that *cinema does which no other medium does*, and that specificity, in his account, is the "imprinting of time."

Tarkovsky is not shy when it comes to laying down rules, laws and principles. He is on the track of an *ideal* cinema which, in his eyes, can come about only through the application of *true* notions about what cinema is, what it does, what it can do, and what it should do – its *vocation* as an art form. He stakes everything on this intuition, almost fanatically.

He defines the essence of cinema thus: "Time, captured in its factual forms and manifestations." The *shot* – preferably held for an extended period – swiftly becomes the chief building block in his conception of cinema, because a shot captures "blocks of time," from the moment the machine is turned on to the moment it is turned off, over and over – at least when running at "normal" speed. Time imprinted! This "unit" of cinema guarantees for Tarkovsky the *unity* of its form. The metaphor of the *block* easily suggests the notion of filmmaker-as-sculptor. But the shot-block already contains much more content, much more complexity and "reality" (however staged) than the raw slab of material that a sculptor initially faces.

Every shot has what Tarkovsky calls *time-pressure*: we witness something in the shot, some action, some movement, inscribing itself in a circumscribed time and space. At this level, Tarkovsky's theory is a *realist* one – even as so little in his films seems realistic in any conventionally naturalistic sense. "The cinema image is essentially the observation of a phenomenon passing through time." That's why his own films so often created physical situations of endurance or a gauntlet, like the writer-artist-hero (Oleg Yankovsky) who must successfully carry a lit candle over the course of a nine-minute take in *Nostalghia* (1983).

Naturally, these blocks are not entirely raw, grabbed straight out of the camera and hurled onto the screen. They must be "trimmed" at the start and end – usually very decisively, not just to omit the stray frames before and after the calls of "action" and "cut" – and they have to be placed in an expressive sequence. "The filmmaker, from a 'lump of time' made up of an enormous cluster of living facts, cuts off and discards whatever he does not need, leaving only what is to be an element of the finished film." There are other processes that also often intervene: the laboratory work of grading, the reconstruction of a soundtrack, perhaps reframing of images (as even Classical Hollywood regularly did via animated refilming of the footage – see Samuel Fuller's films for many examples of this). In the reality of his filmmaking practice, Tarkovsky worked with some of these processes. However, it is fair to say that, in his theory, he plays down the significance of post-production treatments (the digital age would have horrified him!). It is interesting to note, in this regard, that a prime and self-avowed "disciple" of Tarkovsky, Alexander Sokurov (born 1951) – who crafted an entire feature, *Russian Ark* (2002), in one mind-bogglingly elaborate shot – deviates greatly from his Master in both his use of reality-warping lenses and filters in shooting, and further treatments of colour in post-production.

Another contemporary filmmaker-writer, Olivier Assayas (born 1955), alludes to the realist film theory of André Bazin (who had begun making his first film near the end of his life at 40), in an enthusiastic 1997 interview-commentary with Bérénice Reynaud on Tarkovsky's *Mirror* (1975).

> *Mirror* is based on the idea that the truth lies in the duration of things. It is not driven by montage, but by the juxtaposition of units. And these units draw a certain legitimacy and truth from the Bazinian elements they contain: respect for the passing of time, respect for the real, respect for the spectator – it allows you to feel the pulse of the world.

Although some directors – including Rivette, Dušan Makavejev, Todd Haynes, Věra Chytilová and Godard – would certainly include "juxtaposition of units" within their personal conception of montage ("large-scale" montage, the form of the ensemble), it's clear what Assayas is referring to within Tarkovsky's theory and practice: not "chopping up" each shot and redistributing it into smaller units (as Hitchcock routinely did), but labouring to sustain and preserve it, possibly all the way to the level of the *sequence-shot* (an entire scene contained in one shot). In Tarkovsky's lecturing and writing, he made it clear that, in the hierarchy of cinematic units, the shot comes first, the scene second, and the entire film third – and it was at this largest level that, intriguingly, he would allow a higher degree of "manipulation" and experimentation (moving the blocks around in different orders) in order to find the ultimate shape of the film.

A perusal of Tarkovsky's preferred metaphors will leave no doubt as to his predominantly *organic* aesthetic vision. A film is a living body with cells (that must correspond with and reproduce the whole) and a bloodstream; if it is based on the interaction or tension of opposing principles, it must find its equilibrium in the manner of the physical principle of "communicating vessels"; much imagery of "brook, river, waterfall, ocean" is called upon, with "the entire world reflected as a drop of water."

As a corollary to the centrality of the shot and its capturing of time in Tarkovsky's thinking, he (like Béla Tarr today) insisted that the "figures" of symbolism, allegory and metaphor should be banned from *mise en scène*: meanings must be "natural," arising from "the things themselves." It was his update on a famous remark by Roberto Rossellini: "Things are there, why change them?" But be warned: whether uttered by filmmakers or anybody else, invocations of "reality" and "truth" are notoriously slippery, and often fairly meaningless, constructs: their force is rhetorical rather than concrete.

Tarkovsky, even though he (necessarily) used editing within his own scenes and constructed large-scale montages, waged a fierce campaign against theories and practices of cinema based *primarily* on montage, that locate the essence or specificity of the medium there – and Eisenstein emerges as his special, distant nemesis in this regard. Tarkovsky regarded the reliance on montage as a sign of manipulation and artificiality – the opposite of his conception of "truth." Eisenstein didn't fragment his shots Hitchcock-style but, as in Tarkovsky's favourite negative example of the grand battle-on-the-ice in *Alexander Nevsky* (recall Chapter 1), he did keep them relatively short, and subordinated them to the conjoined rhythm of cutting and music (by Sergei Prokofiev). This particular "classic" sequence sent Tarkovsky into such polemical rage that he somewhat misdescribed the scene as he remembered it (in his time as a lecturer, he always stood alone on stage with a microphone, and had no film-clip demonstrations for back-up).

> Eisenstein's own work vindicates my thesis. If his intuition let him down, and he failed to put into the edited pieces the time-pressure required by that particular assembly, then the rhythm, which he held

> to be directly dependent on editing, would show up the weakness of his theoretical premise. [...] Ignoring the need to fill the frames with the appropriate time-pressure, he tries to achieve the inner dynamic of the battle with an edited sequence of short – sometimes excessively short – shots. [Note: they are not quite so short!] [...] [Viewers are] dogged by the feeling that what is happening on the screen is sluggish and unnatural. This is because no time-truth exists in the separate frames. In themselves they are static and insipid. And so there is an inevitable contradiction between the frame itself, devoid of specific time-process, and the precipitate style of editing, which is arbitrary and superficial because it bears no relation to any time within the shots [...] The event is not recreated but put together any old how.

Tarkovsky presented an elaborate philosophical justification for his essentialising of time in cinema. In the history of civilisations, he argued, humanity needs to "increase its mastery over the world." Spatial mastery – seeing as apprehending and possessing, the "pleasure of seeing" as Max Ophüls eulogised it – is not enough to satisfy the Russian filmmaker's dream. Tarkovsky believed that in the act of watching films we seek to regain "lost time" – his reference point here being Proust's novels, but today it could be the films of Apichatpong Weerasethakul (who has often described his work as "sealing" memories about to be lost) or Orson Welles (1915-1985), who once evoked film as the medium providing "pieces of time we'll never forget."

Finally, it's a poetic and melancholic vision – upon which an entire theoretical system was erected. But note the ultimate, cautionary word from Andrei himself at the end of *Imprinted Time*.

It is for the artist both to devise principles and to break them. Artistic texture is always richer than anything that can be fitted into a theoretical schema. I begin to wonder if my own rules are becoming a constraint…

Source: Andrei Tarkovsky's two books are *Sculpting in Time* (University of Texas Press, 1989) and *Time Within Time: Diaries 1970-1986* (Seagull Books, 2019). There is also a Spanish translation of a selection of his lectures in *Atrapad la vida: Lecciones de cine para escultores del tiempo* (Errata Naturae Editores, 2017). The dialogue between Olivier Assayas and Bérénice Reynaud about *Mirror* is "Tarkovsky: Seeing is Believing," *Sight and Sound*, January 1997, pp. 24-25.

24
Mythical, Infantile Substratum

Pier Paolo Pasolini (1922-1975) had no resistance to theory. The activity of theorising came as naturally (and prolifically) to him as the activity of filmmaking, writing poetry, or whipping up journalistic pieces for Italian newspapers. Although his 1960s semiotic/linguistic framework may seem forbiddingly sophisticated and hyper-intellectual at first glance, he would have doubtless dubbed all his endeavours – theory, poetry, film, and the rest – as, at some fundamental level, *savage*, intuitive, impulsive, driven. For he was animated by an often ambiguous attraction for the "primitive," and the outlawed, in every realm of life and culture, from language and sex (like Eisenstein, Martel, Epstein, Child and Akerman, he was queer) to art and thought.

Some of Pasolini's major ruminations on film theory (as well as literary theory) are collected in a book whose title already says a lot: *Heretical Empiricism* (1972). Empirical philosophy is often assumed to be rational, controlled, verifiable, sensible; Pasolini means us to understand that an excess of empiricism, taken all the way to extreme conclusions, is heretical! That shows a love of paradox similar to Godard's mode of thinking and creating. Pasolini was forever on the track of what he called a "scandalous reality" – which has nothing to do with aesthetic realism. It is an exacerbated, provocative, convulsive vision of the real.

One must also note the tricky, embedded title of his most famous essay: "The 'Cinema of Poetry'," which will be discussed in detail here – even some reprintings of this text drop the added quotation marks around "cinema of poetry." It is as if, in the very moment of proposing and defining the term (the first version of which appeared in 1965), Pasolini is already questioning, doubting, deconstructing it. And, indeed, the text fairly burns with internal equivocations, self-contradictions and paradoxes. It would be wrong to try to reduce it to a clear-cut "statement"; it is, rather, the exploration of a possibility, unfolding in the present tense of Pasolini's experience of the then new cinema. Pasolini was an extraordinary writer, and we must make the effort to read his theory text just as we would analyse a film: sensitive to its flows, breaks, leaps, shocks, surprises, provisional closings and openings.

Is there – as some researchers of the time (including Christian Metz and Roland Barthes) eagerly sought – a "language" of cinema that can be defined, like everyday or literary language, in terms of signs, codes, structures, signifiers and signifieds? Pasolini's first intervention in this field was to disrupt that assumption, and for his pains in doing so, he found himself cast out of the annals of film theory for many years to come as a "naïve" participant – just a filmmaker dabbling in semiotic concepts. (By the same token, Luc Moullet, a fellow filmmaker whose debut feature *Brigitte and Brigitte* [1966] Pasolini had admired, launched his own public critique of the essay in 1966 and the analytical trend he assumed it represented, a diatribe wonderfully titled "On the Harmfulness of Film Language, on Its Uselessness, and on the Means to Combat It." Godard tipped his hat to that one!)

So Pasolini's opening move was to dispute that cinema is founded on the "arbitrary" relation that pertains to (for instance) marks forming letters on a page and a living body uttering words. Cinema is not "instrumental" in that way, and resists being instrumentalised (in the education system, for instance). The wild, savage aspect of the cinematic medium is that it communicates inchoately, drawing upon a "language of gestures" and, ultimately, the "language of reality" itself. Once again, not to be confused with naturalistic realism! In a challenging reversal of creative chronology and cultural hierarchy, Pasolini states that cinema is *stylistic* before it becomes *grammatical* – its immediate carnival of *appearances*, coming first and foremost, trump its elaborated *forms*. Paradoxically, it is a fully formed language *preceding* the sophistication of aesthetics. Wow!

To combat the intellectual reign of "lin-signs" (linguistic signs, i.e., words), Pasolini thus posited *im-signs* – raw, brute images. "The filmmaker does not take his signs from a shrine [...] but from chaos, where they are nothing more than possibilities or shadows of a mechanical, oneiric communication." Note in this formulation the same duality or shotgun wedding we will find in Jean Epstein, where the indifferently *mechanical* nature of the cinematic apparatus is yoked to its intimate affinity with *dreaming* (the realm of the oneiric).

Pasolini offers a distinction (once again re-appropriating or coining his own semiotic terms) between *syntagma* and *stylema* in cinema. This bears some similarity to the couplets horizontal/vertical (Deren) and metaphor/metonymy – in other words, the linear, connective, narrative function (syntagmatic) versus the lyrical, poetic, metaphoric function (stylematic). But Pasolini adds a value judgement to this distinction: in his view, syntagma are transitory and short-lived in cinema (whereas they may last longer in other media), because "the world is exhausted each time in description." So much for syntagma!

In fact, it is good to be jolted and reminded in this way that many conventions in filmmaking – for example, our current obsession with "subjective immersion" in a fictional character's "journey" – are indeed ephemeral, coming and going with the fickle tides of cultural fashion. Whereas, in Pasolini's system, stylema have a better shot at enduring because they are unique and personal, a matter of specific filmmakers and their vision of the world. (Moullet's critique of Pasolini asserts, in fact, exactly the same thing.)

Pasolini places a high premium on what he perceives as the *irrational* core of the cinematic medium.

> The linguistic instrument on which film is predicated is, therefore, of an irrational type; and this explains the deeply oneiric quality of the cinema, and also its concreteness as object.

This evokes the "unreally real" formulation of Deren – and resolves (at least provisionally) the tussle that many filmmakers debate, within themselves or with others, between "film as faithful recorder of documentary reality" and "film as projection of inner dream/fantasy." However, Pasolini returns to reckon with syntagma when he launches his theory of the "cinema of poetry" – as opposed, naturally, to the cinema of (narrative) prose.

First, let's pause for a semantic map or two. When Pasolini compares literary language to cinematic language, these are some of the opposed terms that respectively appear: order/chaos, cultivated/instinctive, rational/irrational, abstract/concrete, human/pre-human, civilised/animal, language of signs/language of reality. His fervent wish for cinema language is that, by all rights, it "*should be* expressively subjective and lyrical" (i.e., poetic) – but that it has been subject, in cultural history, to a "rather foreseeable and unavoidable rape" that reduced it to the controlled, regulated, constrained state of prose. All the same, such "naturalistic and objective" repression can never be total: Pasolini evokes the drama of a "mythical and infantile" substratum that intermittently bursts to the surface, in reassertion of the medium's prime irrationality.

A second semantic map becomes necessary for the latter part of Pasolini's long essay. The cinema of prose is contrasted with the cinema of poetry in the following ways. Where the former is into narration (telling stories), the latter is into *monstration* (showing) – a fabulously suggestive word. Prose is the realm of the conscious mind; poetry springs from the unconscious. Where prose cinema trades in "aesthetic naturalism," poetic cinema discloses a "mystic sub-film." Objectivity/subjectivity, convention (especially of genre)/invention, classical/modern, epic/lyrical: this is the kind of map of cinematic styles that we can network with many similar statements and lists. Ultimately, simply making this distinction – even placing a value judgement on one side of the divide over the other – is not the crucial point of the operation for Pasolini.

The big question for Pasolini becomes: how, by what mechanism, does the primitive, mythical and infantile substratum of film emerge? Must it be left to pure chance? Bernardo Bertolucci (1941-2018), a protégé of Pasolini in the early to mid 1960s, feigned a casual approach to this challenge in the course of a 1967 commentary on Godard.

> The shots, whether static, panning or tracking, are autonomous, with an autonomous resonance and an autonomous beauty; we must not be overly preoccupied with previsualising their montage, since, anyhow, their order will automatically emerge the instant we place one shot beside the other. Moreover – as Rossellini knew – any shot is basically as good as any other; all of them contain a poetic force, and the relation obtaining between them will appear no matter what we do.

Pasolini might have replied: that is all very well, but *how* can we ensure that the shots will be "charged with poetry"? His implicit answer is the invention of a theoretical, methodological and analytical tool he names (once again with reference to linguistic and literary categories) the *free indirect* mode of discourse. In written fiction, the free indirect occurs when the normally objective third person narration "slips into" (and then out of) the subjective thoughts or feelings of a character, clearly and efficiently, but without needing to add "he said" or "she thought": "Kate shuddered. Why had she given in?" It is a very common literary device – so common that we hardly notice it. Although I won't go into it here, Éric Rohmer (1920-2010) was also drawn to the practical theorising of what he labelled the "three levels of discourse" in film: direct, indirect and hyperdirect. However, his concern (in a 1977 essay) was essentially to enable a flexible, non-realistic approach to voice, speech and dialogue in cinema. The free indirect path of images was not his goal, as it was for Pasolini.

Transplanting the free indirect mode of discourse into cinema is, for Pasolini, a way of playing with fire. For his intent goes far beyond the most basic, conventional form of this figure in cinema: namely, the POV (point-of-view) shot, where we "see through the eyes" (usually for a quite short duration) of a character. Hitchcock, De Palma and many other filmmakers have used POV systematically, always as an integrated part of a *découpage* syntax: shot of character / their POV / back to the character. Pasolini, by contrast, is after a looser, less constrained, less syntagmatically moored or connected "takeover" of the character by the stylistic functioning of the film itself. And not just the character's literal, optical vision, either; rather, their entire mental space of perception, emotion… all the way to the point of hallucination.

If there is something strangely amusing in Pasolini's theorising about this matter, it is his enthusiastic embrace of various states of mental illness (neurosis, psychosis, schizophrenia, and so on) as paths to uncorking the cinema of poetry! For him, it's no doubt part and parcel of the modern *zeitgeist*: the heroes and heroines in Godard, Antonioni, Varda, Bertolucci, Bellocchio, Polanski and so many other contemporaneous filmmakers in the 1960s are deeply troubled souls, whose grip on external reality is vacillating and uncertain.

Ultimately, the free indirect is less a narrational technique for Pasolini (as it is in classical cinema) than what he proudly calls a mask, alibi or pretext: by "entering the mind" of a neurotic character in this way, the film can liberate its own stylistic (or stylematic!) procedures. Pasolini defines it as "simply the immersion of the filmmaker in the mind of his character and then the adoption on the part of the filmmaker not only of the psychology of his character but also his language" – understanding "language" in the full Pasolinian extension as sensibility, feeling and expression on all levels. There is no formula or routine to this in his account, for the personal styles of filmmakers always win out: the psychic agitation conveyed frenetically by one filmmaker may be translated through disquieting stillness or "stuttering" in another. Some filmmakers will propose a new idea, a new camera position in almost every shot (Welles, Rocha, Oshima, Lynne Ramsay); others will work with repetition and reprise (Erice, Varda, Resnais, Christian Petzold).

To the very end of his epic (and highly influential) essay, Pasolini resists the possibility of "rationalising" all that he has proposed, turning it into an intellectual system. In fact, he might well have agreed with the thrust of Moullet's critique of any attempt to discern and regularise the ways of cinema into a set language.

> One could say that good cinema starts where language ends and dies where language is reborn. [...] Language is theft. Art is individual, communication of a single instant, it's what can exist only once. Language is that which can only exist from the second time onwards, when an associate has transformed art into signs. There is no more creation, only mechanical reproduction. Art can never be reused. Language can only be reused. [...] In film language, the thing expressed is no more than a vulgar symbol, a sign that robot-filmmakers use and which robot-spectators understand.

Similarly, Pasolini halts his meditation on the free indirect before it ascends to "higher" levels of (as it were) pure, lofty "ideas." He forbiddingly states that, as "interior monologue," the free indirect in cinema lacks "both the explicit conceptual element and abstract philosophical element." Rather, it gloriously remains an "extreme stylistic articulation."

> [It] frees the expressive possibilities compressed by traditional narrative convention through a return to origins until the original oneiric, barbaric, irregular, aggressive, visionary quality of cinema is found through its technical devices.

Source: "The 'Cinema of Poetry'" appears in Pier Paolo Pasolini, *Heretical Empiricism* (New Academia Publishing, 2nd edition, 2005). Other references: Bernardo Bertolucci, "Versus Godard," *Cahiers du cinéma*, no. 168, January 1967, pp. 28-30; Luc Moullet, "On the Harmfulness of Film Language, on Its Uselessness, and on the Means to Combat It," included in his splendid collection *Piges choisies* (Capricci, 2009) and translated into English at https://theseventhart.info/2019/10/21/on-the-harmfulness-of-film-language-on-its-uselessness-and-on-the-means-to-combat-it>; Éric Rohmer, "Film and the Three Levels of Discourse," included in *The Taste for Beauty* (Cambridge University Press, 1989).

25
Asynchronised Strike

In August 1928, Sergei Eisenstein, Vsevolod Pudovkin and Grigori Alexandrov composed a stirring "Statement on Sound" (often republished under the title "A Statement"), scarcely two pages long but action packed. Note the time and place: the technical breakthroughs in sound technology for film had yet to appear, especially in Soviet Russia. Nonetheless, they asserted, "it is opportune to state a number of principal premises of a theoretical nature" – especially as early experiments with film sound, particularly in the United States, were informed by "misconceptions" that "threaten to destroy all present formal achievements" of the silent era of cinema.

Here again, we see the prevalent assumption that, by the end of the 1920s, cinema had reached an aesthetic peak, and was menaced by a possible backsliding decline once sound was married to image. All the same, the possibilities of sound beckoned to the writers of this manifesto as being of "vast significance" as compared with the pale insignificance of "colour and stereoscopic film"! (Eisenstein, for his part, would later be re-drawn to the dream of stereoscopy, and colour became part of his aesthetic palette in several segments of *Ivan the Terrible* [1944].)

For this trio, the aesthetic triumph of cinema up to 1928 was indelibly linked with montage. In fact, they brandish the primacy of montage as an "indisputable axiom," a law, "the basic and only means that has brought the cinema to such a powerfully effective strength," enabling "the best means to affect the spectator."

Yet how will montage, in all its proud discontinuity and fragmentation, work alongside the often continuous *flow* of sound, whether voices, music or atmospheres? This is the unspoken dilemma that the Soviet theoreticians faced. They rejected what they (correctly) foresaw as the "novelties" allowed by the coming of sound: "a certain 'illusion' of people talking, of audible objects, etc." Like for Vertov, "people talking" or the "photographed play" aroused, in these theorists, the spectre of a hated form: "bourgeois theatre." One hears the distant echo of this still today, when directors such as Brian De Palma oppose their ideal of "pure film" to mere "pictures of people talking" – which is now associated primarily with the medium of television, rather than the "antiquated" mode of classic theatre!

This gives us a fascinating moment of historical relativity: who, today, would refer to the standard recording and synchronisation of speech, or the sound emitted by an object (such as a phonograph) accompanying its image, as an *illusion* – even if that's exactly what it is, a reconstruction aligning different levels of technical registration? Only avant-gardists such as Isou and Frampton returned, decades later, to the frontal attack on this specific, constitutive illusion of the sound film.

The Russian statement rails against the "big problem of synchronisation" (the frequent use of capitalisation is part of the original text).

> To use sound in this way will destroy the culture of montage, for every ADHESION of sound to a visual montage piece increases its inertia as a montage piece and increases the independence of its meaning – and this will undoubtedly be to the detriment of montage, operating in the first place not on the montage pieces but on their JUXTAPOSITION.

For these artists, this simple *juxtaposition* of image and sound – block against block or track against track, as it were – will not solve the core problem, for these layers will tend to cleave apart, "independently" (a phenomenon we can observe today, for instance, in many modern musical and/ or Foley accompaniments to silent films). What is required is genuine *counterpoint*: "Only a CONTRAPUNTAL USE of sound in relation to the visual montage piece will afford a new potentiality of montage development and perfection." And this process of counterpoint must begin from "DISTINCT NONSYNCHRONISATION."

Many debates around the coming of sound in cinema turned around the question of how *natural* or *artificial* this "add-on" was. Eisenstein, in much of his theoretical speculation, opted for a natural or *organic* model to explain the evolution of this art (and, indeed, all the arts, in their intertwined, historical development). In the "Statement on Sound," this new aural factor was greeted as the organic solution that would resolve certain impasses that had congealed in the "cultured cinematic avant-garde" – including, presumably, their own prior work.

The first impasse noted is the presence of written *intertitles* inserted between images. Despite the dynamic experiments with fonts, sizes, timing and so on (very evident, for example, in Vertov's classic *Man with a Movie Camera* of 1929), it proved impossible to fully and successfully integrate intertitles into a montage flow. The second impasse is what they referred to as *explanatory* elements, such as "certain inserted close-ups" that "burden" the montage and "retard the tempo." One can detect in this a temperamental suspicion of overly psychological and sentimental drama (as embodied in the cult of the facial close-up) – a tendency that, for this manifesto, had already led to "decadence." What they referred to as "tasks of theme and story," in a fairly classical mode, were deforming the vocation of montage, leading it away from its more abstract and intellectual functions.

"Statement on Sound" concludes by bringing in another reigning obsession of the late 1920s: *internationalism*, the cinema as a universal, "Esperanto" language comprehensible to all peoples of the world.

> Sound, treated as a new montage element (as a factor divorced from the visual image) will inevitably introduce new means of enormous power to the expression and solution of the most complicated tasks that now oppress us.

> The CONTRAPUNTAL METHOD of constructing the sound film will not only not weaken the INTERNATIONAL CINEMA but will bring its significance to unprecedented power and cultural height.

Such a method of constructing the sound film will not confine it to a national market (as must happen with the photographing of plays) but will give a greater possibility than ever before for the circulation throughout the world of a filmically expressed idea.

There is an evident paradox here: the "filmically expressed idea" of sound cinema envisaged must, presumably, not be reliant on dialogue – the spoken word bound to its national or regional language. Internationalism in sound will rely on other aural dimensions: music, noise, voice as pure emanation (cries, grunts, and so on).

Almost two decades on from this collective Statement, and well into the period of the "talkies" worldwide, Eisenstein was still looking for a theoretical basis on which to formulate the inviolable "principle" of non-synchronisation in film sound. He rails against the "rebirth of mechanical synchronism" in "bad sound films" that lack the long-desired *audiovisual counterpoint*. He opposes the "narrowly material aim of reproduction" (which, it seemed, had already triumphed) to its true, "magical" aim: "the way it impacts the viewer."

In this quest, Eisenstein's appeal to the natural, organic realm became even more pronounced. He proceeds by endeavouring to "make strange" the familiar experience of synchronism: "One can read the principle of 'synchronism' (even on the everyday level) only after having understood, having seen, after having encountered occurrences of asynchronism." To ground this "natural" history of asynchronism, Eisenstein spins a historical tale of the role of the *drum* in ancient cultures, and its associative relation to *thunder* in the sky. "Thunder in connection with absolutely the strongest effect of light in nature – blinding lightning, flashing through the darkness of the night or of a storm!"

This close link between cinema and the fundamental alternation of light/darkness is a recurring theme in film theory – Josef von Sternberg's memoir *Fun in a Chinese Laundry* (1965) offers another, more whimsically expressed but deeply earnest reflection on this. Eisenstein's inspired reasoning runs as follows.

> These days even a child knows that the burst of thunder and the flash of lightning do not occur simultaneously (synchronously) as an audio and visual embodiment of one and the same natural phenomenon. […]
>
> But everyone also knows that in reality – in our apprehension – they almost never occur simultaneously.
>
> I.e., to be precise – they do come together once – in what is for us the culminating moment of the storm, producing in us a fear unequalled by any other natural phenomena.
>
> Up to this synchronised strike and after it there are phases of asynchronised strikes and flashes – gradually growing closer and closer together to the point of culmination, after which they grow gradually distant from one another.

Therefore, the "difference between the speed of light and that of sound" places the "revelation in storm and thunder" as the basis for audiovisual counterpoint. What a splendid moment of filmmaker thinking this is! The phenomenon of thunder and lightning provides not merely a metaphor but a *dynamic model* for the workings of cinema: gradually phasing and dephasing in their interrelation of image and sound.

Source: The "Statement on Sound" can be found under the title "A Statement" in Elisabeth Weis and John Belton (eds), *Film Sound: Theory* *and Practice* (Columbia University Press, 1985). A PDF can be found at https://italiancinema525.files.wordpress.com/2013/11/sound_reader.pdf. Eisenstein's later reflections on non-synchronisation, gathered under the title "Revelation in Storm and Thunder," appear in his posthumously published *Notes for a General History of Cinema* (Amsterdam University Press, 2016) edited by Naum Kleiman and Antonio Somaini, pp. 207-222. Sternberg's pondering on light occupies the entire Chapter 12 of his *Fun in a Chinese Laundry* (Secker & Warburg, 1965), pp. 309-325.

26
In Suspense

How many different metaphors for cinema can co-exist in one paragraph of description? Jean Epstein (1897-1953) went for the record at the tender age of 24, in a passage titled "Magnification" from his immortal book *Bonjour Cinema* (1921).

> Point blank. A head suddenly appears on screen and drama, now face to face, seems to address me personally and swells with an extraordinary intensity. I am hypnotised. Now the tragedy is anatomical. The décor of the fifth act is this corner of a cheek torn by a smile. Waiting for the moment when 1,000 metres of intrigue converge in a muscular *dénouement* satisfies me more than the rest of the film. Muscular preambles ripple underneath the skin. Shadows shift, tremble, hesitate. Something is being decided. A breeze of emotion underlines the mouth with clouds. The orography of the face vacillates. Seismic shocks begin. Capillary wrinkles try to split the fault. A wave carries them away. Crescendo. A muscle bridles. The lip is laced with tics like a theatre curtain. Everything is movement, imbalance, crisis. Crack. The mouth gives way, like a ripe fruit splitting open. As if slit by a scalpel, a keyboard-like smile cuts laterally into the corner of the lips.

Of what, exactly, is this a description? You may well ask. Epstein prefaces it by exclaiming: "I will never find a way to say how I love American close-ups." No – he finds at least 20 ways! He is fixed on a moment, a movement, an anticipation of something that is about to happen on the screen: a face, in sublime close-up, is about to smile. That's it, that's all. But just look at the vast range of phenomena Epstein sees and detects in the fleeting, grainy frames leading up to this great event. A smile is anatomical and bodily, a matter of wrinkles and orifices (the mouth), muscles and blood vessels. It is dramatic and emotional. It follows the processes of "movement, imbalance, crisis." The face on which the smile happens is a landscape (static or during an earthquake), a film or stage set, a mountain (orography). The beginning of a smile is the bustle of wind, shadows, insects, waves. A toothy smile is a piece of sliced fruit and a keyboard. The action of a smile is at first a tremor, a vacillation, a bridling; then it is a tearing, a cutting, a cracking, a scalpel slitting. And the entire operation happens like a musical crescendo.

Epstein not only piles up his metaphors; he likes to mix them, too, like a true, intoxicated poet of his modern times. Bodies are like the earth and the earth is like a body; objects are people and people are objects; humans are machines and machines are human; emotion is like waves and breezes, and those waves and breezes are already emotions in themselves... Just take a look at Epstein's own extraordinary short film *Le Tempestaire*, made 26 years later in 1947, to get a measure of how completely all the realms of metaphor had interpenetrated each other in his fervent imagination.

We could go on analysing that single paragraph from *Bonjour Cinema* practically forever. But it suffices to note that this entire carnival of metaphors is cranked up into motion by Epstein because he wishes to stage a conceptual displacement or, more powerfully, a *conversion*, a genuine and felt *metamorphosis*. His remarks are framed by the overarching notion that "drama," i.e., conventional narrative, is not really, in his view, the province of cinema. And it should never become so. For him, cinema exists microscopically, in frames, in split-second changes and movements – hence his title here, "Magnification." The movie camera, this extraordinary invention of the 20th century, is a microscope; through its eye, poetry and science are effortlessly combined. (Later, he became fascinated with technological possibilities such as slow and reverse motion, both for image and sound.) So he needs to demonstrate that the smallest, most extraordinary gesture – like a smile – can be everything that "grand drama" is said to be and to deliver… everything, and more. Hence the incredible, delirious "performance" enacted by his imagistic prose.

Cinema, for Epstein, is at once a new sensual realm and a new intellectual realm, one that he will never stop theorising for the next 32 years, even as cultural fashions cruelly abandoned and mocked him as the dinosaur of an ancient, long-surpassed avant-garde, a pitiful "eccentric" all at sea making unusual documentaries about fishermen (his Brittany cycle, now the object of widespread veneration). A sad obituary in *Positif* magazine (written by the poet Charles Ford) noted that, by 1953, "his name means almost nothing to today's cinephiles." Beyond his death, critics dismissed his adaptation of Edgar Allan Poe's *The Fall of the House of Usher* (1928) as a stuffy, museum-piece classic of yesteryear (in truth, it is nothing of the sort). Even an admirable surrealist such as Jacques Brunius, in his wonderful survey *On the Margins of French Cinema* (1954), indulged in some retrospective, not-very-subtle, homophobic gay-bashing of Epstein (whose writings on queer history and culture appeared in print only in 2014).

It would be another two decades after the filmmaker's death until his work was collected and reprinted (with some subtle censorship prevailing) in the mid-1970s, and yet another two decades before the present-day Epstein revival began accelerating. This tale tells us a lot about the wayward shape, and sometimes the wholesale oblivion, of film history and culture. There is always someone like Epstein whose legacy needs to be recovered, remembered, redeemed and revivified. Don't forget it!

Let us return to Epstein's prodigious theorising. Although he laboured to displace the role of narrative in cinema, he never rejected it outright; virtually all his own films have some narrative pretext or line. Rather, he sought to unearth other levels, other potentialities, other micro-intensities inherent in cinema as a visual (and later audio-visual) medium; it was these that he grouped and investigated under the term *photogénie*. Narrative was (as it were) too large-scale a parameter to grip his interest and imagination – not to mention that it was mainly derivative from the novel and theatre. Stories were old-fashioned, dead husks; in the final lines of the pamphlet-like *Bonjour Cinema*, he answers an imagined "old gentleman" (bourgeois, no doubt!) who finds all screen stories stupid: sure they are, Epstein responds, but that's what is great about them. Because, beyond story, "emotion remains. But emotions don't interest you anymore." By contrast, small things mattered to Epstein as bearers of high energy and emotion – every gesture that functioned as that smile did.

> Cinema, by and large, doesn't do justice to the story. And "dramatic action" here is a mistake. The drama we're already watching is half-resolved and unfolding on the curative slope to the crisis. The real tragedy is in suspense. It looms over all the faces; it is in the curtain and in the door-latch. Each drop of ink can make it blossom at the tip of the pen. It dissolves itself in the glass of water. At every moment, the entire room is saturated with the drama. The cigar burns on the lip of the ashtray like a threat. The dust of betrayal. Poisonous arabesques stretch across the rug and the arm of the seat trembles. For now, suffering is in surfusion. Expectation. We can't see a thing yet, but the tragic crystal that will turn out to be at the centre of the plot has fallen down somewhere. Its wave advances. Concentric circles. It keeps on expanding, from relay to relay. Seconds. The telephone rings. All is lost.

The real tragedy is in suspense. It is eternal present of the infinite instant: cinema exists to "photogenically" expand the spectacle and sensation of such moments. (The ideas, as well as the metaphors, are close to Martel's here.) Plot (ushered in by that pesky telephone call) hurries everything along too quickly; we must, rather, strive to luxuriate in the split-seconds, the seized-on frames. "*Photogénie* has a value that lasts for mere seconds," he declares; "if it goes on too long, I don't experience continuous pleasure" – quite an aesthetic challenge for any filmmaker, to resolve this conflict between the fragment and the whole! Epstein demanded "a *découpage* a thousand times more detailed than that of most films, even American ones." Here is another passage from "Magnification."

> Even more beautiful than a laugh is the face preparing for it. [...] I love the mouth which is about to speak and holds back, the gesture which hesitates between right and left, the recoil before the leap, and the moment before landing, the becoming, the hesitation, the taut spring, the prelude, and even more than all these, the piano being tuned before the overture. *Photogénie* is conjugated in the future and in the imperative.

The constant suspense of *photogénie* is closely tied to *movement* – sensed or virtual as much as active and dynamic – and, on this point at least, Hitchcock could well have agreed with Epstein: true cinema "does not allow for stasis," its "essence… is movement," and even the seemingly still close-up of a face depends on "temporal dissonance."

Curiously, Epstein was a prophet of a type of aesthetic *immersion*, as distinct from the clashing, self-conscious, fragmented intervals of the montage-is-king school. Epstein may have praised a hyper-*découpage* in editing as necessary "mincemeat" in the 1920s, but he essentially came to preach the importance of flow and dissolution of successive shots one into the other, "relay by relay," as in a dream or trance.

> In order for the spell within which the spectator lives another existence to persist, the look should be allowed to move from one image to another smoothly, without even being aware of the cut. It is a question of harmony between the dimensions, angles, directions and speeds of juxtaposed movements. And any shared form – a memory of the shot in the reverse shot, even just the smoke of a cigarette – acts as a bridge on which the eye glides from one shot to another without feeling disoriented. When that turns out to be impossible, the hyphen is given to the ear in the form of overlapping sounds. Here, as in dreaming, a hiatus in the fabric of representations constitutes a prodrome, the threat of waking.

Even Epstein's earliest, fully achieved films realised this *harmonic* goal. By 1947 he had developed the theoretical notion of "visual fabric," "a paralogical continuity, visual or visual/sonic" (by this stage, Epstein had coined *phonogénie* as the aural counterpart to *photogénie*). This is decidedly not a call for spatio-temporal realism, but a different kind of continuous, woven flow of image and sound. Seemingly disparate images can form a "sentimental concordance"; films require a "guardrail" of paralogical continuity in order to channel emotion to the spectator, "a guardrail suited to dreaming, a dream-guard." The "emotional connection dominates all others." And all this in the context of an article nominally designed as advice for establishing the "shooting scripts" of films!

The category of *rhythm* is all-important to Epstein's theory and to his work, but not the machine-rhythm of Soviet montage; rhythm must be manufactured as an undulating wave in order to produce gradual and unceasing metamorphoses. However, on this ever-shifting ground of metamorphosis, Epstein was not an avowed surrealist (he even fiercely rejected the umbrella terms of experimentalist or avant-gardist). He was frequently at war with the surrealists, and vice versa (hence Brunius' rude invective against him as a boxed-in representative of the filmic "impressionism" school of the 1920s in France, alongside Germaine Dulac, another significant filmmaker-theorist, Abel Gance and others). Epstein's fundamental disagreement with surrealism had two key aspects. First, exactly like Maya Deren, he rejected the surrealist embrace of Freudian psychoanalysis as a "legend" or interpretive key that could decipher dreams and fantasies as expressive of unconscious "complexes" and "syndromes"; this was too closed a system for him, "alien" and "foreign" as Deren described it, not at all attuned to the messy realm of drives and desires. Second, Epstein's theory had a material (and materialist) basis: for him, it was never a matter of conjuring another, imaginary world, but of discovering the marvellous levels and properties within *this*, our shared world. The following passage is from his *The Cinema Seen from Etna* (1926).

> The camera lens is an eye which Apollinaire would have called surreal (without any relationship to today's surrealism), an eye endowed with inhuman analytic properties. It is an eye without prejudices, without morals, exempt from influences. It sees features in faces and human movements that we, burdened with sympathies and antipathies, habits and thoughts, no longer know how to see.

In the "existential" terms that became increasingly political for Epstein in the 1940s, this crusade for a cinematic vision "without prejudices, without morals, exempt from influences" was a cry against the influence of oppressive, internalised ideologies, and against industrial standardisation in the manufacture of culture and its commodified "dreams" (he liked some special Hollywood silent films, such as those of Cecil B. DeMille in the early 1920s, but positive references to the American movie system virtually disappear from all his subsequent texts).

In filmic and aesthetic terms, Epstein's anti-surrealist position meant that nothing needed to be staged or contrived, "tricked up" with filters, superimpositions, or various overtly deforming treatments. It was enough to use the camera to uncover a deeper, hidden, secret reality, and all subsequent cinema form had to be in the service of bringing this vision out, underlining it. The cinema had the power to reveal patterns, correspondences (Baudelaire's guiding idea was a clear influence on this thinking), physical interrelationships that the naked eye (and human mind) could not grasp alone. And this experience through cinema further opened the door to our metaphoric and poetic reflection, our grasping of the true complexity of things – what he had baptised, at the tender age of 25, as *lyrosophy*.

Source: The richest English-language collection of Epstein's writings is *Jean Epstein: Critical Essays and New Translations* (Amsterdam University Press, 2012) edited by Sarah Keller and Jason N. Paul. It is from the 1947 "Visual Fabric" that I quote here, plus the extract from *The Cinema Seen from Etna*. The essay "Magnification" is not included in that book but can be found in *French Film Theory and Criticism: A History/Anthology* (Princeton University Press, 1988), edited by Richard Abel. *Bonjour Cinema* exists in Spanish translation as *Buenos días, cine* (Intermedio, 2015), along with *El cine del diablo* (Cactus, 2014). In French, Epstein's indispensable *Écrits complets* is currently being rolled out across ten scrupulously edited volumes. Six have so far appeared, the first two from Independencia and the rest from Les Éditions de l'Œil.

27
Past the Photographic

"If we can't get past the photographic screen and reach something deeper, then cinema just doesn't interest me." Those could be the words of an avant-garde filmmaker of the 1970s, or a cosmopolitan, digital, New Media artist of today. But the declaration was in fact made in 1951 in France, by a Romanian-born Jewish polymath named Isidore Isou (1925-2007), early in the course of a 150-page manifesto titled "Aesthetic of Cinema" published in the magazine of his artistic circle, *Ion* – a sustained, rigorous piece of theorisation almost unknown today beyond a small number of specialists. It has existed, for 70 years, entirely outside the institutions of most universities, festivals and cinémathèques.

In this text by Isou, the term *post-photographic* appears often – and prophetically. Let us take in the shock of this historical context: Isou composed it in between the publication of André Bazin's often anthologised "Ontology of the Photographic Image" essay in 1945 and the first period of *Cahiers du cinéma* magazine in the early 1950s. Bazin, even though we take him today to be the absolute defining point of mid-century European film theory, does not rate a mention from Isou, not even as an explicit nemesis to be vanquished.

Who is Isou? Some will know that he was the founder and leader of a movement in art and thought named Lettrism. Some may know the remarkable film he made a year before he wrote his manifesto, the *Treatise on Slime and Eternity*, a breakthrough work of feature-length experimentation that was to win fans including Stan Brakhage – Isou himself would coldly remark, many years later, that Jean-Luc Godard and Guy Debord (to name only two luminaries whom he considered his mortal enemies) stole everything from it. Others might have come to the legend of Isou through the fond passage devoted to him in Greil Marcus' book on the distant origins of punk music, *Lipstick Traces* – a book whose subtitle evokes a "secret history of the 20th century."

Isou was precocious. He published his first Lettrist manifesto when he was 16. By the age of 25 he had written over half a dozen books, covering an amazing diversity of fields, and all under an increasingly unified system that he did not hesitate to call *Isouian* theory. These books include *Introduction to a New Poetry and a New Music*, *Treatise on Nuclear Economics*, *Youth Uprising* (in 3 volumes), *The Making of a Name and a Messiah* (the name and the Messiah both being Isou), and *The Mechanics of Women*, which presents itself as a learned, lived testimony to the science of "erotology." Inevitably, Isou was not shy when it came to declaring the importance of his own film production.

> There is no work in the entire history of cinema comparable to *Treatise on Slime and Eternity*, in terms of the richness of its creations. Preceding film creations were only particular applications from more advanced aesthetic domains, while Isouian creations are the straightforward promises or presentiments of a total transformation of knowledge.

Isou's artistic works covered many media – and combined many media in the same gesture, as in his *hypergraphic* collage images – but a special place was reserved for his theorising, which was of a vaulting, indeed messianic ambition, because it aimed to interrelate all major areas of human and social activity: art, technology (which he called "mechanics"), science, mathematics, economics, sexuality, and so on. He wrote: "In the period circumscribed between 1931 and 1945 [i.e., basically the period since his own birth], nothing new has been revealed in poetry, the novel, philosophy, economy or cinema." Isou gave himself and his Lettrist comrades the task of revealing this something new.

In "Aesthetic of Cinema," Isou proposes that the first projection of a film is its fatal consummation, its "wedding night," where its destiny is set and fixed for evermore. The Lettrist mission, by contrast, was to sneak in and interfere with the bride before that malign, conservative, suburban destiny could occur. Isou, it should be clear, was an anarchist and a provocateur – and his (deeply gendered) language of metaphor followed suit.

At the start of the 1950s, cinema as we knew it was dead for Isou, the mission or vocation of its heroic era over. In the course of "Aesthetic of Cinema," he fulminates against such filmmaker-theorists as Jean Epstein, Louis Delluc, Germaine Dulac, Sergei Eisenstein and René Clair, as well as neo-realism (which he viewed as a regressive movement), and the animation experiments of Walt Disney!

Such wiping-off of all previous achievements in a field is the founding *tabula rasa* gesture of many an avant-garde manifesto, but in Isou's Lettrist system, it has a particular and special coherence. In a striking move, Isou stakes the claim early on in his text that his definition of cinema "is the result of an *invention*, not a *given*." And his definition is, in the first place, that any bit of film is the *unfurling* or *unwinding of a reproduction*. He extends this to the soundtrack as well as the image track, which were for Isou always two different, separate, *discrepant* things. Cinema is thus a multiple object which is, above all, printed, then copied (reproduced), thus fundamentally serial in nature, and its original (the film's negative, in those celluloid days) is always hidden away, occulted, secreted from the interfering hands of true, subversive artists.

So, for Isou cinema is, in the first place, *a strip of film*, and as such has the status of a *found object*, even when the artist generates its images and sounds. This emphasis on the mechanical, on printing and serialisation, immediately does away with any sacred ontology of the photographic (or cinematographic) image, any "redemption of physical reality" – and in this founding, definitional moment we can measure the distance between Isou and Bazin as well as a large, international army of post-Bazinians. We can also sense Isou's proximity to our present-day digital moment in culture. Isou set himself against the theories of his time that based themselves primarily in the photographic – which he posits as neither the *origin* nor the *destiny* of cinema, but something more like a limiting "historical accident" of its development and exploitation.

In terms of artistic strategy, Isou's theory led him to the cavalier disrespect of the image in *Treatise on Slime and Eternity*: he scratched on it, flipped it upside down, blacked it out for long periods, and so on – gestures that have a long history in experimental film and beyond. Bear in mind, though, that this provocation had a particular edge in 1950, since many of the people who had agreed to appear in his film were Parisian celebrities, and at the Cannes Film Festival they saw on screen their eyes and mouths being scratched out by marks on the film frame, while reams of Lettrist phonemic-nonsense poetry cascaded discrepantly on the soundtrack.

Let us return to the theoretical argument – very elaborate and detailed – of "Aesthetic of Cinema." Isou had a global theory of artistic creation. Each medium, he argued, passed through its *amplic* phase of expansion – its conventionally expressive novelistic, pictorial or musical phase – until this classicism becomes "sclerotic" (Isou's corporeal and medical metaphors run high). Then the medium arrives at its *chiselling* phase, its state of breakdown. Lettrism, as a practice and an idea, always installs itself at this chiselled point, the phase of a violently happy *negation* of the medium at hand. A negation but also a *purification*, since Isou was always after what was essentially specific to each medium, and abhorred what was simply lazily "imported" from other media. A chiselled medium dissolves into its smallest and purest particles: its letters and phonemes, its dots and lines. In terms of cinema, Isou insists that we must find its "primary particle," and that particle is the individual film frame, or what he calls the film medium's *physico-chemical base*.

All film theories can be divided and classified in relation to whether they attend to the frame as an essential unit of cinema – as in animation or some experimental cinema traditions – or whether they bypass this primary particle to begin at a higher level of representational abstraction, such as the shot, the take, the scene or the narrative as a whole: all the things that Isou relegates to the category of "secondary elements" in cinema. Here is a crucial passage of his text.

> Once we reach the primary particle [of film], we must halt the kinetic élan [explored by previous filmmakers] and reverse the "movement" towards (and on behalf of) the photographic. Thus, it's above all a question of provoking an *anti-cinema*. Then we will be able to touch the image that usually passes us by at each of its 24 frames per second, and we will be able to imprint our stamp on an element [i.e., the frame] that is usually turned toward reality, thus ignoring us.

Once again, the sovereign Lettrist ethos of getting in, breaking in, and touching, imprinting, interfering with the medium comes to the fore here – along with the disdain for being ignored, rendered a passive, witnessing spectator by the film apparatus. Isou takes this orientation in a striking metaphoric direction when evoking film's "secret flesh."

> We must discover the *secret line* of the particle and work with it. This is how we will render our presence visible within the secret flesh of a representation. The negative of the film is the *foetus* of the work, the monstrous element of the beautiful image of reality. We must incrust our individual presence, our act of creation, within the palpitating somersault of this "virtuality."

What a passage! First, the horror-movie imagery: Isou's celebration of the filmic negative as the monstrous foetus that subverts the formed, finished, "beautiful image" of reality-based, photographic cinema. And second, his association of this foetus-negative with the *virtual* – a gesture that is prophetic of our digital age in both its technology and its aesthetic philosophies.

It is not a matter, finally, of locating Isou in the grand narrative of 20th-century art history, jamming him into a preordained Lettrist slot between Dadaism and Surrealism on one side and Fluxus and the Situationism on the other side. Rather, the secret history represented by "Aesthetic of Cinema" can make a sudden, surprise appearance in our present context, speak to us and shake us up in its eruption. For, like Isou in 1951, we too, today, are still in search of the "palpitating somersault" of the virtual.

Source: Jean Isidore Isou, "Esthétique du cinéma," first published in *Ion*, no. 1, April 1952, pp. 7-153. A facsimile reproduction was published by Jean-Paul Rocher, 1999. A meticulous transcription and English translation of Isou's major film, its title rendered as *Treatise on Venom and Eternity*, is available from Annex Press (2019).

28
Featureless White Screen

> Films are made out of footage, not out of the world at large.
>
> Hollis Frampton, 1968

The American avant-gardist Hollis Frampton (1936-1984) had a huge intellect and a far-reaching theoretical ambition. A true conceptualist, it was doubtful that he saw much difference (if any) between his film works and his written essays, which were posthumously collected in *On the Camera Arts and Consecutive Matters* (2009).

Frampton took very seriously the mechanical or *apparatus* basis of what he termed the "camera arts" – where this apparatus, in its totality, expands to include not only the camera and the editing bench, but also the projector, the architectural set-up of the movie theatre, and the position (in all senses: biological, psychological, social) of the spectator. All these "given" elements had to be understood in their complexity, before any individual artistic expression really mattered. A decade after his death, the long-delayed French translation (in the cosmopolitan magazine *Trafic*) of key statements by Frampton, "For a Metahistory of Film: Commonplace Notes and Hypotheses" (1971) and "A Pentagram for Conjuring the Narrative" (1972), influenced Jean-Luc Godard during the period of completing his *Histoire(s) du cinéma* series in the 1990s.

Frampton belongs to a 1960s generation of artists deeply formed by the philosophy and aesthetics of structuralism, and by various branches of science. Like Deren in an earlier generation, he sought to synthesise artistic production, speculative philosophy, mathematics, physics, optics... Like many of his time all around the world (such as Kurt Kren in Austria and Peter Gidal in UK) in various *structuralist-materialist* groups, he was drawn to the conceptual procedures of generating art through precisely numbered and graded formal procedures relating to the shot, the frame, image-sound synchronisation, and so on. Everything was (as we say today) on the *meta* level, ceaselessly drawing attention to the concrete, material basis of film form, and to its effects on you, the spectator.

Representational illusion was not a priority for Frampton, unless it was intended to be placed in quotation marks and then dismantled. He applied the same attitude to narrative, which was something that could be *conjured* but was not to be considered or treated as some irrefutable or inevitable *essence* of cinema as a medium. Story was just one *possibility* in what had turned out to be a restrictive, repressive history of cinema's development as a medium.

> A spectre is haunting the cinema: the spectre of narrative. If that apparition is an Angel, we must embrace it; and if it is a Devil, then we must cast it out. But we cannot know what it is until we have met it face to face.

Granting the seriousness of all this, it must also be said that Frampton – like his Canadian friend, Michael Snow (born 1928) – was a joker. Wit and humour (sometimes of a very "low" sort) were rarely absent from his experimentation. Word games and unexpected "punchlines," reflexivity, sudden surprise-turns in a work's structure, everyday references, eruptions of unconscious associations: all became part of his approach, thus helping to create a bridge between "pure" formalism and the more politicised games of Yvonne Rainer, soon to follow on the road of American experimental art.

The 1968 performance-piece "A Lecture" is an exemplary demonstration of Frampton's praxis, situated somewhere between and across art and pedagogy. In its initial presentation, Frampton, standing in front of a bare white screen, simply turned on a tape recording (of Snow reading Frampton's lecture) and retired to the back of a room to work – using extremely elemental manœuvres – a movie projector. With no film in it! The performance has since been recreated (using the original audiotape) in, for example, the Criterion DVD *A Hollis Frampton Odyssey*.

"A Lecture" is Frampton's own playful attempt to define a basic essence of cinema. As he attests right near its end, in a witty third-person flourish, "self-expression interests him very little. He's more interested in recovering the fundamental conditions and limits of his art." For him, this condition-limit comes down to the bare, "featureless white screen" (in its industrial "carefully standardised rectangle"), and the light of the projector that pierces a theatre's darkness. As a mechanical gesture, movie projection or screening is repeatable, predictable, programmable, "infallible" (and, occasional catastrophes aside, has become even more so in the digital age). But Frampton is pitching at a level higher than the merely exploitable economics of the film industry. When he invokes "our rectangle of white light" as "eternal," he is tuning into a different kind of speculative and psychic process.

> So it seems that a film is, first, a confined space, at which you and I, we, a great many people, are staring.
>
> It is only a rectangle of white light. But it is all films. We can never see *more* within our rectangle, only *less*.

In the oft-pondered theoretical relationship of cinema as a medium to individual instances of film – comparable to the relationship of language as a general human capacity to speech as specific utterances – Frampton here poses an extreme formulation. The empty screen contains *all* films, pure cinema; to watch a particular film is already a diminution, a loss of possibility. Frampton is after the essence of cinema within the blank *void* that, in some sense, gives rise to it, or acts as the indispensable support to it. This idea is comparable, in the same era of the arts, to John Cage's eulogy of silence as the primal "bed" from which all sound (musical or verbal, deliberate or accidental) arises. One task of experimental art, then, becomes the effort to *return* us (sometimes via deconstructive steps) to these essences of silence and emptiness. "There's too much here, I want to see less": a typical piece of Framptonian humour.

The playfulness continues with a definition that generates certain performance-actions: a film is a devising of "things to put into a projector," things like a hand, a brush, and so on. "It seems that a film is anything that may be put into a projector, that will modulate the emerging beam of light." "A Lecture" goes on to approach the realm of ordinary, generic films, via the example of an anonymous (indifferent) Lana Turner movie. It is, like any film, "a narrow transparent ribbon," "uniformly perforated with small holes along its edges." Here Frampton turns his attention to the illusion of movement that is created from many thousands of discrete frames projected in succession. "We can *learn* to see" these frames as they stream past us: this is Frampton's radical, pedagogical hope.

Like Raúl Ruiz, Frampton loves logical (and sometimes surreal) syllogisms that "prove" a point. He advances the idea that what any film is primarily *about* is what becomes "most visible" in it: a print of a Lana Turner movie that is completely scratched from start to end, for instance, will be about the scratch, not the star. This leads to the following logical demonstration.

> Now suppose that we project all films. What are they about, in their great numbers?
> At one time and another, we shall have seen, as we think, very many things.
> But only one thing has *always* been in the projector.
> Film.
> That is what we have seen.
> Then that is what all films are about.

Frampton has taken us back to the zero-point of cinema. Perhaps he would see that not so much as anti-cinema, but a necessary stage of purification. He concludes "A Lecture" with the reflection: "There is still time for us to watch our rectangle a while. Perhaps its sheer presence has as much to tell us as any particular thing we might find inside it. We can invent ways of our own to change it." Yet where can an artist go after reaching zero, while still remaining within the type of meta-consciousness of cinema that Frampton enacted and embodied?

"Making a film is one thing, viewing a film is another." The American artist Robert Smithson (1938-1973), known primarily for his "land works" including *Spiral Jetty* (to which he also devoted a film), begins his short 1971 meditation "A Cinematic Atopia" with this distinction between viewing and making. But, as he proceeds, it becomes clear that whatever film he might or did make arises from a specific way of conceptualising the viewing experience. Smithson thus shifts the medium-specific definition of Frampton (of which he was well aware) into the more "virginal," psychological realm of the spectator – while nonetheless retaining a similar sense of the cinema as a *magma*, an amorphous blob, being greater (and better) than individual films.

Smithson's text is finally neither a reflection on his real practice, nor an exercise in "workable," practical theory or poetics; it is more like a speculative *thought experiment* bordering on science fiction or today's "weird" horror genre. To imagine it, and to write it, is enough for Smithson; there is no need to execute it in reality. On this level, it comes close to Alexander Kluge's collection of *Cinema Stories* (2007), musings likewise only existing, finally, as words on a page – not as real film history or applicable theory.

Smithson begins his reverie by conjuring not the special type of spectator known as a cinephile, but rather a more ordinary moviegoer, with whom he prefers to identify. Smithson is not a "specialist" of film, but rather somebody who, as an artist, derives a particular type of perceptual experience from his dim, accumulated memory of cinema.

> My memory becomes a wilderness of elsewheres [...] I will allow the elsewheres to reconstruct themselves as a tangled

> mass. Somewhere at the bottom of my memory are the sunken remains of all the films I have ever seen, good and bad they swarm together forming cinematic mirages, stagnant pools of images that cancel each other out. A notion of the abstractness of films crosses my mind, only to be swallowed up in a morass of Hollywood garbage. A pure film of lights and darks slips into a dim landscape of countless Westerns.

Cinephiles love to imagine a vast crowd of individual films "talking" to each other – or, as in an even livelier metaphor suggested by Jean Rouch (1917-2004), "begetting" or giving birth to each other, as happens within saturated movie genres. Smithson's imaginary spectator experiences something different. Indistinct perception plunges him or her into a *limbo*. "If there ever was a film festival in limbo," he suggests, "it would be called 'Oblivion.'" The type of radical possibility that Smithson, as an artist, senses in the midst of limbo is the disordering of all rational logic, all systematic means or ordering and categorising phenomena.

> A kind of aphasia orders this teetering realm. Not one order but many orders clash with one another, as do "facts" in an obsolete encyclopedia. If we put together a film encyclopedia in limbo, it would be quite groundless. Categories would destroy themselves, no law or plan would hold itself together for very long. There would be no table or contents for the Table of Contents. The index would slither away into so much cinematic slime.

There is much in common between the avant-garde reflections of Smithson, Frampton, Isou, and a philosopher who briefly dabbled in experimental filmmaking, Jean-

François Lyotard (as recorded in his 1973 essay "Acinema"). A particular historical period, crossing minimalist and conceptual art, defines this loose network: from the early 1950s to the mid-1970s. After that – as we shall see – a different set of reference points takes hold.

Like Isou, Smithson is drawn to the metaphors of film as garbage, mud and slime, and of the spectator as heavy, listless, torpid, tepid, blurry. Like Frampton, he returns to the blank, white screen as the holder of all possible films: "The simple rectangle of the movie screen contains the flux, no matter how many different orders one presents." Like Lyotard, he is fascinated by extremes, by excess, by the kind of delirium that is triggered by the waste-product of film, its leftovers, a sea or swamp of "rejected film clips." Smithson inverts what previous theorists including Siegfried Kracauer celebrated as cinema's invitation to the viewer to enter and (re)discover the real world; here, that same viewer is immersed in a dull abstraction, minimalist art taken to its logical endpoint of pure blandness. Smithson's affinity is, in fact (and whether he knew it or not), more with the Russian writer Maxim Gorky who described, in the earliest days of cinema, a projection session as an abominable "kingdom of shadows." Smithson thus invokes the vision or perception of a "cinematic borderland."

> The ultimate film goer would be a captive of sloth. Sitting constantly in a movie house, among the flickering shadows, his perception would take on a kind of sluggishness. He would be the hermit dwelling among the elsewheres, foregoing the salvation of reality. Films would follow films, until the action of each one would drown in a vast reservoir of pure perception. He would not be able to distinguish between good or bad films, all would be swallowed up in an endless blur. He would not be watching films, but rather experiencing blurs of many

> shades. Between blurs he might even fall asleep, but that wouldn't matter. Sound tracks might hum through this languor like so many lead weights. This dozing consciousness would bring about a tepid abstraction. It would increase the gravity of perception.

But Smithson adds a special obsession of his own to the list offered by Isou, Frampton and (a little later in time) Lyotard. This artist of place – *topos* – dreams precisely of *atopia*. A non-place, or at least a place with no clear borders. Cinema represents for him, and triggers in him, a half-paradisal, half-hellish fantasy of physical space. Smithson's fantasia of *scale* takes us backward to Eisenstein, and forward to Raúl Ruiz.

> Tangled jungles, blind paths, secret passages, lost cities invade our perception. The sites in films are not to be located or trusted. All is out of proportion. Scale inflates or deflates into uneasy dimensions. We wander between the towering and the bottomless. We are lost between the abyss within us and the boundless horizons outside us. Any film wraps us in uncertainty. The longer we look through a camera or watch a projected image the remoter the world becomes, yet we begin to understand that remoteness more. Limits trap the illimitable, until the spring we discovered turns into a flood.

Smithson's reflection here touches upon the philosophical: in the same period of the early 1970s, Stanley Cavell's first book on film, *The World Viewed*, also discussed both the joy and disquiet involved in our witnessing, as spectators, this "remote world" on the screen.

Some of the most extreme imaginings of what cinema is or could be include a cautionary note: we cannot, perhaps should not, go this far! Lyotard says exactly this in "Acinema": "We are not demanding a raw cinema […] We are hardly about to form a club dedicated to the saving of rushes and the rehabilitation of clipped footage." An early 1980s Australian manifesto of radical Super-8 filmmaking by artist Mark Titmarsh, whose reasoning is indebted to Lyotard, reaches the same point: "Without wishing to invoke an out-of-focus aesthetic" … Likewise for Smithson, who concurs: "But ultimate movie-viewing should not be encouraged, any more than ultimate movie-making."

What is clear in every case, however, is that the idea of the extreme is a spur to creation and invention, what literary critic I.A. Richards called a "machine to think with." For Smithson, as for Frampton, the abyss of cinema is an oblivion that we do well to approach.

Source: The text of Hollis Frampton's "A Lecture" is reprinted in *On the Camera Arts and Consecutive Matters* (MIT, 2009), as well as an earlier, less complete anthology, *Circles of Confusion: Film, Photography, Video – Texts 1968-1980* (Visual Studies Workshop, 1983). A great many of his texts and interventions are accessible at http://hollisframpton.org.uk/links.htm. Robert Smithson's "A Cinematic Atopia" appeared in the special film issue of *Artforum*, edited by Annette Michelson, September 1971, pp. 53-54. It is reprinted in *Robert Smithson: The Collected Writings* (University of California Press, 1996). The English translation of Lyotard's essay "Acinema" has most recently appeared in *Acinemas: Lyotard's Philosophy of Film* (Edinburgh University Press, 2017), edited by Graham Jones and Ashley Woodward.

29
The Proper Spectator

> If you're interested in Plato, you're reading the wrong book. If you're interested in difficult childhoods, sexual misadventures, aesthetics, cultural history, and the reasons that a club sandwich and other meals – including breakfast – have remained in the memory of the present writer, keep reading.
>
> Yvonne Rainer, *Feelings Are Facts: A Life* (2006)

Yvonne Rainer (born 1934) is a major figure in modern art, spanning dance, performance, film and video. Her groundbreaking work in minimalist choreography in the early 1960s (as part of the Judson Dance Theater in New York) led her, gradually, into an investigation of narrative – and then into cinema. At the same time, the issues of identity raised by this engagement with narrative coincided with a growing political consciousness tied to matters of gender, sex, class, race and bodily ability.

In a sense, Rainer's trajectory can be understood in retrospect – and she certainly discusses it in these terms – as negotiating the tension between two positions. As a modern artist developing through the 1960s and '70s, Rainer sought to dissolve the linear, rational certainty of stories, statements, characters, space and time, social values and ideological beliefs. Her central strategy in this quest has long been the *separation* of voices from bodies – and the sinuous problematisation of both as "vessels" of meaning.

In the 1970s, her "talking pictures" were praised for their thoroughgoing use of "shifters" – a dizzy multiplication of the supposedly anchoring points of "I, you, he, she, we, they" … It is no coincidence that Chantal Akerman's *Je tu il elle* ("I you he she") from 1974 was hailed as one of the masterpieces of radical 1970s cinema – and that it is a film organised in clearly signalled, separated parts, levels and episodes. Fragmentation, multiplicity, heterogeneity, radical montage: these are among the keywords informing Yvonne Rainer's work on form and signification.

At the same time, Rainer's deepening commitment to leftist feminism, ecology, disability militancy and other causes took her in the opposite direction: identity politics, embodiment, agency (i.e., individuals taking action), the claiming of direct speech as public intervention. How could she continue to dissolve the sense of speech and gesture, story and history, in a new political era that stressed the urgency of engagement over playful deconstruction? It is the adventure of the constant negotiation between these poles of commitment that Rainer's career gleefully explores.

In 1965, Rainer's approach was strongly based on an ethic of denial, negativity, subversion, destruction – "culture jamming," as it later came to be known. In her famous "No Manifesto," we learn (telegrammatically) what she judged to be worth denying.

> No to spectacle.
> No to virtuosity.
> No to transformations and magic and make-believe.
> No to the glamour and transcendency of the star image.
> No to the heroic.
> No to the anti-heroic.
> No to trash imagery.
> No to involvement of performer or spectator.
> No to style.
> No to camp.
> No to seduction of the spectator by the wiles of the performer.
> No to eccentricity.
> No to moving or being moved.

To fully understand this manifesto in its specific time and place, we would need to extensively illuminate its horizon of implied references and allusions – a horizon that includes everything from the Martha Graham "school" of dance choreography (in which Maya Deren participated) and Susan Sontag's 1964 essay on camp, to the spectacular "trash imagery" of Jack Smith's underground classic film *Flaming Creatures* (1963) and mainstream Hollywood's embrace of the (predominantly) male anti-hero figure. By the time she began making feature films, in 1972 (after experimenting with short projections as part of dance performances during the 1960s), with *Lives of Performers*, her horizon of reference had somewhat shifted – we could say it was triangulated between Hollywood, Godard and the burgeoning women's cinema of figures including Akerman.

Rainer's published writings, often beginning as performed lectures, adopt an unusual mode of address. On the one hand, they are usually posed as reflections arising from her own practice, not an attempt at pure theorising; on the other hand, they are deeply informed by the work of theorists from Laura Mulvey and Teresa de Lauretis to Meaghan Morris and Judith Butler. Above all, they resemble her artworks: regularly subverting the protocols of academic presentation, her talks/texts multiply digressions, puns, montage "cuts" to different levels, run-on poetic word associations, ambiguous quotations, "inappropriate" subjects (like that club sandwich she refers to above) and performative effects. Just a little taste here: a 1986 essay is titled, in full: "Some Ruminations around Cinematic Antidotes to the Oedipal Net(les) while Playing with De Lauraedipus Mulvey, or, He May Be off Screen, but…"

Rainer often returns to muse on her "basic assumption" of necessary negativity in art practice. When occupying the terrain of cinema, what is she fighting against?

> The necessity for digressing from and undermining a coherent narrative line driven by characters, or simply refusing to comply with its demands for spatio-temporal homogeneity, uninterrupted flow of events, closure, etc., has always been a basic assumption in my scheme of things.

Homogeneity, smoothness, flow, closure: all different ways of describing the *unity* – the unified illusion – of classical narrative film. To many artists of the 1970s, this unity did indeed constitute an enemy, to be subverted at all costs and in all possible ways. Rainer's films offer a rich catalogue of *digressions* and *interruptions* to such a norm, just as Godard's or Yoshida's do. At the same time, Rainer realised that some involvement, some psychic or emotional investment on the viewer's part, was probably necessary to get the "machine" (or swimming pool!) of cinema moving at all. Many filmmakers found themselves treading this tightrope wire of involvement and distance – or, as Rainer put it, *hooking* and *unhooking* the spectator. The moment that an actor opens their mouth and talks, it is hard (Rainer reflects), to "destroy the coherence of this speaking moving fictional subjectivity." In her view, even Godard failed at truly or consistently subverting this aspect of the cinema-machine.

For Rainer, film narrative is not only condemned by its hermetically sealed, ultra-smooth, well-oiled surface. She also associates it with psychoanalytically inflected terms like *sadism, irreversible history* or *destiny*, and *death-drive*: terms and metaphors we shall find echoed from Godard and Wenders through to Pedro Costa and Albert Serra today. The road of narrative, if taken without question or diversion, is the straight, direct road to closure, death, nullity, non-contradiction. Today, we need to project ourselves, in our imaginations, back to a time and a culture when this belief, this sensibility, was so passionately held. Rainer, for her part, has largely stuck to it all her working life, as her autobiography *Feelings Are Facts* shows.

Rainer resents a certain type of commonplace, common sense, everyday reaction to films: when people sum up their response with a plot summary like "it's a film about a guy who..." (one of her own films is ironically titled *Film About a Woman Who*, 1974) – exactly the kind of summary Hitchcock craved in his viewers! – or throw out an observation on the order of "that kind of woman wouldn't behave like that...," according to the logic of some unspoken, fully ideological code of verisimilitude. To hell with believability! Rainer embraces, in her thought and in her art, the possibility for people in her films to behave weirdly, perform inappropriately, "break character," contradict their given, social role. This becomes a prominent tendency in her cinema in the 1990s, in *Privilege* (1990) and *MURDER and murder* (1996).

> Will anyone ever come out of the movie palace saying, "It's about this man you see and this woman you hear. He has been given a name; she hasn't. When he speaks of her, he calls her 'she' or 'my wife'; whereas she never refers to him as 'my husband.'" This proper spectator has given equal attention to the fictions and the production of those fictions, to the social relations and the representation of those relations.

Of course – and she well knows it – this "proper," perfect spectator is a dream, a wishful projection on Rainer's part. But that does not mean she will ever stop hoping and looking for this spectator, which could even be us.

Source: Apart from her 2006 memoir *Feelings Are Facts: A Life* (MIT Press, 2006), Rainer's major essays and lectures are collected in *A Woman Who... : Essays, Interviews, Scripts* (Johns Hopkins University Press, 1999).

30
Denuded Music, Moving Positions

Abigail Child (born 1948) is a prolific American avant-garde artist who has devoted much energy to critique and an engagement with theory. Deeply involved in experimental, collective projects of writing, especially through her commitment to feminist and queer art practices, Child's essays, reviews and poetry books also provide an invaluable chronicle of the various cultural places and spaces she has passed through: San Francisco in the 1970s, New York in the '80s, Boston (where she has taught since 2000), Rome (where she made the project *A Shape of Error*, 2011). Her 2005 essay collection *This is Called Moving: A Critical Poetics of Film* is not as well known or often cited as it should be.

Although she intersected, at different points, with the punk and No Wave movements in American art, it would not be entirely correct to align Child with the most extreme anti-film or anti-cinema impulses. To be sure, motifs of jubilant destruction and violent negation are frequently (as we shall see) in the foreground of her thinking and of her film work (see the classic *Mayhem* of 1987). But Child rarely razes it all to ground zero in the programmatic spirit that Laura Mulvey announced (but did not herself grimly follow) in the concluding, provocative lines of her 1975 "Visual Pleasure and Narrative Cinema" manifesto: "Women, whose image has been continually stolen… cannot view the decline of the traditional film form with anything much more than sentimental regret."

Child began from a different point of ambivalent fascination. Melodrama, *film noir*, historical romance, Gothic fantasy: all these forms and genres may well have stolen and imprisoned the (image of) women, but they should not now be simply thrown into the dustbin of patriarchal cultural history. Child holds onto and celebrates powerful, ecstatic moments of cinema wherever she experiences them – in Vertov, Godard, Len Lye (1901-1980), *Kiss Me Deadly* (1955); indeed, we could say she tears these moments out of their context as one might tear especially beloved pages from a book before discarding the husk of the whole.

A prime focus is on lively montage procedures applied to found footage. In re-editing, re-staging, recombining the fragments of the culture around her, Child aims to redeem and recharge whatever she can – to bring out their potentialities of cinematic energy and reroute that force along other political tracks and concerns.

Frampton evoked the grasping of cinema's "conditions and limits" as a goal of his praxis. In a less scientific, more rhizomatic way, Child also aims at this: a crucial motif in her writing is the need to deal with the *illusion* of film, not in the sense of either smashing or somehow bypassing it, but precisely to show it up *as illusion*, to put it in a frame, to clearly outline and dramatically demonstrate its limits. And the same for *image* – image of woman, of man, of wealth, of sex, whatever – where the point is not to do without images, or get beyond them, but to harness the spectacular, imagistic quality of cinema in another way. (Child could never write a manifesto titled, like Roger Munier's, *Against the Image*!)

The crucial strategy is always to *denaturalise* what is assumed as natural in every sphere of life – and thus to make it available for use in another way. So Child embraces artifice, theatricality, playfulness – all juiced up by an ever-present sense of urgency, threat, danger. Child's thinking and art is ultimately about "staying alive," staying afloat in a complicated, stormy, at times asphyxiating sea of images, stories and values. We grab what we can to keep breathing, to get some oxygen into our lungs. And to keep moving. For Child, as for Marco Bellocchio (see Chapter 33), stasis represents death.

I will concentrate here on Child's reflections on film sound – or, as she puts it in her 2000 essay "Deselective Attention," the "combinations and recombinations, dismantlements and dismemberments of image and sound in a number of historical and contemporary films." Already, the negativity of dismantling is twinned with the positivity of recombining. The tone is given in the opening sentence: "I speak to a genealogy of distortion, interruption and breakdown [...] that seek[s] to introduce new, *impossible* rhythms and worldviews." Child cross-refers between avant-garde film (Martin Arnold, Bruce Conner, Arthur Lipsett) and experiments in the audio arts of music and radio, as befits her horizon of experience.

Child has always waged war against *smoothness* in art and thought: everything that is "seamless," too glossy, too comfortingly artificial or synthetic. "It seems we need a more differentiated reality on screen, more differentiated than these conventions can speak to, or of – a vision more inclusive of parts, of the half-seen, remembered or overheard." So there must always be a fracture, a crack that allows us to get in and interfere with the mechanism – an echo here of Isou's metaphors, but rewritten for feminism.

Drawing from the legacy of modern movements across media including Scratch Video, Glitch Art and Cyberpunk, Child celebrates the happy accident whereby "the increased mechanisation of daily life guarantees a series of breakdowns (and breakups), eruptions that upset and destabilise the (synthetic) flow." Note the affinity with Yvonne Rainer's word play: breakdowns in the technological sphere trigger immediate association with breakups in interpersonal relationships. But what has to be "broken up" is also everything that conventional cinema hands to us as already "naturally" fused or married – such as image and sound in flawless synchronisation.

On this level, Child connects with Eisenstein and his comrades, a history she explores in various parts of her book. In fact, historical *slippage*, the unexpected communication between times, places and contexts, becomes a central part of her theorising. For the present time of the "ongoing," the now, is also an illusion to be punctured and re-knit.

> The dislocation and multidimensionality that results – via counterpoint, static, percussion and silence – upsets, discharges and redefines the space of investigation. What *is* disappears so that what is under (or beside or below or inside another

> outside) appears. There is, to paraphrase [Marcel] Duchamp, a "delay" in the quotidian. It is a historical passage, with cultural repercussions. Breakdown enacts a hole in the ongoing; it *denaturalises* the present and, thereby, alerts us. Before the closure of repair, breakdown announces dismemberment, a disturbance of norm.

Straddling media, Child makes the link between the sound-art experiments at the end of the 20th century and the radical montage traditions that preceded them in cinema, as well as in Brechtian theatre – as always, she seeks to establish a "continuing moving-image impulse."

> Restringing moments, *maiming them*, performing stoppage, shares ideas with Eisenstein's montage of "collisions," Russian "defamiliarising" techniques, and Brechtian alienation and separation effects. These strategies variously create new measures, revealed through what we might call a *denuded music*, creating a play of meanings, as well as a critique of meaning. Even as it obstructs, breakdown instructs: the stoppage forces a new beginning, which is the promise and site of creativity.

Child goes so far as to suggest – referring now to the basic, mechanical apparatus of film – that the very condition of single-frame animation to give the illusion of projected movement makes cinema "the paradigmatic interruptive form." But the given apparatus, in its limits and conditions, is not quite enough; it needs a push and a shove from motivated artists.

Surveying various cases of militant image/sound desynchronisation in avant-garde films, Child hails the birth of "ludic critique." The levels cross-penetrate from form to content: the loops and dephasing of the tracks seemingly trigger the breakdown of a heterosexual couple in Frampton's *Critical Mass* (1971), or the cacophony created inside an "American kitchen" (a fragment pilfered from the Hollywood classic *To Kill a Mockingbird* [1962]) by Martin Arnold in *Passage à l'acte* (1994).

Then Child moves onto the even freer terrain of what she calls (after Canadian experimental composer R. Murray Schafer) "split" or "schizophonic" sound. "Here there is a free connection between image and sound, a commentary created through rhythmic and musical, indeed poetic, contrapuntal adjacencies." Montage comes into its own, on all its imaginable levels and extensions: horizontal, vertical, tonal, overtonal, graphic, contrapuntal, interruptive, disintegrative…

What grabs Child in all this is the "aim not to be realistic but to enter into the emotional vibrancy of the thought/event. I suggest this is the appeal of sound dislocations, both synchronistically and contrapuntally, to allow the viewer/listener entry 'inside the energy.'" But there is always the danger of sensory overload, and Child is acutely aware of it. We must find a way to navigate the stream, to ride the flows.

> We can be "overwhelmed and incapacitated by rootless images and amplified voices," warns [video artist] Bill Viola, but we can at another moment rejoice in the constructed conjunctions that force a thinking mind into action, giving us tools to deal with the welter of images, "not the formal structures of efficient info management" but the creative welter of images and sounds, a vision of a world from within moving positions.

Source: Abigail Child, *This is Called Moving: A Critical Poetics of Film* (University of Alabama Press, 2005). Other key theoretical essays in this collection include "Melodrama and Montage" and "Sound Talk." Several of Child's best films can be viewed at https://ubu.com/film/child.html.

31
Occult Alternative

The brilliant and playful meditations of Chilean-born Raúl Ruiz (1941-2011) in his *Poetics of Cinema* book series (Volumes 1 and 2) are fairly well known and often cited. Indeed, Ruiz's entire œuvre as an artist is probably primarily associated with his critique in Volume 1 of the mainstream, Hollywood narrative principle of "central conflict theory." However, in my opinion, the essay that is the centre and pinnacle of Ruiz's theoretical reflections is his "The Six Functions of the Shot" from 2003.

In the general use of Ruiz's theoretical ideas, we find the same aporia as in much of the analytical commentary on his films: it stays at the level of generality and evocation, an auteurist genuflection before everything that is somehow vaguely strange, crazy and "Ruizian." However, I believe that Ruiz's meditation on the shot and its functions is a major, extremely concrete contribution to film theory.

Ruiz's writing on cinema is unique in its style and manner. He often proceeds via what philosophy calls a *thought experiment*: imagine if X were Y... He has always used, in his writing, the rhetorical form of the logical demonstration – with its assertions and syllogistic proofs – even as he spins it into surreal conclusions. He reserves his right to freely generate concepts from the world over and from the depths of time, drawing in (and recombining) ideas from the Latin American Baroque, Arabic culture, ancient Sophist philosophy, Chinese aesthetics, advances in contemporary neuroscience and mathematics, the annals of film theory, and so on, *ad infinitum*! Above all, he begins from the felt need to re-energise or re-enchant our living relation to films, both as spectators and as makers.

Cinema for Ruiz has precious little to do with the norm of common-sense viewing or perception of cinema (such as, for instance, cognitive theory seeks to establish): the assumption that films are, first and last, basically stories about human beings who feel things, struggle against and overcome obstacles... Cinema should be, rather, a machine that allows us to attack all common sense and commonplace assumptions, inside a movie theatre as well as outside of it. Like Yvonne Rainer, Ruiz too seeks the "proper spectator."

Ruiz's "Six Functions" essay returns us to the basic thrust of his books: it methodically proposes a *poetics*, which he defines not so much as a set of basic principles (as in Aristotle) but a working method, a way of doing or making things, a means of generating images, sounds, and the connections between them. The notion of the six functions therefore has an eminently practical, and indeed pedagogical application (Ruiz used it extensively within his filmmaking teaching). On this level, it can be compared with the (very different) system proposed by a more classical filmmaker whom Ruiz greatly admired, Alexander Mackendrick. Unlike Mackendrick, however, Ruiz's ultimate aim is not craftsmanship, but to imagine an ideal, liberated cinema – as he avows, the goal is to "awaken the imagination" of both viewers and makers of film, and to establish (through careful, practical steps and exercises) a whole new way of creating. In direct contradistinction to Hitchcock, Ruiz seeks to inspire the production of "films that cannot respond to the question, 'What is this movie about?'"

Is there an enemy lurking in the background of this picture painted by Ruiz? We must take him at his explicit word: the enemy is narrative (indeed, the "dictatorship of narrative" as he named it in 1981). This can strike many devotees of Ruiz as an odd, unlikely, paradoxical or contradictory position: isn't the joy of pure fiction more evident in Ruiz's work than in that of almost any other contemporary filmmaker? Isn't Ruiz a born storyteller, a spinner of tales – no matter how devious or baroque – in the tradition of Luis Buñuel?

Ruiz, for his part, always publicly played down such a characterisation of his project. He is not interested in telling, for each of his films, *a* story, one single or particular story. Above all, he does not wish to achieve the imaginary *coherence* or plenitude of a story. Narrative is just a pretext for him – but a pretext for what? He is interested above all, he declared, in the *passage* between diverse worlds (real or imaginary), or between different narrative levels; it is those bridges, those suspension points, those difficult moments of *connection* or *disconnection* that he seeks to understand, explore and work with.

"Six Functions" is Ruiz's most sustained meditation on cinema because it offers, precisely, a theory of connection and disconnection within the filmic medium. And it does so by grounding itself in a particular syntactical *unit* of cinema: the shot. We can relate Ruiz's choice of this fundamental cinematic unit to many filmmakers' theories, beginning at least with Eisenstein and Vertov in the 1920s and working through to Tarkovsky (of whom he was no fan). As these earlier Russian filmmakers proposed (each in their own manner), there are visible shots in cinema but also, as we have seen, the less visible *intervals* between shots, or the fleeting *interstices* joining them – not only, technically, the literal black spaces between film frames on celluloid (so much a part of cinema's peculiar metapsychological effect for the spectator), but also conceptually. This expandable interval (both material and immaterial) between shots is a crucial factor for Ruiz.

There are two essential properties that Ruiz ascribes to any shot, all shots. First, it is *discontinuous* in relation to all its neighbours in a given film; it is therefore an autonomous unit – an autonomy that Ruiz takes to the extreme in his oft-repeated declaration: "When we see a film of 500 shots, we also see 500 films." Second, the shot must be conceptualised as a *force-field*, a complex (and even mysterious) interplay of energies and intensities.

Ruiz proposes a novel definition of what is contained within any shot – although, at first, it may seem quite conventional. A shot is comprised, he suggests, of *events* (things staged or found within the pro-filmic field) and a *point-of-view* that is imposed by the camera's position and perspective (an idea reminiscent of Mackendrick's "winged witness"); these events are "settled" (determined, shaped) by a change in the camera's viewpoint (such as a reframing due to camera movement). A shot is, furthermore, a set of *objects* (including humans as objects) linked by *actions*. So far, we have nothing that could not be accommodated within a reasonably classical definition of filmic style, form or *mise en scène*.

The novelty of Ruiz's idea becomes evident when we reach the following provisos: first, that each shot, in its autonomy, also contains *provisional openings and closings* – a more radical notion than that a shot may modulate itself, or have successive stages – and second, that every shot possesses *microfictions* that are "struggling to draw attention to themselves," the busy sum of which constitute the "unconscious of the shot." On this second proviso, a parallel can be drawn with video artist Thierry Kuntzel (1948-2007) and his influential notion of the *other film*, polymorphous and unbound, hidden within every seemingly normal film – a theory generously documented in his 2006 multimedia book *Title TK* (Éditions Anarchive/Musée des Beaux-Arts de Nantes).

What are filmic microfictions? Take a look at the opening street shot, pregnant with enigma and suggestiveness, at the outset of his *Hypothesis of the Stolen Painting* (1978): it's up there on screen long enough for us to wonder about its dark impasse, the open windows that face each other, all the tiny objects and events that flutter in the breeze, the random street sounds… not to mention (in retrospect) the puzzling relation of this so-called "establishing shot" with any visualised space that follows it. Or recall Ruiz's impromptu proposal for his ideal art installation (offered from the stage of the Museum of Contemporary Art Australia in 1993): a film set after everyone has left, a dim light streaming in from outside (some of Michael Snow's sculptural installation work approximates this idea)… In such *dispositifs*, all the elements present in a pro-filmic situation are left free to interact with each other in imaginary scenarios.

What, for Ruiz, are the *functions* involved in his categorisation of shots? What is a function for, what action does it perform? These functions are twofold: they mark both the *potentialities* in the shot – the latent or dormant energies or capacities that can be made manifest, sparked into action – and the possible ways it can be *linked* to the surrounding shots. Therefore, while holding to the principle of each shot's autonomy, Ruiz is also seeking to establish the *ensemble* that a group of successive shots can form, and the (extremely variable) logic, rules/principles or poetics of these ensembles.

The function of a shot, in short, is what determines its various (to return to the first proviso) "openings and closings" – as well as the destiny of its numerous microfictions. "The microfictions told by the set are hierarchised with the appearance of a point-of-view." Any hierarchy, for Ruiz, performs a dual action: on the one hand, it closes down the field of possibilities (by brutally deciding on some over others) and, on the other hand, by this very act of elimination, it implies and even outlines the presence of all those other options – and therefore inadvertently sets them loose, sets them to work throughout the body of the shot or the film.

This conceptual and aesthetic logic, whereby elimination is also a kind of perverse procreation, was expressed as early as 1981 in Ruiz's piece "Three Thrusts at *Excalibur*" (which prefigures many themes of "Six Functions"). "Every story, to the extent that it narrates, also at the same time excludes – and thus makes obvious – not the rest of the world, but its counterpart... its occult alternative."

Generally, however – within the context of the dominant, mainstream trend in filmmaking practice – the hierarchical nature of cinema is, for Ruiz, an impoverishment that he subsumes under the banner of a "subordination to the strategic model." *Strategic* is the opposite of a key term for Ruiz, *recursive* (to which we shall soon return); the "strategy" in question is to form a strictly functioning, streamlined narrative machine.

So here are the six functions as outlined at various times and in various ways by Ruiz, both in the essay and in the useful summary included in the interview given as a bonus on several DVD editions of his films.

1. A shot is a *paradigm* and an *allegory* for the whole film – as when it provides a "poster image," or what has been called a summary "narrative image."
2. It is a *reflexive* or *critical* image. This is what Ruiz calls the recursive function (opposite to the strategic function of "always going forward"), the function of doubt that makes a viewer want to immediately "rewind" or re-see an image in order to verify the enigma of its contents.
3. It is *centripetal* (independent, autonomous).
4. It is *centrifugal* (it "reaches out" to connect with the following and preceding shots).
5. It is *holistic* – it can "replay" the entire movement or deep logic (not the superficial plot) of a film in microcosm.
6. It has *combinatory* potential – it suggests ways in which it can be "remixed" into an alternative sequence of the given shots, resulting in different semantic and syntactic (or, for Pasolini, stylematic and syntagmatic) associations.

When we try to categorise the shots of any film using Ruiz's schema, we must remain faithful to his underlying assumption that any shot potentially contains, or performs, *all six* functions. Indeed, his Utopian goal as a filmmaker – rarely achieved in practice, as he hastens to point out, perhaps impossible to achieve in its totality – is to enable all the functions to figure in every shot for a whole film, the whole time. So, in the less ideal production circumstances of the real world, what determines a shot's dominant or characterising functions? Precisely the connection it makes – or does not make – with its neighbours.

I will dare to propose a hierarchy of these functions, from the top down. Ruiz might have disagreed, but of the six functions, two of them seem to me the major categories: centrifugal and centripetal. The critical or recursive function is the next most significant. The paradigmatic and the holistic functions offer variations on each other (it is easy to confuse them conceptually). And the combinatory opens a set of possibilities that are not fully explored within the "Six Functions" essay itself, since they fall somewhat outside the field delimited by the centrifugal/centripetal opposition – but these possibilities frequently form the substance of Ruiz's remarks about his own filmmaking practice, since they call up non-successive, non-linear, non-syntagmatic, properly *diachronic* dimensions of cinema.

The centrifugal/centripetal duo completely opens up the realms of cinema theory, analysis and criticism. It offers a conceptual step beyond Deren's longstanding distinction between horizontal (narrative) and vertical (poetic) dimensions. In terms of the dynamic force-field approach, Ruiz describes the difference between his two posited tendencies in the following way: where the energy of a centrifugal shot seeks to exhaust itself, to "die," so as to lead on or hook into the successive shot – a basic principle of classical narrative economy and efficacy – the energy of a centripetal shot seeks its "central core" in order to assert and demonstrate its autonomy. As Ruiz has noted in interviews, the elaborate long takes of modern cinema (Theo Angelopoulos, Béla Tarr, Tsai Ming-liang, etc.) are clear examples of centripetal autonomy in action – shots that are, in a palpable sense, films in themselves. (There is an evident overlap here with Tarkovsky's theory of *time-pressure* in a single shot, except that he would not have entertained the "provisional openings and closings" idea.) But it is crucial to add that even a temporally brief shot can be centripetal in its function and effect. And this is not an opposition, either, as is sometimes mistaken, between static shots (whose literal force-field centre may be quite visible, as in a film by Hou Hsiao-hsien or Jia Zhang-ke) as centripetal, and in-motion ones as centrifugal; for Ruiz, a shot that opens and closes many times over, constantly settling, unsettling and resettling itself via elaborate camera movement, can also be a model of centripetality – as is frequently the case in his own films.

The key element is the shot's "will to connect" – or its refusal to do so in conventional terms. The traditional syntactic connection between successive shots can be summarised, within psychoanalytically oriented film theory, under Jean-Pierre Oudart's influential idea of cinematic *suture*: the editing join (such as shot/reverse shot, graphic match, or *raccord* on movement) that stitches or repairs the always potentially gaping interval or discontinuity between shots, creating the illusion of a single, seamless, fictive space. (Even Epstein, as we have seen, had his own version of the suturing idea.)

Ruiz's total view of the ensemble of a shot's relations strongly resembles a comment once made by American filmmaker-comedian Jerry Lewis (1926-2017): the centripetal urge is all about "hanging here" – sticking to the time and action of a shot, exploring it, opening out all its dimensions – while the centrifugal drive is about "groping there," restlessly setting up and leading on to the next plot-point, the next event. And richness may result from the co-existence and intermingling of these functions – not the polemical privileging (whether for classicist or modernist ends) of one over the other.

There is much more that could be said about "The Six Functions of the Shot": its concept of "specifically cinematic emotion"; its views on the systematic organisation of sound (which constitute another kind of viewpoint on a scenic ensemble); its adaptation of pictorial principles from Chinese painting that allow "ways into the shot, strolls inside the frame"; its idea that the *weak* or *secondary* elements (very different to how Isou conceptualised *useless* secondary elements) in successive shots can build strong chains – a principle evident in the comedies of Ernst Lubitsch, Luc Moullet and Stephen Chow.

Ruiz's theory of the centripetal has special uses for film critics and theorists. For starters, it serves as a good weapon against all those people (cognitivists, genre buffs, screenwriting advisors) who preach the gospel of classical narrative – often explicitly premised on the purely centrifugal assumption that the question "what will happen next?" is always more significant that what is going on in the here and now (that was a sacred storytelling principle for Mackendrick, for example). Lucrecia Martel's reflections also converge on what we might call the *centripetality of the present moment*.

Overall, rather than a standoff between narrative and spectacle (a constant theme in film study), Ruiz's film theory prompts a new attentiveness to two, simultaneous kinds of involvement inherent in cinematic spectatorship: the *sequential* (centrifugal) and the *immersive* (centripetal). As cinema moves and mutates in the 21st century, we will – as practitioners, cinephiles and critics – need to be increasingly adept at both levels of engagement.

Source: The best version of Raúl Ruiz's "The Six Functions of the Shot" can be found, in Carlos Morreo's superb English translation, at http://www.screeningthepast.com/2012/12/the-six-functions-of-the-shot. Ruiz's *Poetics of Cinema* book series (Volumes 1 and 2) now exists in several languages; the fascinating materials posthumously gathered for the unfinished Volume 3 (lacking, strangely, "Six Functions") exist only in the assembled Chilean edition, *Poéticas del cine* (Ediciones Universidad Diego Portales, 2013). The final essay in that volume, a 2005 award acceptance speech titled variously "Cinema is Another Life" or "Cinema, Art of Shadows," also exists in English at http://lolajournal.com/2/cinema_another_life.html. Ruiz's 1981 text "Three Thrusts at *Excalibur*" can be found in *Positif* magazine (no. 247, October 1981) and in my English translation here: http://www.screeningthepast.com/2015/01/three-thrusts-at%C2%A0excalibur.

32
Short Preface to All Criticism

> I give – not answers, because I don't think anyone can give definitive answers on this subject – but perhaps the elements of an answer.
>
> Jacques Rivette, 1999

In late 1998 and early 1999, Jacques Rivette (1928-2016), then 70 years old, called upon a privileged interlocutor, the writer Hélène Frappat (author of a superb 2001 book titled *Jacques Rivette, secret compris*), for a special dialogue. He wished to express himself on certain matters of a general nature in relation to cinema. And he felt compelled to look back – not over his film work, but his earliest and most famous writings as a young critic. It is a far-reaching discourse, published under the solemn title of "The Secret and the Law."

Some directors use an interlocutor in this way in their later years, especially if they do not wish to sit at a desk and write their thoughts, preferring to speak them to another. Buñuel did it with Jean-Claude Carrière for his 1983 autobiography *My Last Sigh*, and Godard did it with Youssef Ishaghpour for the book *Cinema: The Archaeology of Film and the Memory of a Century* to accompany the *Histoire(s) du cinéma* series in 2000. In part, I believe this method provides a way for these filmmakers to say very serious things whilst maintaining a certain lightness of tone – to both announce a few things once and for all, and yet remain on the side of whimsy, spontaneity and even (at times) frivolity. The presence of the interlocutor makes the eventual work of transcription, editing and publication more efficient, and also gives the proceedings a pleasantly human air.

Frappat set the scene of this exchange with Rivette in her 1999 introduction to its initial publication in the influential *La lettre du cinéma*, a magazine that launched a new generation of critic-filmmakers (including Axelle Ropert, Sandrine Rinaldi and Serge Bozon) in France.

> What you are about to read is not an interview, but more exactly what Rivette prefers to call a "dialogue," a form that, according to him, is more interesting than the usual "Q & A," more open and closer to his customary working method when he writes, prepares and shoots a film with the members of his team. And the stake of this dialogue will be more general and theoretical (what is a film?) than specific and circumstantial (how to judge this or that film?). Perhaps that's why – given that, most of the time, he had no desire to discuss his past writings – Jacques Rivette here returns to two seminal texts published by *Cahiers du cinéma*, one in 1953 and the other in 1955: "The Genius of Howard Hawks" and "Letter on Rossellini." At the heart of these two articles, Rivette interrogates two cases of evidence: the evidence of Hawks' genius, and of Rossellini's modernity. A question all the more crucial in that, in a certain way, it puts the very activity of criticism in peril: how can one prove this evidence (when it is not demonstrated, but only asserted)? And under what conditions is it possible to assume the feeling of evidence that often founds our critical judgements?

So, this is a form of reflection poised somewhere unique between film theory and film criticism. It does not deal very much with matters of medium essence or specificity; nor, at the same time, does it presume to discuss very many individual films and filmmakers. By returning to his own earliest critical texts – which, it becomes clear, had never left his mind or his sensibility – he seeks to interrogate the very *foundation* of all critical judgement, evaluation and opinion of film. It is a topic that few directors, to my knowledge, have ever pondered in such depth.

At the beginning of "The Secret and the Law," Rivette associatively wanders from Frappat's initial question about "filming work" – the labour of filming labour, that Pedro Costa often speaks about – to get to his true starting point.

> Forty-five years later, I want to return to the sentences at the start and end of my old article on Hawks: "That which is, is" – where the second "is," all going well, does not mean the same thing as the first "is"! … It's not a pure tautology but, by the same token, we must not run away from tautology. For example, a tautology worth reclaiming is this: films are films. That implies many things, particularly that a film should be a film: i.e., something that exists in space and in time, on the screen, before our eyes, but also the imprinted celluloid, sensitised by procedures both optical and chemical that we must take account of. Light is not something magical; it's also part of the work.

Rivette address the tension, present (as we have seen) in many filmmakers' reflections, between the machine and artistic intervention.

> There's a detour via this machine which is the camera… The photographic process intervenes between the eye and what will appear on screen: that's also a process of work that we must not refuse by taking recourse to the words, "It's magical"

Rivette, on the basis of his idea about tautology and truth, then arrives at the major question on his mind: "What allows us to say that this film exists, and some other one doesn't?" Some films are important, some endure – and many others do not. "A film exists" is not a bare statement of banal fact for Rivette, for it must win the *right* to exist – while many others do not, and cannot. What is, is – but we must know what that second *is* is!

Rivette is concerned to pin down this process of what we might call "natural selection" in the arts, a historical process that, by and large, he accepts – at least when he agrees with its result. Embedded in his question is the staunch belief that some films are obviously, incontrovertibly *cinematic* – i.e., they activate, to the fullest extent, at least one of the many "essences" of film. "This is the fundamental question," he asserts, "the question that everybody avoids." When is the cinematic evident? And what is cinematic evidence?

Rivette stakes a great deal – as, in a sense, every artist must – on his own *temperament* and convictions. Indeed, the famous assertion in his 1953 essay is all about the intractable certainty of personal conviction.

> The evidence on the screen is the proof of Howard Hawks' genius: you only have to watch *Monkey Business* [1952] to know that it is a brilliant film. Some people refuse to admit this, however; they refuse to be satisfied by proof. There can't be any other reason why they don't recognise it.

Or, as the inspired critic-scholar Bill Routt rephrased this in his (English-language) essay "L'Évidence": "Those with eyes to see need no arguments to convince them, and those who cannot see are not worth convincing" – a "rhetorical technique" that, as he persuasively and positively argues, "represents the radical assertion of new vision common to many contemporary critical postures." Chris Marker (1921-2012) stated almost exactly the same thing at the conclusion of his 1995 reflection on Hitchcock's classic *Vertigo* (1958):

"Obviously, this text is addressed to those who know *Vertigo* by heart. But do those who don't deserve anything at all?"

Frappat rightly points to the duality inherent in Rivette's original investigations of this theme: a zany, cartoonish Hollywood comedy (*Monkey Business*) on the one hand, a highly modern example of art cinema (*Viaggio in Italia*, 1954) on the other hand. Both, taken individually, were contentious cases in their time: the Hawks film was (and probably still is!) at risk of being dismissed as merely quasi-infantile entertainment, while the status of Rossellini's 1950s work with Ingrid Bergman was then in wildly debated flux, as yet far from the "classic" status comfortably conferred on it today. Considered *together* – as a consolidated expression of the sensibility of Rivette and at least some of his colleagues at *Cahiers du cinéma* – the films constitute a shotgun marriage of high and low culture.

It's a provocative gesture, but not *only* provocative or polemical, and not in the slightest bit perverse. Rivette is tenaciously forcing the issue, in the late 1990s as in the mid-'50s: how do both these films, at once, impress us deeply *as cinema*, across all their superficial differences? "There was something we admired, at the same time and on the same level – not in the same way, but just as strong – in Rossellini and in Hitchcock" (much to the puzzlement of the tutelary figure, Bazin!). "That's what we tried to resolve." And in a sense, 45 years later, Rivette is still trying to resolve that matter fully, in his mind.

Like Kané, Rivette is not impressed by the work of most film critics. He expresses his exasperation at the critiques he reads from day to day: "Where is the film in what you have written?" The mundane discussion solely of a narrative component could just as well be applied to novels, plays or TV programs. He is equally unimpressed by the unanimity of acclaim that many ordinary films receive. "It's generally true that the works so instantly well received by everybody interest nobody ten years later." On the other hand, critics should not seek to spark artificial, contrived conflicts over this or that current movie. Twenty-first-century scuffles over the quality and intent of, say, Harmony Korine's *Spring*

Breakers (2012) or Sofia Coppola's *Lost in Translation* (2003) are of a lesser intensity – and are less lasting in their cultural effects – than the mid-1960s war over Carl Dreyer's *Gertrud* (1964), a masterpiece scandalously crucified on its initial release.

Rivette's fond horizon of reference, in this dialogue with Frappat, is the one formed (as it is for many of us) in his young-adult days: in his case, the now almost forgotten philosopher known publicly as Alain (real name Émile Chartier, 1868-1951), and the arts critic-cum-publisher Jean Paulhan (1884-1968), particularly his wonderfully titled book *Short Preface to All Criticism* (1951), as well as another with a great (this time extended) title, *The Key to Poetry, Allowing us to Distinguish the True from the False in Every Case, or: A Doctrine Dealing with Rhyme, Rhythm, Verse, the Poet and Poetry* (1945).

From Alain, Rivette adopts the "that's just how it is" attitude of evidence, "refusing argument and discussion" and relying only on the presentation of examples. This is the "principle that opinions, just like works, must be uttered as clearly as possible: take it or leave it." Rivette finds this "evidentiary" quality in the films of Hawks, John Ford and Cecil B. DeMille.

From Paulhan, Rivette draws, once more, the central, impelling question: why are some works of art rightly remembered (even if they were severely attacked in their day), and others rightly forgotten (even if they were ephemerally acclaimed by the majority)? How do we arrive, over time, at "true" judgement – where true judgement is indivisibly linked to the "truth in film, in the way that Cézanne spoke of the truth in painting" (which is also the subject of a 1978 book by Jacques Derrida).

There is a process of self-critique going on here. Looking back over the animating, enabling concepts from the 1950s of *auteurs* and their *mise en scène* (which certainly consumed him at the time), Rivette now finds them sorely lacking. Cinema, he concurs (at Frappat's prompting), "requires different criteria of judgement than those traditionally used." But in what can these criteria be based?

> To posit *mise en scène* is just to replace one problem with another! That's effectively what we did at *Cahiers*, and I'm among those responsible for this putting on a pedestal of the term *mise en scène*. Because it allows us to make a point about mystery. But once we say *mise en scène*, what do we mean by it? The problem is merely displaced – well, let's say it's named, but not resolved. It's all about the *mise en scène*, sure, but what is *mise en scène*? Big question!

Likewise, in Rivette's retrospective gaze, the "auteur policy," the hailing of the "director as superstar," as a consistent and identifiable artist, failed. (His own career certainly benefitted, at particular points, from the popularity of celebrity auteurism, as we saw with the funding of his mid-1970s *Daughters of Fire* project.) Referring to the guiding intuition of the time that Hitchcock (or Hawks) and Rossellini were profoundly connected by the existence of "truth in cinema," and could somehow be interrelated, Rivette rued the eventual result.

> Yes, but the auteur policy very quickly became a retreat, because it was saying: alright, [Hitchcock and Rossellini] are very different, but what they have in common is that they are "auteurs." OK, but from this moment on, suddenly everybody became an auteur! Now, it's true when it comes to Rossellini and Hitchcock, it's always true of Ford and Renoir, it's still true when it comes to Hawks and, naturally, always true of Lubitsch or Dreyer. But is it still true when we get to [Vincente] Minnelli, and how can it possibly be true for Richard Fleischer?

Strong words! (Especially to this fan of Minnelli and Fleischer.) Furthermore, "some undoubted auteurs, such as René Clair or [Joseph] Mankiewicz, are not, for all that, great filmmakers." (Ouch again!) Rivette reiterates what he considers the question "suspended" by *mise en scène* and auteur criticism: "What is it that we admire on the same level – because of their coherence, because of (let's say) their logic, but that's not enough – of filmmakers as different as (to keep the same names) Rossellini and Hitchcock?" This circles back to the major question: what do we expect from a "true" film? Rivette turns again to Paulhan and his *Short Preface*.

> The authors that we feel the need to talk about and discuss are those who write with a clear recognition of the problem posed: the relation between words and what we can call ideas, thoughts, feelings, emotions – the two faces of language.

In his *Key to Poetry*, Paulhan arrived at what Rivette describes as an "algebraic formula" (mathematics metaphors once again): "Any just theory must be reversible; i.e., a theory of poetry that speaks of words should stay the same when speaking of ideas." On this now recognisably Godardian terrain of rhetoric and suggestive argument-by-association, Rivette plays with substituting *time* and *space* for *word* and *idea*: "Theories of cinema that speak of time are just, if we can apply them in terms of space" – and vice versa. For cinema is the art of *space-time* (an echo of Deren and several others).

> It's true that all existing film theories have a tendency, like older theories, to privilege space. This leads to the overestimation of films that are collections of beautiful images, and then people confuse Ford with [prolific Mexican director] Emilio Fernández (it was another world…).

> And others privilege time, i.e., in that era when montage was considered in the most mechanical way, and therefore Pudovkin becomes the equal of Eisenstein…

For Rivette, the danger in the current cultural climate is to end up seeing cinema solely within a pincer movement of *time* and *narrative*.

> [Cinema is seen as] purely and simply narrative unfolding, and thus under the umbrella categories of the novelistic, of stories, of fiction – all of which are important, but at the risk of forgetting that we're dealing with projected images, photographic images reproducing places, bodies, gestures, and that is not the kind of thing that can be "told in words." I believe this is the current tendency in criticism, as much in the newspapers as in Gilles Deleuze [in his *Cinema* books], who clearly privileges what he calls the time-image.

Ultimately, Rivette arrives at his own, obviously long-nurtured theory: that in filmmaking there is the presence of the *Law* and the *Secret*. The Law is constraint, convention, the "rule of the game" in both content (storytelling, genre) and form (standard, cemented procedures of *mise en scène*). Whereas the Secret is a mysterious, existential "hidden truth" about humanity and the world, a truth that the artist bears and expresses without being entirely in control of it, or having mastery over it. This truth is "bodily, unthought" – and not strictly a matter of autobiographical memory or experience. We are very close here to Kané's understanding (Chapter 9) of an auteur's true, underlying *theme*.

"The Secret is individual; while the Law is society." Picking up a suggestion from Frappat, Rivette begins to talk in terms of constitutive, generative *relations* and *tensions*.

"The richer the relation between the Law pole and the Secret pole, the more intense the film will be." And he finally adds a third term.

> There's a third word that I'd want to put upfront in order to speak of those films that truly deserve to be called films: *danger*. They are all films that have faced danger, all of them were difficult to make, risky films for everybody, and not just the director, but for everyone involved, most of all the actors. There are films where a real danger was faced – sometimes unconsciously, sometimes consciously – by those undertaking the task, and they brought it home safely; and there are those where, consciously or unconsciously, they put at risk (more or less voluntarily, more or less strongly) one or another fundamental element of film (narration, camera, acting, whatever) that only wanted to be left undisturbed… And we're talking about not only sole, solitary filmmakers like Bresson, Sternberg or Eisenstein, but the entire group of people who are part of the adventure. It's a series of surmounted dangers; there is perhaps no great film without the sense that it could have been a catastrophe, that it should have failed, without this type of miracle that saved everything, through the combined force of work, calculation and persistence. But to put it that way is maybe a more modern approach, which takes us far from the great classicism of the pioneers. For them, the danger was that they were obliged to completely invent everything.

Source: The dialogue between Jacques Rivette and Hélène Frappat, "Le secret et la loi," is reprinted in full (with its original introduction) in the collected writings of Rivette, *Textes critiques* (Post-éditions, 2018), scrupulously edited by Miguel Armas and Luc Chessel, pp. 381-421; it constitutes the entire fifth and final section of the book. A serviceable English translation by Srikanth Srinivasan appears as "Secrets and Laws" at https://theseventhart.info/2021/03/01/secrets-and-laws-interview-with-jacques-rivette. Rivette's key essays of the 1950s (including the two he discusses here) appear in English translation in *Cahiers du cinéma – The 1950s: Neo-Realism, Hollywood, New Wave* (Harvard University Press, 1985), edited by Jim Hillier. Bill Routt's essay "L'Évidence" can be found at https://wwwmcc.murdoch.edu.au/readingroom/5.2/Routt.html. Chris Marker on *Vertigo* is included in *Projections 4½* (see Chapter 7) and at https://chrismarker.org/chris-marker/a-free-replay-notes-on-vertigo.

33
A Dream is a Thought Expressed in Images

With the psychoanalyst Massimo Fagioli (1931-2017) in the 1980s, Marco Bellocchio (born 1939) developed a personal theory of cinema that he has used, ever since, as a loose, flexible working method for creating and elaborating his films – including those projects he does not originate, but which are presented to him initially by a producer, such as the adaptation of a book (*Sweet Dreams*, 2016).

This is not the only occasion when a director has worked creatively – and on an ongoing basis – with their personal psychoanalyst: Abel Ferrara with Christ Zois (*The Blackout*, 1998) and Blake Edwards with Milton Wexler (*That's Life!*, 1986) offer equally fascinating examples. As in those instances, Bellocchio's analyst moved, by degrees, from the clinical situation to a recurring role as co-writer.

In Bellocchio's case, this unusual collaboration, lasting a decade (until his adaptation of Fagioli's dramatic text *The Butterfly's Dream* in 1994), did not proceed without controversy and even ridicule in the media. It began with a bang in *Devil in the Flesh* (1986), in the midst of which Bellocchio experienced a severe psychological crisis, doubting whether he could continue at all as a film director. After discussing this "on the couch" in his private sessions with Fagioli, it was then agreed that the latter would come onto the set and work therapeutically with the actors, who were having trouble coping with the project and its emotional demands.

This move by Fagioli was not altogether unprecedented in the context of his own work since, in the radical "post-psychiatry" period of the 1970s, he had pioneered a practice of collective therapy enacted publicly – often with large groups of people sharing their dreams and opening them to response and discussion. (In the more conservative American context, Milton Wexler also promoted group therapy – a curious overlap with collective film production!) Bellocchio had attended many of these public sessions before engaging in private consultation with Fagioli.

At a certain point in their work on film projects, Bellocchio involved Fagioli in most of his public appearances (interviews, press conferences, festival screenings). And even when their direct collaboration ceased, a film such as *The Wedding Director* (2006) seemed – certainly to Fagioli himself – to be an oneiric recapitulation of everything they had discovered and elaborated together.

Here is an outline of the theory postulated between director and psychoanalyst. As Fagioli explained it in a seminar of 2006 where he shared the stage with Bellocchio (who mainly remained silent!), cinema uses three types of imagery. (Naturally, the dimension of sound is not lacking from the films that have resulted from this thinking but, conceptually at least, the duo stick with the visual-pictorial realm.)

First, the habitual images of the *everyday* world that arise from "conscious memory." This type of imagery is involved with *orientation*, familiarity, routine, ritual: we take the same path to work each day, we eat meals at the set times with our family, and so on. It is a matter, quite literally, of a *status quo*, repeated and unchanging.

On a second, deeper level, there is *dream* imagery, which records, restages and rearranges material emerging from the unconscious. For Fagioli, "a dream is a thought expressed in images" – which is why he was increasingly drawn, in his life, to the possibilities provided by the various arts. In film, this imagery can be rich, fanciful, disturbing, even ecstatic or horrific; Bellocchio's work is full of such dream imagery, which leads to some of his most powerfully realised sequences. However, for Bellocchio and Fagioli, dream imagery does not truly go beyond a level of "description." Dreams (as the pair interpreted them) point to important things, but go no further; they do not yet provide an analysis, nor do they offer a resolution. But they "make strange" the elements of everyday existence, dislodge the habitual paths of orientation, and thereby provide a way forward in the overall process.

In the third category, there are genuinely "new or novel" images that manage to "instrumentalise the human body, its movement and expression" in a surprising, generative way *within reality itself* (thus surpassing the "nudging" or dislocating realm of dreams). This is harder to grasp in the abstract, but easy to identify in Bellocchio's cinema. His films since the mid-1980s are characterised, above all, by an exploration of bodily movements in space (whether natural or built environments), movements that are variously blocked, destabilised, groping, or liberated. Passages of walking, running or dancing are the most expressive implement in his *mise en scène* toolbox, not just symbolising but more profoundly *enacting* a process of personal renewal, and what the Surrealists called "permanent revolution." Bellocchio himself described the idea succinctly: "Rigidity is fatal."

In Fagioli's view, Bellocchio's significance and immensity as an artist arise from the fact that he is a "great depressive" who risks the "destruction of his individual identity" – rather than seeking to stabilise it in an unchanging way (this more traditional stance is one that Fagioli contemptuously ascribes to Bernardo Bertolucci, another filmmaker deeply involved with psychoanalysis as well as Buddhism). In fact, depression – like in the films of Nanni Moretti – usually forms the emotional baseline of Bellocchio's characters at the outset of their stories. In order to break out of a morose cycle – frequently fixated on the past and/or their childhood – they have to find a way to free themselves, to once again live in the present and open up their future.

This process leads, in cinematic terms, to both a *dramaturgy* and a *choreography*. In a 2011 interview, the director commented on these "movements."

> In my films there's always the attempt to get out of closed spaces, the willingness to break through walls and liberate oneself... In imagining a story, we cannot disregard the movements of change. We begin from a substantial dissatisfaction with our conditions of departure, and this results in an attempt to become different from

> who we originally were… I feel this very strongly in myself as well as, in a very natural way, the call of transformation, which I always try to achieve as a necessity. Far from being an obligation, this necessity becomes, rather, the identity of my work.

Perhaps this all might be considered a case of *personal poetics* – a means to help one director (Bellocchio) create his own work, by facing and working through his own crises and problems – rather than a generalisable film theory applicable to anything beyond itself. There is no doubt that the personal element here is extremely important – and leads to extraordinary, vital, dynamic cinema (remember that, when making *The Traitor* in 2019, Bellocchio was nearly 80). That is already sufficient justification for the theory to exist.

Yet this book, *Filmmakers Thinking*, wants to suggest something more radical. What if we did take the Bellocchio/Fagioli model seriously as a theoretical proposal? Where might it take us, both in relations to films already made, and films still to be made? What new appreciations of cinema might it offer? What creative mutations might it produce in other people's hands? I believe there are many generative possibilities open.

Recall the axiom coined by Isidore Isou: the definition of cinema is not a *given*; it is – it can be or should be – an *invention*. To invent means not to merely describe, but (as in the above model) to strike out in a new direction, to *instrumentalise* the nominated elements of the medium in a new and creative way.

This is what all of the filmmakers discussed in this book, in their own ways, have done. It is up to each one of us, now, to take further the adventure of filmmakers thinking.

Source: The 2006 seminar by Marco Bellocchio and Massimo Fagioli is transcribed in a French translation as "Les images nouvelles," *Marco Bellocchio/Carmelo Bene* (Le Magic Cinéma, 2009), pp. 26-29. The passage quoted from a 2011 interview is translated from an Italian thesis on Bellocchio by Marina Pellanda of University of Padua, accessible at http://paduaresearch.cab.unipd.it/4236/1/TESI.pdf. An audiovisual essay by Cristina Álvarez López and myself inspired by this interview, *Into the Void* (2020), can be viewed at https://vimeo.com/433912296.

Index

Adachi, Masao, 91
Aesthetics (of cinema), xiv, 3-4, 20, 31-32, 46, 53-54, 78, 92-93, 120, 134-136, 150, 152-154, 159, 168, 173-176, 181, 191, 194, 195-200, 201, 209, 211, 223, 227
Akerman, Chantal, 19, 75-81, 99-103, 112, 134, 161, 173, 211, 213
Alain (philosopher), 238
Alexander Nevsky (Eisenstein, 1937), 1-5, 169
Alexandrov, Grigori, 181-186
Almayer's Folly (Akerman, 2011), 99-103
Almodóvar, Pedro, 17
Althusser, Louis, 143
Altman, Robert, 41
Álvarez López, Cristina, ix, 249
American cinema (classical), 12-13, 24, 55, 64, 117-118, 143, 159, 187, 191, 194, 217-218
An Anagram of Ideas on Art, Form and Film (Deren, 1946), 84, 146, 149-150, 156
Analogy, 57-58
Anderson, Paul Thomas, 38
Anderson, Wes, 39
Angelopoulos, Theo, 229
Animation, 34, 95, 139, 197-198, 220
Anthropomorphic cinema, 20-22
Anti-cinema (or: anti-film), 33, 91-96, 128, 199, 204, 217
Anticipation (in film), 55-56, 187-188
Anti-intellectualism, 37-43, 142-145, 154-155
Antonioni, Michelangelo, 21, 62, 113, 142, 178
Aoyama, Shinji, 91
Apichatpong Weerasethakul, 11, 75-76, 170
Apparatus (see: Dispositif)
Arkush, Allan, 61
Armstrong, Gillian, 116
Arnoul, Françoise, 70
Artaud, Antonin, 34
Assayas, Olivier, 146, 168, 171
Astruc, Alexandre, 79
Atopia (or: non-place), 205-209
Aumont, Jacques, xvi, 68
Auteurism, 27, 39-42, 64-65, 72, 124, 144, 158, 223, 238-241
Avant-garde (arts), 80, 93, 109, 146, 154, 156, 183, 189, 195, 197, 206-207, 217, 219-220

Balibar, Jeanne, 124
Balzac, Honoré de, 58-59, 124
Barthes, Roland, 64-65, 174
Baudelaire, Charles, 194
Bazin, André, ix, xvi, 17, 19, 53-54, 168, 195, 197, 237
Bellocchio, Marco, 178, 218, 245-249
Benayoun, Robert, 61-62
Bergman, Ingmar, 60, 86
Bergman, Ingrid, 113, 237
Bertolucci, Bernardo, 146, 176-178, 247
Bigelow, Kathryn, 45, 144
Bitomsky, Hartmut, xiii-xviii
Bitsch, Charles, 100, 111
Boetticher, Budd, 116
Bonello, Bertrand, 10-11, 13
Bonheur, Le (Varda, 1965), 80
Bonitzer, Pascal, 94-96
Bonjour cinéma (Epstein, 1921), 187-194
Boorman, John, 9, 26, 63
Brakhage, Stan, xvi, 165, 195
Brecht, Bertolt, 141-142, 220
Bresson, Robert, xvii, 33, 39, 86-87, 113, 134, 165-166, 242
Brunius, Jacques, 189, 193
Bull, Lucien, 34
Buñuel, Luis, xvi, 62, 142, 146, 224, 233
Burch, Noël, 93
Butor, Michel, 21

252 Filmmakers Thinking

Cage, John, 93, 203
Cahiers du cinéma (magazine), 53-60, 62, 69, 78, 81, 114, 142, 195, 234, 237, 239, 243
Calvino, Italo, 3-4
Campbell, Joseph, 26
Campion, Jane, 146, 153-154
Carax, Leos, 100
Carrière, Jean-Claude, 27, 121, 233
Casino (Scorsese, 1995), 56
Cassavetes, John, 123, 157-158, 163
Cave, Nick, 116-117
Cavell, Stanley, xvi, 208
Cayatte, André, 48
Centrifugal (function), 228-231
Centripetal (function), 228-231
Chabrol, Claude, 61
Chance (role of), 3, 30, 53-60, 68, 72, 93-94, 115, 123-125, 176
Child, Abigail, 19, 138, 146, 217-221
Childhood, 29, 64, 85, 95, 105-106, 138, 185, 211, 247
Chow, Stephen, 230
Chronophotography, 34
Chytilová, Věra, 168
Cinécriture, 75-81, 126, 137
Cinematography, 10, 99, 106, 120
Cinephilia, xv, xvii, 61-62, 103, 113-114, 116, 118, 189, 205-206, 231
Clair, René, 197
Classicism (in cinema), 12-13, 24, 26, 37, 50, 54-55, 64, 80, 91-92, 138, 143, 147, 167, 176, 178, 182, 183, 198, 214, 223-231, 242
Colpi, Henri, 53, 58
Comolli, Jean-Louis, 37, 138, 140
Conner, Bruce, 219
Conrad, Joseph, 101-102
Core idea (of a film), 7-13, 80, 99, 115, 229
Corman, Roger, 27
Costa, Pedro, x, 31-36, 100, 103, 157, 214, 235

Counterpoint (audiovisual), 121, 127, 182-185, 219
Cox, Paul, 9
Craft (of film), xiv, 22, 38, 40, 45-50, 56, 69, 91-92, 115, 121, 143, 163, 167, 224
Craven, Wes, 144-145
Creative process, 1-5, 21, 24, 26-27, 40, 46, 53, 57-58, 66, 68, 91, 99, 121, 140, 142, 174, 220-221, 245, 248
Cronin, Paul, xii, 45, 51
Cukor, George, 12-13, 38, 42-43, 80
Culture (of film), xi, xvi, 17, 19, 113, 173, 182-183, 193, 197, 212, 214, 218, 223, 227

Daney, Serge, 62
Danger (in cinema), 39, 102, 118, 143, 218, 221, 241-242
Dante, Joe, 61, 143
Dardenne, Luc, 77, 81
Daughters of Fire series (Rivette, 1976), 123-129, 239
Death (in cinema), 21-22, 95, 214, 218, 247-248
Debord, Guy, 195
Decay, 21, 206
Découpage, 59, 93, 178, 191
Deframing (in cinema), 94, 96
Degas, Edward, 35
Deleuze, Gilles, 142, 241
Delluc, Louis, 197
Demenÿ, Georges, 34
DeMille, Cecil B., 194, 238
Denis, Claire, 100, 125, 144
De Palma, Brian, 123, 178, 182
Deren, Maya, xvi, 16, 84, 146, 149-156, 165, 175, 193, 201, 213, 229, 240
Derrida, Jacques, 238
Desire, 11, 32, 35, 54, 62, 73, 94, 99, 105, 184, 193, 234
Desynchronisation, 181-186, 201, 219-220
De Toth, Andre, 38, 47
Dialogue (in films), 24, 27, 47-48, 59, 127-128, 177, 184

Digital media, 115, 146, 162, 167, 195, 197, 200, 203
Dinesen, Isak, 30
Dispositif (or: apparatus), 78-79, 226
Documentary (film), xiii, 31-33, 40, 61, 62, 77-78, 108, 113, 123, 124, 151, 158, 161, 176, 189
Donohue, Walter, 51, 63
Douchet, Jean, 65
Dream, 2, 7, 11-12, 29, 66, 84, 101-103, 153, 162, 170, 175-176, 181, 191-193, 208, 215, 245-249
Dreyer, Carl, x, 33, 238, 239
Duchamp, Marcel, 220
Dulac, Germaine, 153, 193, 197
Dumont, Bruno, 107
Duration, 59-60, 168, 178
Dwoskin, Stephen, 103, 137, 140
Dynamism, 3-5, 15, 49, 55, 116, 121, 158, 163, 170, 183, 185, 191, 229, 248

Editing (see: Montage)
Editing (technology), xiii-xiv, 11, 41-42, 127, 162, 201
Edwards, Blake, 39, 143, 245
Eisenstein, Sergei, x, xv, xvi, 1-5, 19-20, 29-30, 35, 46, 53, 136, 141, 145, 146, 150, 158, 169 170, 173, 181-186, 197, 208, 219-220, 225, 241, 242
Eléna et les hommes (Renoir, 1956), 54
Ellis, Bob, 41-42
Epstein, Jean, ix, 32, 150, 173, 175, 187-194, 197, 230
Erice, Víctor, 61, 103, 179
Erotology, 196
Essence (of cinema), 29, 31, 53, 114, 134, 138, 165-166, 169, 191, 202-204, 234, 236
Ethics, 33, 76-77, 80, 134, 212
Everyday, the, 112, 174, 184, 202, 214, 246
Evidence (of cinema), 30, 76, 88, 234-238

Experiment (of thought), xiv, 88, 138, 202-205, 217, 223
Expressivity, 46-47, 56, 59, 109, 121, 151-152, 167, 176, 179, 193, 198, 247

Fagioli, Massimo, 245-249
Fantasy (unconscious), 12, 176, 208
Fantasy (genre), 126, 128, 217
Fascination, 85, 217
Fassbinder, R.W., 146
Feeney, F.X., 39, 43
Fellini, Federico, 7-13, 46
Feminism (in film), 91, 146, 212, 217, 219
Ferrara, Abel, 143, 245
Fiction, 3, 25, 31-32, 37, 48-49, 53, 55, 77-78, 108, 113, 126, 135, 151, 158-159, 175, 177, 191, 214-215, 224-227, 241
Field (concept), xvi, 4, 15-18, 19, 84, 86, 139, 150, 161, 174, 196-197, 225, 227, 229
Flaherty, Robert, 103
Fleischer, Max, 95
Fleischer, Richard, 239-240
Flor, La (Llinás, 2018), 128
Ford, Henry, 34
Ford, John, 33, 116, 238
Form (in cinema), xiv, xvi-xviii, 2-5, 8, 9-10, 15, 17, 20, 29-30, 31, 37, 39, 40, 42, 46, 54, 56, 61, 63-65, 76, 78, 80, 85-88, 93, 99, 112, 120-121, 128, 133-138, 149-156, 160-163, 165-171, 174, 177-178, 181-186, 192-194, 202, 212, 217, 220-221, 226-229, 241
Frame (or: photogram), 29-30, 69, 80, 93, 162, 167, 170, 188, 191, 198-199, 201, 204, 220, 225
Framing (by camera), 39, 41, 71, 94, 106-109, 160, 170, 230
Frampton, Hollis, 138, 139, 146, 150, 182, 201-209, 218, 220
Franco, Francisco, 17
Frappat, Hélène, 129, 233-243

Frears, Stephen, 39-40, 46-47, 51, 142
French Cancan (Renoir, 1955), 69, 70, 72
Freud, Sigmund, 34, 142, 193
Fuller, Samuel, xii, 24, 116, 167

Gabin, Jean, 70
Garrel, Philippe, 27, 142
Genre (in cinema), xii, 21-25, 39-40, 84, 102, 109, 115-118, 123, 125-126, 128, 133, 134, 176, 205-206, 217, 230, 241
Ghatak, Ritwik, 140
Giallo, 134
Godard, Jean-Luc, x, xiv-xvi, 30-32, 48-49, 53-60, 61, 77, 86, 91, 93, 95, 100, 111-114, 123, 126, 141, 151, 157, 168, 173-174, 177-180, 195, 201, 213-214, 217, 233, 240
Gomes, Miguel, 61
Gorin, Jean-Pierre, 91
Gorky, Maxim, 207-208
Gossip, xvii
Grace, Helen, 4-5
Grammar (of film), 47-51, 79, 92-93, 174
Grandrieux, Philippe, 33-36, 77, 102, 105-109, 142
Grant, Cary, 24
Gray, James, 143
Green, Eugène, 147
Greenaway, Peter, 136, 140, 146
Griffith, D.W., 33
Grüss, Alexis, 37

Hawks, Howard, 24, 234-239
Haynes, Todd, 100, 145, 168
Hellman, Monte, 116, 123
Henderson, Brian, 139-140
Heterogeneity (in film), 56, 211
Hillcoat, John, 100, 115-122
Histoire(s) du cinéma (Godard, 1988-1998), 30, 57, 201, 233
Historical field, 15-18
History (of cinema), xi, xiii-xviii, 19-20, 23, 29-36, 53, 78-79, 91, 100, 117-118, 123, 152, 155, 165, 176, 184, 196, 198, 200, 201-202, 205, 211, 217, 219
Hitchcock, Alfred, 20, 22-26, 38, 47, 49, 50, 54, 55, 123, 168, 169, 178, 214, 224, 236-237, 239-240
Homogeneity (in film), 213-214
Horizon of reference, 17-18, 103, 113, 136, 213, 238
Horizontal/Vertical (concept), 16, 152-156, 175, 221, 229
Horror, 25, 33
Hou, Hsiao-hsien, 103, 229
Humour, 24, 112, 202, 204
Hypothesis of the Stolen Painting (Ruiz, 1978), 226

Illusion, 15, 37, 80, 85, 93, 95, 120, 181-182, 202, 204, 214, 218-220, 230
Image (in cinema), 2-5, 7-13, 19, 21-22, 25, 29, 47, 48-49, 55, 59-60, 64, 72, 77, 83, 85-89, 93, 100, 105, 112, 120, 139, 141, 154-155, 158, 160-163, 166-169, 174-177, 181-185, 189, 192, 195-199, 202, 206, 208, 212-213, 217-221, 224, 228, 240-241, 245-249
Imagination (creative), xi, xvii, 2, 12, 29, 48-51, 55-56, 100, 117, 125, 188, 190, 193, 205, 206, 209, 223-224, 226, 247
Imagination (historical), 16-18, 30-32, 117
Immersion (in cinema), 25-26, 85, 175, 178, 191
Imperfection (in art), x, 214-215, 219
Improvisation, 30, 54, 59, 73, 123, 125-127
Impurity (of cinema), 53, 133-140
Inscription (within drama), 28, 64, 102, 127, 167
Inspiration, 32, 34, 61-68, 99, 113, 139
Intermediality, 136-137
Internationalism, 25, 38, 137,

183-184, 197
Interval (concept), 56, 158-162, 191, 225, 230
Intrigue, 25, 187
Intuition, xiv, xvii, 46, 49, 58, 84, 142, 166, 169-170, 239
Invention, 1-5, 11, 15, 20, 30, 35, 46, 54, 59, 88, 117, 128, 140, 142, 150-151, 163, 176, 177, 188-189, 197, 205, 209, 242, 248
Irrationality, xi-xii, 139, 175-176
Isou, Isidore, x, 17, 91, 150, 155, 182, 195-200, 206-208, 219, 230, 248

Jones, Amy, 61
Jones, Kent, 61
Jung, Carl, 26

Kané, Pascal, 27-28, 40, 62-68, 72, 85, 99, 139, 237, 241
Kaplan, Jonathan, 61
Kaplan, Nellie, 61
Kazan, Elia, 40
Keaton, Buster, 57
Kelly, Grace, 24
Klossowski, Pierre, 160
Kluge, Alexander, 205
Kracauer, Siegfried, 140, 207
Kubrick, Stanley, 39, 134-135, 141, 144
Kuntzel, Thierry, 226
Kurosawa, Akira, 26

Lang, Fritz, front cover, 24, 40, 123
Lambert, Mary, 61
Larbaud, Valery-Nicolas, 58
La terra trema (Visconti, 1948), 20
Leone, Sergio, 27, 116, 118, 121
Lettre du cinéma, La (magazine), 233-234
Lettrism (art movement), 195-200
Levinas, Emmanuel, 77
Lévi-Strauss, Claude, xiii
Lewis, Jerry, 24, 230
L'innocente (Visconti, 1976), 20
Lipsett, Arthur, 219
Loach, Ken, 37

Location (of shooting), 75, 79, 102, 105-106, 136
LOLA (online film journal), 81, 103, 163, 231
Lola Montès (Ophüls, 1955), 113-114
Look (see: Regard)
Lookbook, 10, 100
Lost in Translation (Coppola, 2003), 238
Lovers of Verona, The (Cayatte, 1949), 48, 55
Lubitsch, Ernst, 24, 230, 239
Luhrmann, Baz, 135
Lumet, Sidney, 40, 143, 147
Lynch, David, 153
Lyotard, Jean-François, 207-209
Lyricism, 32, 77, 121, 153, 175-176
Lyrosophy, 194

Mackendrick, Alexander, 25, 45-51, 55, 80, 224-225, 231
Maclean, Alison, 145
Mad Max series (Miller, 1979-2015), 25-28
Magic, 4, 9, 58, 63, 65, 69-73, 119-120, 126, 184, 212, 235
Malgré la nuit (Grandrieux, 2016), 107
Mangano, Silvana, 21-22
Manifestos (of cinema), xvi, 20-21, 53-54, 79, 92, 147, 159, 181-186, 195-197, 209, 212-213, 217-218
Mann, Michael, 38-39, 43
Man Who Knew Too Much, The (Hitchcock, 1956), 23, 54
Marey, Étienne-Jules, 34
Marker, Chris, 236-237, 243
Martel, Lucrecia, 19, 83-89, 95, 120, 139-140, 158, 173, 191, 231
Mathematics, 58, 196, 201, 223, 240
Matrixial image, 112
Matsumoto, Toshio, 91
May, Elaine, 24, 61, 123
Mechanics (of cinema), 25, 45-46, 58, 150, 166, 175, 179, 184, 196-197, 201, 203, 220, 241

Mekas, Jonas, x, 79
Melodrama, 22-23, 45, 102, 115, 217, 221
Metamorphosis (or: transformation), 31, 54, 65, 86, 125, 144, 179, 188, 192-193, 196, 212, 248
Metonymy, 153, 175
Metz, Christian, xvi, 174
Microfiction, 226-227
Miéville, Anne-Marie, 95
Miller, Arthur, 149-156
Miller, George, x, 20, 25-28
Minnelli, Vincente, 239-240
Minghella, Anthony, 121
Mira, Merata, 145
Mise en scène (or: staging), 30, 34, 39, 40, 42, 48-49, 54-60, 64-68, 70-73, 77-78, 86, 107-108, 126-128, 133, 147, 158, 160, 167, 169, 188, 194, 218, 225-226, 238-241, 246-247
Mizoguchi, Kenji, 33, 92
Modernism (in cinema), 45, 55-57, 91, 102, 128, 135
Montage (or: editing), xiii-xv, 2, 11, 30, 40-42, 49-51, 53-60, 76-77, 79-80, 92, 106, 114, 125, 127-129, 134, 137-138, 141, 151, 158-163, 168-171, 177, 181-183, 191-192, 201, 211-213, 218-221, 230, 233, 241
Moretti, Nanni, 247
Motivation (in characters), 3, 23
Moullet, Luc, 38, 41, 61, 174-175, 179-180, 230
Movement (in cinema), 21, 23-25, 29, 34, 39, 46, 56, 59-60, 65, 71, 76-77, 79-80, 86, 107-109, 127-129, 133-134, 152-153, 156, 159-163, 167, 187-188, 191-193, 204, 212, 220, 225, 228-230, 246-248
Movements (cultural), 16-17, 56, 91, 93, 112, 135, 193, 195, 197, 217, 219
Mr Arkadin (Welles, 1955) 54, 57

Mulvey, Laura, 145-146, 213, 217
Munier, Roger, 166, 218
Muratova, Kira, 141-142, 147
Murnau, F.W., 54, 60, 103
Music (as metaphor/analogy for film), 57-58, 93, 137, 159, 161-162, 188, 196-198, 203, 217-221
Music (in film), 34, 42, 70, 73, 76, 100, 115, 125-129, 135, 169, 181-184

Narrative (classical), 12-13, 24, 37-38, 50, 54-55, 64, 80, 138, 143, 167, 176, 178, 183, 214, 224, 229-230
Narrative time, 47-50, 55-60, 72, 75, 78, 84, 87-88, 95, 121, 126, 136, 153, 157, 160-163, 165-171, 175, 205, 211, 219, 227-230, 235, 240-241, 246
Narrative experimentation, 24, 45, 88, 95
Naruse, Mikio, 92
Negation, 58-59, 83, 91-96, 128, 140, 169, 198, 212-213, 217-218
New Wave (see: Nouvelle Vague)
Nichols, Jeff, 41
Noé, Gaspar, 33
Non-place (see: Atopia)
Nosferatu (Murnau, 1922), 60
Nostalghia (Tarkovsky, 1983), 167
Notes for a General History of Cinema (Eisenstein, 1947), 19-20, 29-30, 35, 186
Notes on the Cinematograph (Bresson, 1975), xvii, 165-166
Nouvelle Vague (also: New Wave), 56, 93, 243

Oblivion (in film history), 189, 206, 209
O'Brien, Rebecca, 37
Ophüls, Max, 7, 13, 39, 55, 113, 161, 170,
Origin (of cinema), 29-36, 62-63, 159, 179

Oshima, Nagisa, 91, 178
Ossessione (Visconti, 1943), 20
Oudart, Jean-Pierre, 230
Ozu, Yasujiro, 92, 96

Paradox, 33, 53, 59, 91-92, 114, 141, 173-174, 184, 224
Parain, Brice, 114
Parameters (of a film), 75-81, 86, 101, 112-113, 120, 126, 129, 142, 190
Pasolini, Pier Paolo, 16, 35, 79-80, 134, 150, 152-153, 173-180, 228
Passage (between worlds), 77, 157, 208, 219, 224-225, 247
Passion (Godard, 1982), xiv, 30
Paulhan, Jean, 238-240
Pavlenko, Pyotr, 1-5
Peckinpah, Sam, 116, 118, 121
Pelechian, Artavazd, xvi, 158, 163
Petzold, Christian, 179
Phonurgia, 86-87
Photogénie, 190-192
Photogram (see: Frame)
Pierrot le fou (Godard, 1965), 77
Plasticity, 4-5, 12
Poetics, xiv, xvi, 84, 91, 147, 205, 217
Poetics of Cinema (Ruiz), xvi, 147, 223, 231
Poetry (cinema of), 16, 80, 152, 173-180
Point-of-view (also: POV), 49-50, 177-178, 225-227
Polanski, Roman, 40, 63, 178
Polonsky, Abraham, 143, 147
Politics (in/of cinema), 17, 28, 37, 40, 63, 88-89, 92, 95, 102, 159, 193, 202, 211-212, 218
Pontecorvo, Gillo, x
Pornography, 33-34, 76, 134
Positif (magazine), 51, 122, 143, 189, 231
Post-photographic, 195-200
Poussin, Nicolas, 106
POV (see: Point-of-view)
Powell, Michael & Pressburger, Emeric, 56

Pre-cinema, 29-36
Preminger, Otto, 39
Pressure (of sound or time), 86, 120, 167-170, 229
Preston, Gaylene, 145
Prévert, Jacques, 48
Proposition, The (Hillcoat, 2005), 100, 115-122
Psychoanalysts (as screenwriters), 245
Pudovkin, Vsevolod, 134-137, 140, 141, 181-186, 241
Purification (of cinema), 198, 204

Rainer, Yvonne, 91, 202, 211-215, 219, 224
Ramsay, Lynne, 38, 178
Reading against the grain, 92
Realism (in cinema), 17, 20, 24, 32, 38-40, 70, 102, 112, 117-120, 167-168, 173-174, 177, 192, 197, 221, 243
Regard (or: look), 47-51, 57-60, 141-142, 151, 192, 208
Reichardt, Kelly, 100
Rembrandt, x,
Renoir, Jean, 54-55, 58, 69-73, 84, 93, 114, 123, 239
Resistance (of film),
Resnais, Alain, 76, 146, 179
Reynaud, Bérénice, 79
Rhythm (in film), 8-9, 24, 26, 35, 47, 57-58, 75-76, 79, 108, 120, 151, 158-163, 169, 192-193, 218, 221, 238
Richards, I.A., 209
Risk, 11, 61, 65, 93, 125, 157, 237, 241-242, 247
Rivette, Jacques, x, xvi, 16, 100, 115, 123-129, 146, 168, 233-243
Robbe-Grillet, Alain, 21
Rocha, Glauber, xvi, 20, 116, 178
Rohmer, Éric, 12, 146, 177, 180
Rossellini, Roberto, 113, 169, 177, 234, 237, 239-240
Rouch, Jean, 113, 206
Rouge (online film magazine), 36, 103

Routt, Bill, 236, 243
Rozier, Jacques, 58, 69-73, 84, 123
Ruiz, Raúl, xv-xvi, 62, 92, 100, 103, 146-147, 165-166, 204, 208, 223-231

Sade, Marquis de, 34-35
Sanders, George, 113
Sayles, John, 61
Scénario du film Passion (Godard, 1982), 30
Schnabel, Julian, 120
Schrader, Paul, 61, 146
Science, xiv, 15, 58, 63, 88, 150-151, 163, 188, 196, 201, 223
Scorsese, Martin, 38-39, 46, 56, 133
Screening the Past (online film magazine), 73, 109, 122
Screenwriting, 8-10, 27, 31-33, 79, 101, 107, 230
Scutenaire, Louis, 95
Semantic map, 15-18, 176
Semiotics, 152-153, 173-175
Sennett, Mack, 30-31, 33
Senso (Visconti, 1954), 20
Serendipity, 3
Seriality, 30, 109, 197
Serra, Albert, 214
Sex, 28, 33-35, 154, 173, 196, 211, 218, 220
Sexism, 149-156, 211-215
Sharits, Paul, 139
Shea, Katt, 61
Shining, The (Kubrick, 1980), 135
Shotgun Stories (Nichols, 2007), 41
Shots (in cinema), 2, 10, 35, 39, 41, 49, 56-60, 66, 70-72, 76-80, 92-94, 106, 119, 137, 159-163, 166-170, 177-178, 191-192, 199, 201, 223-231
Silent cinema, 11, 23-24, 30-31, 54, 64, 112, 127, 155, 159, 181-182, 193-194
Slide, Anthony, 38
Slippage (of history), 103, 219-220
Slow Cinema, 112, 157

Smithson, Robert, 205-209
Snow, Michael, 202, 226
Sokurov, Alexander, 167
Sombre (Grandrieux, 1998), 105-109
Sound (in cinema), xiii, 5, 8, 10-12, 19, 23, 48, 50, 54, 69-70, 76, 78, 83-87, 93, 99, 115, 120, 127-128, 141, 167, 181-186, 189, 192, 197-198, 201, 203, 208, 217-221, 224, 226, 230, 246
Space-time (in cinema), 240
Specificity (cinematic), 19, 113, 134-135, 138, 151, 159, 166, 169, 198, 205, 230, 234
Spielberg, Steven, 27
Spring Breakers (Korine, 2012), 237-238
Staging (see: Mise en scène)
Statement of Intention (also: Vision Statement), 10, 99-129
Sternberg, Josef von, 24, 143, 185-186, 242
Storytelling (in film), 13, 19, 25, 49, 80, 95, 116, 224, 230-231, 241
Style (in cinema), xv, 37-43, 50, 64, 67, 76-80, 86, 112-113, 115-122, 128, 134-136, 142, 147, 154, 165, 169-170, 174-179, 212, 226, 228
Sunset Boulevard (Wilder, 1950), 66
Surrealism, 61, 95, 126, 150, 189, 193-194, 200, 204, 223, 247
Suspense, 22, 25, 187-194
Suture (in cinema), 230
Svilova, Elizaveta, 158-159, 162
Sweet Smell of Success (Mackendrick, 1957), 45
Syntagma (of film), 175-178, 228-229
Synchronism (of image and sound), 93, 181-186, 201, 219-221

Tabu (Flaherty/Murnau, 1931), 103

Tarantino, Quentin, 134
Tarkovsky, Andrei, xvi, 12-13, 53, 165-171, 225, 229
Tarr, Béla, 169, 229
Tashlin, Frank, 24
Teaching (of film), ix, xvi, 1, 4, 45-48, 64, 145, 158, 224
Technology, xiv, 32, 34, 95, 150, 154, 181, 189, 196, 200, 219
Test shots, 106
Theatre (stage), 17, 47, 135, 138, 141-142, 154, 161, 187
Theatre (cinema), 26, 29, 34, 93, 159, 182, 190, 218, 220
Theme (in cinema), xii, 2, 37, 39, 40, 46, 64-68, 72, 99, 101-102, 106, 114, 119, 121, 126, 150, 183, 237, 241
Theory (of cinema), xvi, 19, 32, 42, 53, 59, 92-96, 114, 125, 133-135, 138-140, 145-147, 149-156, 158, 160-163, 165-171, 173-180, 185, 192-194, 195-200, 205, 217-221, 223-231, 234, 240-241, 245-248
Theory (resistance to), 62, 140, 141-145
Thomas, Dylan, 149-156
Time (philosophy of), 13, 47-49, 55-60, 72, 78, 84-89, 95, 106, 121, 126, 136, 151-153, 157-158, 160-163, 165-171, 175, 179, 191, 205, 208, 211, 219, 223, 228-230, 235, 240-241, 246
Titmarsh, Mark, 209
To, Johnnie, 27
Trailers from Hell (website), 61
Transformation (see: Metamorphosis)
Trash (cinema), 195-196, 205-209, 212-213
Treatise on Slime and Eternity (Isou, 1950), 195, 198, 200
Truffaut, François, 47, 61
Truth, xv, 1, 5, 15, 20, 22, 28, 29-30, 39-40, 47, 54, 64, 68, 72, 107, 116, 118, 133-134, 150, 166-170, 184, 188, 191, 194, 197, 235-241
Tsai Ming-liang, 60, 120, 229
Two-Lane Blacktop (Hellman, 1971), 123
Twombly, Cy, x
Tyler, Parker, 149-155

Unconscious, the, 2, 26, 29, 34, 39, 64-67, 77, 94, 176, 193, 202, 226, 242, 246
Unity (in film), 166, 214

Varda, Agnès, xv-xvi, 78-81, 126, 137, 178-179
Vasulka, Steina, 139
Vasulka, Woody, 139
Vertigo (Hitchcock, 1958), 236-237, 243
Vertov, Dziga, 56, 80, 95, 150, 158-163, 181, 183, 217, 225
Vibration (in cinema), 85-87, 157
Vigo, Jean, 153
Violence (in cinema), 76, 118-119
Vivre sa vie (Godard, 1962), 59, 111-114, 126
Visconti, Luchino, 20-22, 28, 121
Vision Statement (see: Statement of Intention)
Vocation (of cinema), 29, 61, 133-140, 150, 166, 183, 197
Vogel, Amos, 149
von Trier, Lars, 33

Warhol, Andy, x, 112
Weerasethakul (see: Apichatpong)
Welles, Orson, 30, 54-55, 57, 161, 170, 178
Wenders, Wim, 112, 146, 214
Western (genre), 26, 28, 40, 115-122, 206
Wexler, Milton, 245
Wilder, Billy, 22, 24, 40, 65-66, 143
Wollen, Peter, 145

Yoshida, Kijū, 91-96, 128, 214

www.ingramcontent.com/pod-product-compliance
Lightning Source LLC
Chambersburg PA
CBHW070131080526
44586CB00015B/1642